FIRE UNDER MY FEET

FIRE UNDER MY FEET

A Memoir of God's Power in Panama

Leo Mahon

With Nancy Davis

ORBIS BOOKS

Maryknoll, New York 10545

Founded in 1970, Orbis Books endeavors to publish works that enlighten the mind, nourish the spirit, and challenge the conscience. The publishing arm of the Maryknoll Fathers & Brothers, Orbis seeks to explore the global dimensions of the Christian faith and mission, to invite dialogue with diverse cultures and religious traditions, and to serve the cause of reconciliation and peace. The books published reflect the views of their authors and do not represent the official position of the Maryknoll Society. To learn more about Maryknoll and Orbis Books, please visit our website at www.maryknoll.org.

Library of Congress Cataloging-in-Publication Data

Mahon, Leo T.
   Fire under my feet : a memoir of God's power in Panama / Leo Mahon
with Nancy Davis.
      p.   cm.
   Includes bibliographical references.
   ISBN-13: 978-1-57075-698-6 (pbk.)
   1. Catholic Church—Panama—San Miguelito. 2. Mahon, Leo T.
I. Davis, Nancy. II. Title.
   BX1445.S2M34 2007
   282'.728731—dc22
                        2006033736

CONTENTS

FOREWORD

Leo Thomas Mahon is a West Side Irish Catholic Democrat, the son of a policeman.[1] He is also one of the great missionary priests of our time. One must perceive that these two essential facts about Father Mahon are closely connected if one is to understand the story told in his candid, haunting, and very important book.[2]

I have often thought that the genius of Leo's missionary work, whether among the African Americans in the Woodlawn neighborhood of Chicago or the Hispanic Knights of St. John the Baptist or most notably in the Panama mission in this book or at the two parishes he pastored in Chicago after the Panama interlude, arose out of his experience in growing up in Resurrection parish on the West Side of Chicago. He did not imitate in his missions the structure of Resurrection so much as he understood the basic community instincts of priest and people which held that first- and second-generation immigrant parish together during the Great Depression. "Community" has never been an empty slogan or a meaningless cliché for Leo. Rather it is the warp and woof of the fabric of his vision of the Catholic Church in the world—yesterday, today, and forever.

Moreover, I assume that he learned his toughness and his political shrewdness from his family when he was growing up. "Res" as we called it (from our slightly more lace-curtain bastion two parishes

---

1. Unaccountably he is also a White Sox fan. No one is perfect.

2. Full disclosure: Leo and I have been close friends since 1945. For thirteen years I worked with him as an itinerant Sunday Mass priest at St. Mary of the Woods parish. As G. K. Chesterton said of his brother Cecil, through all those years we never stopped arguing and never once quarreled.

away) was always a tough neighborhood, not violent surely, but rooted in the streets and the boulevards and the conflicts that existed all around and in the street-corner society of the corner of Cicero and Jackson. You learned in Res, if I am to believe the stories, how to take care of yourself.

This is where Leo came from and it has marked his life and work. But most priests with his background—this writer included—could not have survived more than a couple of weeks in San Miguelito. Whence the vision, the courage, the energy that permeate this story?

That's a difficult question. I can point to some influences in his life that are important—St. Mary of the Lake Seminary in the time of the legendary Monsignor Reynold Hillenbrand, Leo's seminary class composed as it was of an extraordinary group of gifted and zealous young men (the last of those who had grown up in the Great Depression perhaps), the influence of older priests in the Archdiocese of Chicago like Jack Egan, George Higgins, and Bill Quinn, the springtime euphoria of the Second Vatican Council. Finally, however, zeal and vision for all of us finally arise from gifts of grace and nature (which is also a grace). God blessed Leo greatly and required greatness in return. I am confident that the deity is satisfied with the arrangement.

I used to think that it would have been useful for Leo to have experienced the rigorous discipline of academic theological research. Now I thank God that he was spared it. Theologians tend, like most of us academics, to hide behind the protective walls of our disciplinary boundaries—barbed wire fences, as John Shea has called them.

Reading this memoir recalled all my anger at the way the church treated Leo. I suspect that I'm far more angry over the harassments and the investigations that marked his two decades in Panama and of the clerical envy he has experienced here in Chicago. The infantile, mediocre, and frightened clerical culture that characterized his persecutors easily survived Vatican II and still defaces the Body of Christ. In any properly run corporate body, talent and grace are admired and encouraged, if only because they facilitate institutional survival. The church hasn't quite caught up with that insight and is still busy devouring its own, always folly but criminal insanity in this time of perhaps the most serious—and also the most potentially fruitful—crisis in the last thousand years. Should Leo have been a bishop? Oh yes. But he should have been a cardinal too, a task for which he is better qualified than most of the mediocrities who wear the sacred crimson.

However depressed he may feel at times, I've never known Leo to be bitter, which makes him far more virtuous than I am. Even now, each summer he and John Cusick venture to my vacation retreat in Grand Beach where they dream bright dreams and see dazzling visions. God grant that there be many more years of these visions and dreams.

Andrew Greeley
Feast of Our Lady at Christmas, 2005

PROLOGUE

I stood alone in a sparsely furnished white-washed room of the Commandacia. Colonel Omar Torrijos glared at me with bloodshot eyes and snarled: "You beat me once, but you won't do it again; I promise you. Your life isn't worth a cent. I could have you shot."

Holding my breath and looking him directly in the eye, I spoke with caution so that my voice wouldn't quiver. "I can't stop you, if that's really what you want to do."

"I could put you on a plane and send you back to the States where you belong," he retorted.

Hoping he wouldn't notice my composure was being threatened and my knees were feeling shaky, I responded, "Go ahead, if you think that will solve your problem."

He was silent for a moment, but his eyes never broke contact with mine. Finally he said, "Do you realize, Father, that if all the people of Panama did what you and the people of San Miguelito have done, we could not control this nation?"

"That's just the point, Colonel," I replied.

How did an Irish Catholic boy from Chicago's West Side end up in a confrontation with Omar Torrijos, soon to be general and dictator of Panama? The following pages tell that tale. It is my story from 1963 to 1975 during the years I spent in San Miguelito, Panama, commissioned by the Archdiocese of Chicago to build an experimental church.

1

CHARTING
THE UNCHARTED

*T*he skyscrapers faded into the horizon as the statue of my freedom and what I've known to be my America lost its shape, and with it, a bit of its reality. Leaving the New York port aboard a cargo vessel they called a banana boat, I found myself on my way to Panama, bringing with me all that I possessed. It was a bitterly cold day in late January. We made one stop at Baltimore where the winter cold was so severe I thought we might never get out of the ice-packed harbor. The boat screeched as it fought its way through the ice while the north wind wailed. But as we reached the gray expanses of the Atlantic, our boat picked up some momentum.

I, Leo Mahon, age thirty-four, a Roman Catholic parish priest, along with my peers, Jack Greeley and Bob McGlinn, had been commissioned by Cardinal Albert Meyer of Chicago to build an experimental church in the nondescript barrio of San Miguelito, Panama. I was filled with the pull of hesitancy and the push of excitement, similar to what a seventeenth-century missionary explorer must have felt as he crossed into foreign territory. At the same time, I felt the insane bravery and confidence that an entrepreneur must feel when ready to launch a fledgling company.

It was 1963. There was a hint of upheaval everywhere—Vietnam, Vatican II, hippies, journeys into space, seminaries being built all over the United States, and a Catholic U.S. president in office. And I was turning my entire world upside down—a man of the time, I guess, leaving the comfort of what I had known to be part of an unknown world. And it wasn't that I didn't want it. I did—with a stronger aching desire than anything I had felt—ever. I had wanted this day since the Chicago church had begun talking about missionary work two years earlier. My Spanish was adequate, my energy high, and my drive to succeed, as my peers many times have said, had bishop-status without the title.

The crisp January Atlantic breeze whipped across the cigar I forgot was dangling in my fingers, scattering ashes on my coat. The ritual of brushing off the powdery gray residue while looking ahead into the open water sent me into deeper reverie. I was not sure if it was arrogance or faith or a combination that had me excited. Surely, I could repeat what I had built in Chicago.

I was never one to say no to a challenge. I was west-side Irish and son of a policeman. In those days, that was a winning combination. My position on the streets of Chicago was established. As a youngster I had felt safe and confident, commanding the respect of both my environment and my peers.

Chicago was *my* playland. The order echoed from my mother on a Saturday morning, "Eat your breakfast," was the same as that on every other day of the week. The difference was that on Saturday and other vacation days, my brothers and I would down the usual fruit juice, oatmeal, two boiled eggs, toast and honey, all with a tall glass of milk, and become pioneers in a vast land of unconquered territory. We went out to explore the central hub of our world—the city! The only restriction we had was that of returning home by dusk.

Sometimes we would spent an entire day in the Loop, checking out grand places like the ornate lobby of the Palmer House or the architecture of the Chicago public library; other times we would ride the El all over the city and suburbs; still other times we'd take the Central Avenue bus up to Thatcher Woods where we would bike and make tree houses.

In high school, I didn't need permission to leave the house in the evening. The only question I answered was, "With whom are you going?" and, given that the people mentioned were on my parents' "approved" list, I had freedom many of my neighborhood chums never had.

In the foreground I felt I owned my own life and trusted my decisions, while the background was built with positive, responsive parental support.

Looking back at those early years, I remember wanting to be someone important. I'd rather use the phrase "to do something significant," but back then I couldn't have described what that meant. The most significant and important people I knew were priests. It was pre–World War II. There weren't many openings in our ambient. You could be a teacher, a lawyer, or a policeman. My father was a policeman, but it seemed to be a dead-end job and I wanted something more challenging.

I was bright. The brightest kids, at least the males, went to high school at either St. Ignatius or Quigley. My two brothers went to Ignatius, but I chose Quigley. Ignatius prepared kids for college and big-money careers; Quigley prepared men for the priesthood.

The religious women who taught me in grammar school helped my decision. They had a knack for inspiring young men of eager and quick wit to pursue their "calling." Having a "calling" was the language of the day; the priesthood was a calling from God, and there appeared to be some of us who had it and others who didn't. At age thirteen, I had it, they said, and I gladly took the leap. It felt special to do so; maybe "important" was in my reach.

Initially my mother had grander dreams for me. When I was eight, she took me to Hollywood for a screen audition. I remember the train ride across country. The images of the famous glistened and glowed as I fidgeted restlessly. The time came for my turn to sing and dance in front of the cameras. I was nervous, but pulled out all the stops and showed them what a west-side Irish boy from Chicago could do. I stayed on tune, despite the flutter in my throat; I stayed in step with the music and felt the glory of fame in front of the camera and an audience of three: two talent scouts and my mother. I imagined myself as Andy Rooney's side-kick: Rooney and Mahon, the Irish lads of the Golden Screen. The response from the talent scouts was fast: "Thank you for coming; we'll call you if we have a need for your son's talent." On my way home, as California receded into the distance, I began to plan what I would be doing next Saturday. Goodbye, Hollywood. I'm glad to be back, Chicago.

I must say that I never thought I wanted to be a parish priest. It looked so dull. It didn't appeal to me. I thought maybe I'd be a priest teacher, like a Jesuit; they seemed bigger than life. Or maybe I'd even be a missionary. They converted pagans; that seemed important. My mother had targeted Oxford, but when I said I wanted to be a priest, she, like most Irish Catholic parents back in the early 1940s, was pleased and proud.

M y seminary years went fast and I found myself attracted to missionary work. I was the only one of thirty-nine ordained in 1951 who chose what was considered a "tough" assignment. I volunteered to go to Holy Cross at 65th and Maryland, an all-black parish. I was excited and knew, with the arrogance of youthful enthusiasm, that I was destined to do meaningful and rewarding work. I joined two other young priests at the parish and we worked together and made hundreds of converts.

Holy Cross neighborhood was dressed with the poor and uneducated. We white priests represented everything they weren't—black power hadn't begun! We had the power of education, the power of self-confidence, and the power of God behind us. The powerless found themselves wrapped in our wisdom, inspired to take on our God and embrace our ways of worship. They listened with the attention of the deprived, hungry for hope and the promise of better lives—eternal salvation was certainly better than what they had. We were traditional missioners doing traditional missionary work: when the underprivileged recognized the value of and conceded to our ways, their lives would be transformed.

That style of evangelization worked until I said yes to a group of Puerto Ricans who approached me one day on the steps of the church.

It happened on a Sunday in 1955 while I was greeting parishioners after Mass. Ten young Puerto Rican men gathered around me and said simply, "We have no priest."

"I speak no Spanish," I answered sheepishly.

Smugly, they responded, "We'll teach you."

Puerto Ricans represented a growing minority in the parish. They were to lead me down a whole new road which one day would stretch not only into Chicago's entire inner city, but ultimately to Central America.

I was afraid of the language barrier. I couldn't speak Spanish and they were recent immigrants who knew little English. I was willing to learn the language but realized it would take time.

I had heard of a group of priests on the University of Chicago campus near us who ministered to the Spanish-speaking. They were part of Opus Dei. I went to visit and was greeted at the door by a short and stocky Spaniard priest who, with the presence of a Cheshire cat, seemed to know that he had the biggest and widest grin of his species.

After a brief exchange regarding who I was, I told him my dilemma, "There are Hispanics in this neighborhood and I can't speak Spanish. I intend to learn, but meanwhile, what do I do? Would you help me?"

When he spoke, there was a familiar tone to his voice, reminding me of the voice that had sung lullabies to me as a child—he had an Irish brogue. He told me he had learned English when working in Ireland. I felt a kinship and was encouraged.

"Well," he began hesitantly, and then, picking up the speed of a crane with a loose chain on a downward plunge, he added, "Our congregation is dedicated to elite intellectuals, politicians, and recognized leaders, and so we don't work with the poor."

That moment and other moments that I later experienced with his congregation told me that I was on my own.

It was hard work, but simple work, because the needs of Chicago Puerto Ricans were simple: protection against the police and other predators, jobs, language classes, places to meet and socialize, ceremonies in their language they could understand, and most of all, friends who could bridge the yawning gap between their culture and ours, between the warmth of the Caribe and the cold of the North.

I began as an organizer, as an advocate and spokesperson at multiple police stations when a Puerto Rican was picked up for loitering, drunkenness, or some trumped-up charge and was being intimidated by the bold-mannered authority figure, unable to understand what was being said about him or to him. I worked with the men to find housing for new immigrants, to establish jobs, and to fill out appropriate forms. My ability to speak Spanish improved with each experience.

I continued as leader and guide, as knower of the known, and, as a typical missioner, I evangelized those in need. To evangelize, I understood now, meant to approach people where they were, to give them the necessities of life so that they would be ready to hear the word of God. There were so many necessities that were overlooked. To compound my work, new migrants were coming in every day, so my work grew.

My definition of evangelization had changed. When working with the black community I was the expert guide—"follow me and you will be saved." When working with the Puerto Ricans I was more the servant—"You have needs, I will help you fill them." I was feeling good about the shift in my ministry when, one day, a group of Puerto Ricans approached me.

"You, know, we'll probably never conquer all our problems, but we're Christians; we're Catholics. We don't know anything about our faith and we never talk about it. We are hungry for something more."

"Fine," I said, washed in my own humility. I thought I was doing well, taking care of their physical and safety needs, but they were telling me that helping them gain physical and material comfort wasn't enough. Perhaps I had become just another Saul Alinsky, replicating what he had done in the back-of-the-yards Chicago community, now doing the same for the Puerto Rican community. The energy and efforts I had been extending had a missing element.

I needed an attitude overhaul. I was a priest; I could do more than care for material and physical needs. My understanding of evangelization began to expand.

Certainly I could pull together meaningful and inspirational messages—lead people down a spiritual path. I always had a knack for words; I knew scripture and theology. I had been preaching for a few years at Sunday liturgy. Even though the catechism was prevalent and most formal education began on page 1, "Who is God?" and "Why did God make you?" I knew better than to start there. I took my commission to be a preacher, a deliverer of the Word, seriously and I spent hours preparing. They came to hear. Three sessions later they were still coming. They were there because they liked me. They appreciated my interest in them and the time I gave them. But there was no excitement.

This was a crisis in my own faith. What do I believe, and if it's not exciting, why should I be delivering it? If it isn't exciting, it isn't Jesus, I said to myself. My entire life was dedicated to Him; why wasn't I making Him come alive in them . . . and in me?

I was forced to look for help, mostly from the people themselves. I took the same group and made an agreement with them. I would prepare and deliver. They would tell me whether it was "great" or "blah" or "lousy." Their bluntness led me to understand how little I had known about the people whom I had "converted" earlier in my priesthood, how raw the search for meaning and faith was, and how wise those who searched for it actually were.

M y work, as meager as I felt it was, led to my appointment as director of the Cardinal's Committee for the Spanish Speaking in Chicago. If I was unprepared upon leaving the seminary for the work of a parish priest, especially missionary work, I was doubly ill-equipped to guide and direct the entire apostolate to the Spanish-speaking in Chicago. I had a beginner's knowledge of the language and an almost non-existent knowledge of Latin American culture. I was largely ignorant of how the people thought, what their values were, and what history had formed them. This weakness weighed heavily and I found out it was to be my greatest opportunity. I had to ask lots of questions and listen for hours on end—a new behavior for me, who had been ministering *to* people, not, as I learned to do later, *with* them.

One of the leaders of the community, Juan Sierra, told me about Chu Rodriguez, a street preacher who had been trained by the Redemptorists in the rural hillsides of Puerto Rico; Juan said no preacher could speak like Chu. The problem, my friend told me, was that Chu had "a problem." In those days "a problem" usually meant a family or woman issue.

"Tell him we need him—no matter what the problem," I said.

Chu seemed to avoid my many attempts to reach him. Then one day he appeared while I was leading a group discussion. I tried to make him feel welcome, while wondering if he really was the Chu so many had described: that dynamically articulate, brilliantly inspirational speaker. He was a short man, slight of build and physically unimpressive. His eyes remained downcast, connecting with no one; his hands did not have the discipline of keeping still; his knees and his legs moved like those of an anxious cat waiting to leap from a stranger's arms.

He returned for several sessions and, little by little, I saw the man inside emerging. Later in our relationship when he described himself as a person of small stature, I was ready to argue, since I had all but forgotten his size once his eyes lit up, his composure settled in peace, and his spirit became aflame with excitement. I saw him as a man standing as tall as Michelangelo's David, towering over others in speech and message. But then one day he disappeared. He had gone to Puerto Rico, we soon learned. When he returned, he announced that "the problem" that had shadowed those early sessions with me had been resolved.

He threw himself into his study and worked with abandon. I was soon to hear him preach and, when I did, I was more than astonished. Like his fellow immigrants, he had little schooling. But, oh how he could talk! He was a master at telling stories and a poet in his use of striking metaphors taken from the experience of his listeners and the flora and fauna of his native land. He wouldn't describe

an *esposa* as simply a man's wife; he would give her the attributes of
an angel and raise the respect she was due so that there was a taste
of the spiritual on his tongue when saying the word *esposa*.

Chu became an active member of our leadership team. We organized Puerto Ricans and Mexicans all over the city. They became
the "Hermanos en la Familia de Dios," the Brothers in the Family
of God. Three hundred men! Men only, since the Hispanic culture was one of male domination and we sought to instill a positive domination. We were busy! New migrants came every day with
new problems and new needs. We were still doing the evangelizing and organizing that I had begun, but we had added a vital
faith and spiritual dimension; these men were developing a rich
and deep faith in God and along with it a trust in themselves.

There was a core of us who gathered weekly, planned our work,
but, typical of ministry work, we feared that we would become
stale or trite. We needed more than planning meetings to advance
our work; we needed to advance ourselves in our faith and our
commitment. We talked about a retreat—a time to reflect and pray.
The Cursillo de Christiandad movement had come to the States
and we had scheduled one for Chicago for the following year. But
that was a year away and we didn't want to wait. We could not find a
competent retreat director, so we decided to do it ourselves. I approached Chu with hesitancy to take the talk on "Sin and Forgiveness." I knew the topic would be sensitive and I wasn't sure what he
would do with it, but I had enough trust in him, and I felt desperately in need of a good speaker.

He stared at me as if to say, "Do you know what you're asking?"
The look on his face was like the one Peter must have given Jesus
on that fateful night of the trial, a look of biting remorse.

I nodded indicating that, yes, I did know. I knew he had faced
his own sin and accepted his own forgiveness and that he had come
back from Puerto Rico a revitalized man. I didn't, though, know the
pain of the journey.

We held the retreat at a place outside of Chicago called Childer-
lee, in a lovely old farm house with an English-style rustic chapel.
Twenty men arrived as the sun was starting to set. They carried small
luggage bags, some paper sacks, and armfuls of personal belongings.
Lots of plaid shirts, some blue jeans, and woolen sweaters draped
their arms as they walked up the four gray-painted steps leading to

the door. There was a sense of nervous excitement blended with warm and friendly chatter as friends reconnected. I made sure I was there to greet each one. This was a new experience for them and for me. I had never conducted this lengthy a retreat. How meaningful could we make a weekend of eighteen hours of concentrated prayer, reflection, and dialogue? Most of these men were laborers who were used to the labor of the body, not of the mind and the soul.

In my unpolished Spanish, I gave the opening talk Friday evening. I am unable to recall the theme, much less the words. I suspect no one else who was there could either. All talks were overshadowed by Chu's talk delivered on Saturday morning.

Chu recounted his history—how he was raised in the faith, how he had married his childhood sweetheart, how he had had a large family with her. He described his *esposa* with the sensitivity of an artist crafting the most exquisite porcelain figure. I remember "seeing" her purely through the eyes of a man vividly sculpting the woman he deeply loved. He told us of his call to become a Redemptorist lay preacher, and of how he had preached over the length and breadth of Puerto Rico. He described the shadows of the countryside where the mountains sent seven-minute warnings prior to a summer downpour; how he and his fellow preachers would dance through the raindrops, waiting for the clouds to lift and how again he would seek the people of the village to share the Good News. He described the joy of self-discovery that people of the village experienced when he'd given them a single word or a single message of hope. He hung his head and paused in silence.

Then he told us of his betrayal—how he had gotten involved with another woman and fled Puerto Rico with her, leaving his wife, his children, and so many others deeply hurt and scandalized. As he struggled to describe his actions, tears choked his words, and the tremor I remembered of his early days returned. He slowly, reflectively told us how he struggled after he arrived in Chicago. Each word, each sentence, whispered of the agonizing discovery of the unhappiness he had caused, yet he was unable to break out of his misery. He described how he would avoid the streets when he would leave his house to go the store, lest he be seen by others. He vividly described the smells of Chicago's Puerto Rican alleys and how he began to identify with the decaying smells of old nicotine, of chicken carcasses and human excrement. Although he longed to go to Mass, he didn't out of shame. He had a job, but it paid so little that he and the woman lived in bone-grinding poverty. Things he had taken for granted like soles on shoes and sweaters without holes, he said, were no more. He said he took it all as his "just punishment." Each night he cried himself to sleep thinking of his wife and children alone and hungry.

He described how he hid himself when I visited his apartment. "I was in the house the night Father Mahon came to visit. I hid behind the drapes. If Father had looked down, he would have seen my toes peeking out of my shoes."

But, he continued, he could not avoid everyone and the message began to seep through the blockade of his guilt. He argued with his friends, "But this Father Mahon doesn't know what I have done."

"Yes, he does," came the answer, "but he says to tell you that there is nothing that can't be forgiven and repaired."

After resisting fiercely for so long a time, he said, adjusting himself so that he seemed to scan every eye, he consented to go to one of the evening sessions at the Cardinal's Committee for the Spanish Speaking "just to see."

"I felt ashamed, out of place there—a traitor in a group of loyal people. But they welcomed me and I stayed to listen. What I heard that night and on several other nights was what I needed to hear: God loved me and forgave me. I was his beloved son, no matter what I had done. It struck a chord deep within me, causing a sound that I could scarcely believe—that I hadn't dared to believe with all my heart—that God was not an unforgiving, punishing person, but the One who loved me and understood my pain. All the people there accepted me—not only Father Mahon, but all the others as well. Some of them did not know my story. Most of them did, but all of them accepted me as a brother—as one of their own who belonged in that place."

Chu explained how he struggled to accept forgiveness and finally gave in. Painfully, but graciously, he shared his decision with the woman with whom he was living. He returned to Puerto Rico to beg forgiveness of his wife and children. He came back with them to Chicago—the prodigal son returned.

I know I have not done justice to his talk, but I can recall that it was the most emotional moment of my life. I cried with Chu and all the others. I cried so hard I thought I would physically dissolve. I cried for my sinfulness; I cried for my weaknesses and my own inabilities. I cried for the wife I may hurt, had I ever a wife to hurt. I cried for the child I may have abandoned, had I ever had children to abandon. I was drained, exhausted, emptied, and even frightened by the power of the experience.

Up until that moment I had thought I was an "in-the-head" person with excellent defenses against getting too involved or upset. I had never cried in my entire adult life. I, like everyone in that warm retreat room of browns and creams shadowed by the October hue of autumn beginning to peak, felt bonded to the spirit of everyman and his sinfulness and his struggle to forgive most of all himself.

O ut of that enveloping morning came two insights. The first was that acceptance comes before forgiveness and pardon. I had been taught that one begs forgiveness and then is pardoned and accepted back. I discovered from Chu that the wounded must first feel and be accepted. Those early days before he reconciled with his wife, Chu felt accepted by us; he described it as life being poured back into him. He, a sinner, was accepted in a loving community. It was that unconditional acceptance, he told us, which led him to forgiving himself.

Second, there is no doubt in my mind that what happened that day was a "God-experience"—a personal encounter with God through the intervention of Chu. God touched me, opened me, and left me dazzled, impressed, awestruck. And it came from the people I was serving, not from me. The spirit of wonder and humility stayed with me for a long, long time. As I reflected on that personal experience, I began to see more clearly the face of God. It contained a most gentle, all-embracing look, one that had no raised eyebrow of judgment, no frown of dissatisfaction. It was one of full openness and tenderness. The encounter challenged me in my role of priest. How was I to be for others? I was not to be the overseer, the judger, or even the sower of seed. I was, above all, to be the gatherer, the window opener. Oddly, almost ten years later John XXIII was to encourage the universal church to do the same. Chu taught me that the strength of my ministry was to come by empowering others to tell their story and by allowing the Holy Spirit to work through them. My strength was not to get in the way.

C hu's powerful testimony led me to reflect on another mystery of God's grace. Where others are reared with an overwhelming fear of God, why do I believe in the God who loves me inordinately, who whispers my name at night, who forgives me before I ever say I'm sorry, who believes in me and calls me to freedom and greatness?

Surely one important source of my belief in a God of grace and love is the love of my parents. My father was a gentle, good man who never struck us, never swore at us, and never even raised his voice in anger.

As a little boy I shared a bed with my older brother. One night we had a great pillow fight. Our bedroom shared a wall with the pantry so the clattering of dishes rattled by flying pillows could be heard throughout the house. Mom warned us to be quiet, but we paid no mind. Then she said to Dad, "Go in there and make them stop."

Dad opened the door and in the dim light we could see the belt in his hand. "Take that—and that!" he said as he flayed away furiously. Somehow none of the blows landed on us. We, of course, screamed and hollered, going right along with the game. "That's just a taste of what you'll get if I have to come back," he said as he closed the door. Bemused and grateful, we were quiet after that. I don't know whether or not he fooled my mother. At any rate, there was peace in the house.

Not infrequently my two brothers and I quarreled noisily. Some of the noisiest fights were over what radio program to listen to in the evening. When Dad could take no more, he would get up without saying a word and tear the cord right out of the back of the radio. No one would speak or move a muscle. Cord in hand, he would open the front door and go for a walk. Some fifteen minutes later, much calmer, he would return, kneel down, and fix the radio. All in silence!

I can remember my dad being unfailingly sensitive and respectful. Once I was among a crowd of boys harassing the Jewish people as they came out of the nearby synagogue on the Sabbath day. One of our snowballs hit the rabbi and he chased us. I ran through the alleys, jumped a fence, and entered our house through the back door, thinking I was safe. The rabbi, however, saw where I entered and rang our front doorbell. When my father answered, the rabbi explained what had happened and complained of my atrocious behavior. Even though I knew I had been caught, I wasn't really expecting a big scene. Anti-Semitism, sad to say, was rife in our area and culture in those times. I got the surprise of my life when I saw my father's face; it was livid with shame and anger. There was no punishment. It wasn't needed. Seeing the outrage and disappointment in his face was enough.

My mother was a beautiful lady, tall and slim like my father. She was loving and attentive, yet aggressive and strong-willed. Unlike my father, she could use hard language and colorful words. "If you do that once more," she would shout in her Irish brogue, "so help me God, I'll murder you." It never occurred to me that she might carry out such a threat.

My image of authority, gained principally from the word and example of my parents, was a positive one. I could not imagine God as not being even more kind, caring, forgiving, trusting, and freedom-loving. And as I met people like Chu, some of the harsher images of church leaders I was later to face became anomalies and not models to emulate in my ministry. I, too, could represent the authority images of my youth and be the priest who found answers, not foremost in church doctrine, but in the life and presence of the people, connecting them to the gospel message and, in turn, relating them to the church.

There is not enough oil here for the ceremony, said Cardinal Stritch, looking sideways at his master of ceremonies, Msgr. James Hardiman.

"There's enough, Eminence," replied Hardiman.

"No, there is not," said the old, white-haired bishop.

"Yes, there is, Eminence," said Hardiman, trying desperately to keep the exasperation from surfacing in his tone of voice.

There was a pause and then the Cardinal said firmly, "I said there was not enough chrism; now, go get some more."

Cardinal Stritch had come to the major seminary chapel to ordain thirty-nine classmates, myself included. It was May 3, 1951. During the hiatus in the ceremony hundreds of our parents, brothers, sisters, relatives, and friends wondered what had happened. We almost-priests, pregnant with expectation, lay prostrate on the floor before the altar. The choir filled in the yawning silence with a few hymns. But all eyes were on the Cardinal. He showed no sign of nervousness or impatience. The first young priest knelt before him waiting to have his hands anointed with oil. The rest of us, from our prone position, attempted to peek at the man who would soon become our boss. The Cardinal took the young man's hands in his own and held them there for a long time. Some fifteen minutes later the breathless master of ceremonies returned with a vessel full this time of oil and the ceremony went on.

The picture remains in my mind, like a still-life painted by a long dead master—the Cardinal with the touch of a smile on his face and my classmate, Eugene Faucher, kneeling before him with his head bowed at what we used to call the proper "angle of piety," young hands wrapped gently by the gnarled blue-veined hands of an old man. Better than a tract, that scene told the story of the profound relationship between priest and bishop as we felt it then. At the end of the long ordination ceremony, the Cardinal asked us to promise obedience to him and to his successors. We saw no problem in making the promise. If at that moment he had said, "I want you to go to Tibet," we would surely have answered, "*Beate,*" the Latin word for "gladly."

Ten years later my loyalty hadn't shifted, but it had grown. I no longer spontaneously and gladly obliged; I challenged and questioned. Cardinal Meyer and I respected each other and became friends. It wasn't until later, when I met the likes of John Patrick Cody who followed after the untimely death of Meyer, that I saw how arrogant a church leader could be.

F or Chicago Catholics in the 1950s, the office of the archbishop commanded more respect than that of governor or senator or even mayor. (And with that mayor being the elder Richard Daley, that is saying a lot.) For many years, the archbishop had a long, dark green limousine that bore the license plate #1. Chicagoans thought that quite proper. Back then we priests saw in the bishop a mix of many figures and roles: he was Father, Shepherd, Oracle, the Boss, the One who sometimes had the first word and always the last. He was the Omega point where all ministry, priesthood, and authority met and from which all three emanated. We owed him respect, even veneration and loyalty, then interpreted as submissive obedience. What may be strange to outsiders is that a man got that respect and obedience by virtue of his office, just by being appointed bishop, and that he maintained it permanently unless he was foolish enough to fritter it away.

It was after the death of Cardinal Stritch who had raised respect for the office to the highest level known in Chicago that I began to worry whether it could happen again. Stritch, not only that day of ordination but through my years with him, benevolently encouraged me and knew how to direct my sometimes restless and abounding energy so that not only I but others would benefit. And then along came Albert Gregory Meyer, presently archbishop of Milwaukee, to be the fifth archbishop of Chicago.

The first time I shook hands with him, I found his grip loose and somewhat perfunctory. He smiled, but it was as though his facial muscles had received a message from the cortex of his brain saying "smile now." He appeared to be stern, cold, and even a little arrogant. He had very little social grace and never seemed to master "small talk," something he made no secret about. I was to learn later that his awkwardness, at least in part, was due to his instinct that much of the pomp was irrelevant and that the practice of putting one person in the dead center both of ceremony and decision-making can be quite dangerous.

My work with the Hispanics led me to do things in non-traditional ways and so I found myself sending Meyer multiple messages and requesting non-traditional responses. He called me into his office one day to respond to one of my memos, "Young man," he asked, "you are aware, aren't you, that I am opposed to afternoon Masses?"

"Yes, I am, your Eminence," I said, taking in the magnificent single plank of mahogany embossed by intricate inlays that served as a conference table. Glancing at the Cardinal's matching desk that stood to the left of the long table with its high-back red-plush chairs, I felt a tremor in my stance.

Lifting up the offending memo, he queried, "Then why did you send me this?"

"Because you're the boss, and if you don't wish to grant the permission, then the responsibility is yours and not mine. I did what I could to help those who couldn't attend Mass any other times."

Looking me squarely in the eye, he asked, "Do you really think it's important?"

"Yes, I do," I answered, meeting his gaze and, at the same time, showing the respect I had been trained to deliver.

"Well, then," he said with a wave of his hand, "go ahead. You have my permission."

He was by no means a tyrant or even an ungracious man. Like his predecessor, he allowed his subordinates sufficient autonomy to run their agencies freely. But it seemed difficult to get him to approve new initiatives or listen to new ideas. That didn't stop me from sending him letters and memos about various subjects.

One memo, above all, was to change the course of my life. Pope Pius XII had asked the developed countries to send 10 percent of their human resources—priests and nuns, that is—to help Latin America get through the crisis caused there by enormous population growth and an ever-increasing disproportion in the rate of priests to people. Many dioceses and religious congregations in Europe and North America were responding to the emergency.

Chicago at that time had some three thousand priests. Moreover, the seminary was producing the phenomenal number of forty to fifty new priests each year.

Some of us were afraid that this dynamic generation wouldn't be directed toward the growing number of needs in underdeveloped populations. Chicago's Hispanic population was growing rapidly and, we predicted, might not have priests prepared to serve them. I wrote a memo requesting that the Cardinal begin sending priests to Latin America, suggesting that our mission there would help us understand better how to work with our own immigrants. The Cardinal called me in again to his vast office and pointed to the memo lying on his desk. He didn't call me "young man"; he didn't address me at all.

This time he slammed his fist down, saying, "I'm physically, intellectually, and spiritually incapable of dealing with that issue now." The end!

I didn't expect either his vehemence or the confession of his limitations. There was no small talk, but there never was. I left, believing somehow that the amount of passion *against* this request might mean that there was somewhere deep inside him a passion *for* it.

Shortly thereafter, Pope John XXIII convoked an ecumenical council and, because of his position as the head of the largest diocese in the United States, Cardinal Meyer was appointed to the preconciliar commission. He had to travel back and forth to Rome frequently in those days, before the council ever opened.

After one of his trips to Rome, he beckoned me into his office. He had been hobnobbing with the most influential leaders of the church, expanding and challenging how he looked at the church and its future. I didn't know whether that was good or bad for me or for the Hispanic community. I only knew that he was getting weary of my requests for exceptions to church policy and tradition. I was prepared for him to ask me to resign from the Cardinal's Committee for the Spanish Speaking when he said, "Leo, are you still interested in doing something about the situation in Latin America?"

"Yes," I said, holding the little boy leaping inside of me at bay, "but are you?"

"Well, we have many problems and needs here, but I've heard and seen a lot recently. There's an old saying: if you have just enough food on your table, but you discover your neighbor is starving, then you fast. Would you please develop a full-scale plan that I can study?"

Our boat continued heading south, and after two days of upset stomachs and adjusting to the choppy waves and the biting wind, the slap of winter disappeared and was replaced by the caress of summer. We were feeling the warm breezes of the Caribbean. Our meager vessel finally seemed to adjust and was welcoming the gentle rock of nature's rhythm.

Around midnight, as we were approaching the island of Cuba, Jack, Bob, and I were suddenly awakened by the glare of floodlights streaming through the portholes of our tiny cabin. Out of the shadows cast by an already fuzzy moon, another boat emerged, ready to attack before we were fully aware of its presence. That boat's captain, using a loud and ominous megaphone, called to us.

"Stop your ship. Give us your ship's name, ownership, cargo, and destination."

It was a Cuban gunboat. Since Cuba and the United States were at odds, all American ships were suspect. Warning shots sounded. I was afraid of what my body might do if I dared to stand, peek out the porthole, or even move. I lifted my head half off my pillow, balancing on my elbow and remaining under the covers, all the while telling myself that the Cubans were bluffing; they wouldn't risk an incident with the United States.

Again, the menacing call to stop! Our captain seemed to pay little attention. I heard him give a terse response, offering the boat's name and destination. He didn't stop, or even slow down. In an instant, our boat jerked and picked up speed. The Cuban boat fired more warning shots and, instinctively, all three of us ducked, fearing for our lives. None of us had said a word the entire time.

Our boat doubled its speed, and in minutes we were out of the range of the Cuban boat. I had no idea that what appeared to be a lumbering, easy-paced vessel could take on the energy of a motorboat almost skipping across the water. It took a lot longer for my heart to stop racing and my blood to feel its natural pumping rhythm. Give me the safe streets—with their echoes of gunshots and their smell of gun smoke—of Puerto Rican Chicago anytime, I said to myself. Maybe this mission of God was to be martyrdom and not a missionary assignment. Jack mumbled a sigh of relief, Bob questioned his sanity, and we each retired back to our own thoughts.

I was unable to go back to sleep. Long after the Cuban ship had dropped off and disappeared, I remembered that we weren't traveling on an American vessel. We were sailing on a Nicaraguan boat owned by the Somozas, archenemies of Fidel Castro. Why had the Cubans allowed us to escape?

The sound of guns would be a foreboding of later and even more threatening encounters I would have with Omar Torrijos, general and dictator of Panama, and even with the archbishop of Panama.

S oon I could hear the gentle snores of Jack and Bob keeping rhythm with the boat. I prayed that I was not leading them into martyrdom.

Cardinal Meyer had given me the go-ahead to select my own team.

It wasn't hard for me to begin my search with Jack Greeley. I had known Jack since seminary days. He was gentle, gracious, and fun-loving. As a young man he had been sent to a parish where the pastor was sick. Jack ended up running the parish.

In an era when lay involvement was rare, I had watched him encourage participation—activities we take for granted today. He set up a group to advise him; he sought and encouraged leadership of parish groups; he offered a model of co-partnering where the laity and priest worked together. He seemed able to bring out the best in his people. One time a Chicago parishioner told me, "Father Jack is so refreshing. He wants us to be involved. Everybody loves Father Jack." I was not to be disappointed; Jack brought this same loving attitude to Panama and flourished.

When I approached him, he was just finishing his time as Army chaplain and was looking to do something meaningful. He knew no Spanish, but was eager to learn.

I didn't know Bob McGlinn prior to heading south, but he had taken the time to learn Spanish, and my friend and co-author of the Panamanian proposal, Gil Carroll, encouraged me to interview him. We connected. Bob wanted to do something different; I shared my dreams and expectations. We shook hands and he was on board.

The oft-used phrase describing individuals who march to a different drum may be trite, but explains the Bob I got to know. He would do strange things to get others' attention. One day he came to a meeting late with his pants torn and dirty. Concerned, we asked what had happened.

"I just got in a row with some young Communists," he responded. "They were sitting at a meeting claiming to be faithful parishioners, and I had evidence that they had been attending Communist meetings. I confronted them; they jumped up and attacked me."

"No!" resoundingly filled the room. Bob had dealt with Communists at a sector meeting a few weeks before, so most assumed that the same men had come back to harass him. When prompted, he provided more details and people caringly checked to make sure he was okay. Then we continued the meeting.

This story was not the first that I had trouble accepting. Later I confronted him. "Bob, did this really happen?"

"No," he responded, "But it was a good story and I wanted to get a rise out of people." I never did find out why his clothes were disheveled.

Bob stayed with us for two years, supporting and helping to build our mission. When he left, he said, "Leo, I can't think like you; I can't preach like you. I don't fit."

I couldn't argue. The last thing I wanted was my team to be a clone of me, but, among other unresolved issues, I hadn't been successful in getting that message through to him.

We had heard that it doesn't rain in Panama during the summer, which extends from Christmas to Easter. The three of us, Bob, Jack, and I, with the uneasy anticipation of a new world rushing toward us, stood on the sun-soaked deck and watched the green shoreline of Panama get closer and closer. As the ship slid slowly into its berth in Cristobal harbor, a gray cloud above us opened and poured rain upon us.

On that day, February 22, 1963, we were beginning a voyage through time in a different culture and with a new people, a journey that was to see the barnacles fall away, outmoded ideas and ways disintegrate; a voyage that would include cold and ice, opposition and hatred, nights of danger, trials, and prison; the heavy rainfall of failures and heartbreaks as well as the bright light, warm sun, and gentle breeze of friendship, love, new life, and success.

Memorandum

To: His Eminence Albert Cardinal Meyer
From: Rev. Gilbert A. Carroll and Rev. Leo T. Mahon

Date: February 15, 1962

Proposals for Work in Latin America

Introduction

There are now approximately 200 million people living in Latin America, or one-third of the earth's Catholics. By the end of this century, as many Catholics as now make up the whole church will live in Latin America—as many Catholics as there were from the time of St. Peter up to the early Middle Ages. Latin America, therefore, is an area of primary concern to the Catholic Church.

We frequently hear that if something isn't done to help the church in Latin America within the next few years, disaster will strike and Catholicism will lose its battle there for the minds and hearts of men. Even if we do not accept at face value this message of "gloom and doom" (there are some valid reasons why we should not), still we can hardly doubt that now is a time of crisis. The reasons are many: political, sociological, educational, economic, all of which are important but not precisely within the purview of this memorandum. One factor, however, is apropos —the ecclesiastical, namely, the shortage of priests.

If one uses a ratio of one priest to every 1,000 faithful, Latin America has presently a shortage of 150,000 priests. If *all* the priests in the United States and Spain were to be sent to Latin America now, that area would still have only 65 percent of the clergy needed. One could conclude that in the immediate future this need will not be met; in fact, in the light of population projections that we shall cite later, one can hardly envision a solution within the foreseeable future. Yet, the shortage of priests and attendant problems, because they have reached large proportions, cannot be passed off as impossible of solution. The priesthood and the sacraments are the life of the church. These problems and this shortage must be solved or the church in Latin America may die or, at best, shrink to enclaves in a largely pagan continent.

The shortage of clergy is not a new problem in Latin America, but two important phenomena have brought an older crisis into sharp relief in our day.

1. Population Growth—We are told that much of Latin America before the 20th century had a numerically adequate clergy. The word "numerically" is used advisedly because it was always inadequate by reason of origin (most priests were not natives), by reason of quality (many were morally and educationally inferior), and by reason of structure (far too many were regular clergy). But the twentieth century is seeing and will continue to see a phenomenal population growth. The number of clergy has increased, but not in proportion to the population. "We are worried and preoccupied especially because of the number of priests unequal to the rapid growth of the large cities and the general increase of population in Latin America" (John XXIII—May 7, 1960).

Latin America has the highest rate growth of any area in the world, higher than that of Asia. In 1900 AD the population of Latin America was only 4 percent of the world's population. By 2000 AD the population of Latin America will be 9.4 percent of the world's population. The population of Latin America, today equal to that of the United States and Canada combined, will, by the end of the century, be three times the population of the United States and Canada today, or 600 million. If the ratio of one priest to every 1,000 faithful is to remain the ideal, Latin America would have to produce 600,000 priests in forty years. (These figures are taken mainly from U.N. statistics; even if these projections are off by 100 percent, the problem would still remain enormous.)

2. Urbanization—As frightening as these projections are, the situation becomes even more critical when one considers the direction of the population growth— i.e., moving to the cities. Urbanization in Latin America has a unique feature: a high concentration of people in relatively few cities, usually the national capitals.
-   33 percent of the population of Uruguay live in Montevideo
-   30 percent of all Argentines live in Buenos Aires
-   23 percent of the people of Chile live in Santiago.

Even if 20 percent of the United States population lived in our largest city, then New York would have 36 million people. It is projected that by 2000 AD there will be 500 million people living in Latin American cities and 100 million in rural areas.

This urbanization trend means:
-   Whatever church facilities already exist in Latin American countries will be pathetically inadequate in the face of the sheer numbers of Catholics who should be using them;
-   Whatever visible tie with the church the masses of people from the rural areas may have had is likely to be lost in the city;
-   The rapidly growing urban proletariat is poor in a way no rural dweller ever was. The urban migrant tends to lose his identity and the community that kept alive for him his Christian heritage. The tie that temporally bound him with his church tends to disappear. The urban proletarian is likely to be rootless, isolated, without norms, a lost individual without a spiritual home.

This urbanization poses for the church a very difficult problem, since:
-   No past experience of the church in this area provides the priest with guidelines to follow. The present trend has no precedent and Latin American

ecclesiastical structures were designed for a totally different organization or population.

- The missionary from North America finds nothing in his previous pastoral experience to parallel what he has to face in the Latin American sprawl. True, the church in the United States has had most of its experience in urban areas, but the historical perspective of city growth in the United States is so different (Rome might be a better correlative) and the conditions of urban society in the two continents are so lacking in any adequate basis for comparison that the missionary may find his past experience even detrimental to the accomplishment of his Latin American assignment.

— In a continent where vocations to the priesthood are inadequate, the scarcity of priests in the large urban dioceses is almost incredible. Rio has had an average of three priests ordained each year in the last ten years; Buenos Aires and Mexico City have comparable figures. We can all say with His Holiness that "we are worried and preoccupied because of the growth of the large cities and the general increase of population in Latin America." What can and should be done?

If the United States, Spain, and Canada were to send 10 percent (or 10,000 priests) to Latin America next year, the area would still have only 25 percent of its needed personnel (ideal: one priest to 1,000 people)—to say nothing of future needs. Consequently, it is evident that sending large numbers of foreign clergy to Latin America will not alone solve the problem. Surely they must be sent in as large numbers as possible—but attention must also be given to how the few available priests should be used to handle large groups of people living in urban sprawls. We believe that some thinking (and some validation) must be done along the following lines:

> 1. the training and direction of laymen in functions formerly performed by priests—especially catechesis.

> 2. the use of the liturgy as the main vehicle of instruction and commitment.

I
The Archdiocese of Chicago

We agree that Chicago should send priests to Latin America because:

> 1. As Your Eminence has asked, "even if there is only sufficient food on your table . . . but your brother's family is starving, shouldn't you fast?"

> 2. His Holiness has instructed the wealthier nations of the world to help the poorer countries. Wouldn't this instruction apply, a fortiori, to the wealthier churches (in the sense of vocations and institutions) of the world?

3. A diocese or church is the Christian community of the place united to and directed by its pastor, the bishop—a true family under the care of its father. The family that is a diocese wouldn't think of delegating to someone else its function of charity; but the function of mission is as ancient and as theologically essential to a church as is the function of charity.

But how, where, what numbers, and with what support should these missioners be sent? The needs and resources of the archdiocese must first be considered in the light of primary obligation—viz, to the flock at home. When Your Eminence decides what personnel and what resources can be made available, we propose that a mission to Latin America will surely have one effect—namely, the filling of a need in Latin America for working clergy. This effect would be important no matter how small the contingent. But the contribution would be significant if the mission were designed to produce a possible solution for the problems of the church in Latin America.

If the Archdiocese of Chicago, for example, were to take a parish of 140,000 people somewhere in Latin America, supply twenty priests, and fund up to a million dollars for building parish buildings, the problems of that parish might well be solved, but a truly significant solution would not have been offered to the church as a whole in Latin America.

The answer would come back—"All right, send us a comparable number of priests and money and we'll be able to solve our problems." Such a quantity of priests and money is clearly out of the question. But if, on the other hand, four priests without large amounts of money were able to handle the same parish effectively (using new ideas and techniques), then not only has the parish been cared for, but a possible solution for the church in Latin America will have been proposed.

II
Alternative Plans

We are of the opinion that any help (by way of personnel) given to the church in Latin America by the Archdiocese of Chicago would fall into one of the following categories:

1. Lend–lease plans: The archdiocese could loan priests to an ordinary in Latin America to serve as assistants under local pastors. The Archdioceses of New York and Philadelphia have for some time operated under this plan, loaning young priests for a time to the bishops in Puerto Rico.

2. Controlled-territory plan: One of the major strengths of the North American church is its highly practical concept of parish. The archdiocese could arrange to take over a territory, make it into a parish (or several), and send down a trained team (or teams) of priests who under the ordinary would assume full responsibility for the territory. This plan would be similar to that of the St. Louis archdiocese.

3. Experimental parish plan: This plan would attempt to solve two problems at one and the same time: first, the spiritual care of a specific parish or territory (thus it would be similar to plan #2); second, the care of this parish in such a manner so as to develop ideas, methods, and procedures that might be an answer to some of the problems in Latin America.

4. Loan-the-expert plan: The church in Latin America is in desperate need of quali-fied technicians such as sociologists, educators, seminary professors, theologians, catechetical organizers, etc. The archdiocese has already contributed handsomely to the United States church by sending very qualified men to Catholic University, NCWC [National Catholic Welfare Conference], and other agencies and institu-tions of a national scope. This could be extended to Latin America.

The Archdiocese of Chicago could choose any one of these plans or any combina-tion of the four. It should be noted that plans #1 and #4 involve sending priests as individuals, while plans #2 and #3 would involve teams of priests with the archdio-cese taking on responsibility more formally.

III
Experimental Parish Plan

Plans 1, 2, and 4 hardly need more explanation but, perhaps, plan #3 does. The au-thors of this memorandum are of the opinion that the most important contribution to the church in Latin America would be an effort to evangelize the people and to structure work in the seemingly endless urban sprawls that are burgeoning all over Latin America (they are called *pavelas* in Brazil, *ranchos* in other places). This sort of work, however, would by no means be easy. Practically no ecclesiastical structure now exists to cope with this problem; further, Chicago priests have no comparable pastoral experience which would enable them to confront this situation and to know precisely what to do. But this work is so important that we are of the mind that the Archdiocese of Chicago should undertake it. The project could be signifi-cant if priests were assigned to the experimental parish in a practical Latin American ratio of priests to people—not the ideal but impractical North American ratio—and second, if the area chosen were to contain not only the middle class and/or the rural dwellers but also and most important the Latin American "proletariat."

Understandably, it would be impossible to avoid all risks of failure, but it would be feasible to reduce these risks by choosing an ordinary who would give the fullest and most intelligent cooperation, by selecting the most stable, intelligent, and imaginative priests to work there, and, last, by choosing a people and a place whose cultural frame of reference would not be entirely foreign to the Chicago priest missioners.

IV
Implementation of Plan #3

With all this in mind, we make the following proposal should plan #3 be chosen:

1. That the Archdiocese of Chicago take a parish either in Puerto Rico or Panama. The people of these countries are closer to the spirit and mind of the United States priest than people in any other area in Latin America. In fact, one might say that both the Puerto Rican and the Panamanian are "hybrids"—products of a bi-cultural marriage. American priests are highly respected and valued in both places. Panama would have one advantage over Puerto Rico—namely, Panama is considered to be truly Latin American, while Puerto Rico is thought by many to be a possession and part of the United States.

2. That Chicago priests be assigned to the parish in proportion to the number of people in the parish according to a realistic appraisal of present and future availability of clergy in Latin America—say one priest to every 7,000 people.

3. That the priests be chosen on the basis of their interest, intelligence, knowledge of Spanish, creativity, and ability to work with a team.

4. That the priests (with these qualities) already in Spanish-speaking work in Chicago be given preference if they wish to go and that they receive a regular assignment from the Chicago chancery office.

5. That the parish not get involved in the enormously expensive and truly self-defeatng task of building and maintaining a parochial school. Over 40 percent of the population of Latin America is of school age (under fifteen). Thus, if a parish of 18,000 in Panama or Puerto Rico were typical of Latin America, it would have something like 7,000 students for the parochial school system. Any effort to begin a parochial school would care for only a small percentage (say 15 percent), divide the parish into first- and second-class Catholics, and concentrate a disproportionate amount of time, money, and personnel on a small minority.

6. That the priests assigned to this project adopt the standard of living of their parishioners within reasonable limits.

7. That the priests organize, train, and direct a large group of laymen who would work with the best, most advanced, and most relevant ideas in popular catechesis and liturgy.

8. That a religious community be asked to assign personnel to the parish on the basis, not of conducting a parochial school, but of developing mass-scale catechetical methods. We have reason to believe that several prominent Chicago communities would be very interested in such a project.

9. That the entire team of priests, religious, and lay people work very closely with the ordinary of the place. One of the Latin American church's most grave problems is the failure of clergy, particularly religious, to work with the bishop.

10. That the Archdiocese of Chicago be financially responsible only for salaries—until such time as the parish would be able to provide for itself. We believe it would not be too difficult to find a pastor and people (or several) here in Chicago who would take on this burden as a mission project.

11. That one of the Chicago Catholic colleges or universities be asked to take on the project in its sociology department so that results could be scientifically verified and then written up for publication in both Latin and North America. It is very possible that foundation money would be available for this part of the project.

12. That close cooperation be maintained between the parish in Latin America and the priests working there and the Cardinal's Committee for the Spanish Speaking for the following reasons:
   a. the "experimental" parish would be a valuable training ground for Chicago personnel; we would assume that some of the priests working there might eventually be re-assigned to Spanish-speaking parishes in Chicago.
   b. the possibility of assignment to Latin America would make for greater interest among young priests in working with the Spanish-speaking in Chicago.
   c. some of the lessons learned in the parish might be applicable in Chicago parishes.
   d. the Latin American parish could be used for summer field work for interested seminarians and young priests who desire to improve their Spanish.

13. That close cooperation also be had between this project and the Latin American Bureau of NCWC. We know that Father Considine and Msgr. Quinn are very interested in this type of project and might, if methods prove successful, set up a pastoral institute there for training personnel and evolving new and better methods.

2

MANNING
THE UNMANNED

*D*uring the months of preparation and farewells, I had time to reflect on my motives for going to Panama. I wanted the adventure and the challenge, of course. But I began to realize how angry and unsettled I was. I had come to see, ever more clearly, the ugly face of authoritarianism and clericalism in the church all around me. It was beginning to dawn on me that what I was criticizing so vehemently was not merely in the structures and my fellow clerics—but it was also deep inside of me. Besides adventure, I was looking for a new self as well as for a new church and a new humanity. I had been born and nurtured as a "pyramid Catholic"—looking at the church as a wide-based triangle, with the people on the bottom, with authority and "Christ likeness" rising through priest and bishop to the top of the pyramid, the pope, the embodiment of the Catholic Church. From on top of the pyramid came grace, authenticity, and mission. Little did I realize how the Spirit would work through the people of Panama to turn my pyramid upside down.

Our unremarkable arrival in Panama gave me no clue of the radical transformations in my theology and my faith that would be wrought during my time in that challenged and challenging country. We were welcomed into San Miguelito without fanfare. I was not prepared for the heat that baked the burden of deprivation with no options and little relief. I found men without rank or respect, women bound by the burdens of family, and conditions far poorer than those in the depths of Chicago's inner city. And even more disheartening, no one cared that we were coming. Why should they?

Our "parish church" turned out to be a rickety, shed-like building made out of old boards and topped by a tin roof; it was there that we celebrated our first Mass. Emaciated and scarred dogs made up a good portion of the congregation. During the Eucharistic Prayer, two of them managed to copulate under the makeshift table we used for an altar. No one except us gringos seemed to be disturbed by this "communion." Eighty children, five women, and one man, well into his senior years, attended.

After Mass, the majority of the congregation remained, forming what seemed to be a welcoming line. Feeling warm and invited, I approached them smiling, prepared to engage in the friendly cordiality of a new minister being welcomed by his congregation. I was surprised to find that the children were waiting for their free ticket to the cinema, something they had been receiving weekly for coming to Mass. And a more devout-looking woman approached and asked for *the numero*. It took me several moments to figure out that she wanted the number for the national lottery. She must have figured that since this was our first Mass there, we would have the lucky number.

So, this is what missionary work in Panama was to be like! I was already yearning for the community I had left behind, for people who understood me and I them. Maybe that pyramid church wasn't so bad.

L ate that day, dispirited after our first formal congregational encounter, my companion priests and I walked the dusty road toward our new house, a simple home of cement blocks, much like homes all around us. As we walked, we noticed four men on a small front porch, playing dominoes, what I later discovered was a favorite Panamanian pastime. They seemed to get great enjoyment from slamming the domino pieces on the wooden table. I could see the big bottle of rum and their glasses bounce and totter with each strike. One of them called to us, "*Hola Padres. Bienvendidos.*" They seemed friendly, so we climbed the three cement steps and introduced ourselves.

One of them, Octavio Pinto, said, "We're glad you're here."

"Why?" I asked.

"Because you're going to teach the children catechism." The other men laughed in agreement.

Irked by what seemed to be a patronizing attitude, I said, "We have no intention of teaching catechism to anyone, least of all to children."

"But, then you're going to build a church," someone continued.

"Will you go to Mass if we build one?" I said.

They laughed the boisterous laugh of alcohol mixed with cynicism and dismissal and said "No."

"Then we're not going to build a church."

By now they were having difficulty continuing their light-hearted courtesy. One said, "Well, what did you come for?"

Not aware of where the words came from, but knowing that we had to say something to get their attention, I said, "To start a revolution." It worked.

Pinto sat up. Looking quite alert and sober, he said rather quickly, "This we have to talk about." Taking his lead, the others put down their dominoes and invited us to sit down. Over six-packs of beer and by flickering candlelight we talked about the revolution. The conversation was about hope and despair, expectations and fears, excitement and hesitation. We talked into the early hours of the morning, and when we left we were high—not on beer or rum, but on new friendships and shared dreams.

After our first encounter on his doorstep, Pinto and I were frequently visitors at each other's homes. He asked us if we needed anything for our new house. We said we needed an outhouse. "We will be up this afternoon to make it for you," he said. This was the first—and perhaps the most significant—parish construction.

The two-seater, as it became known, was used not only by us but also by our neighbors and lots of people attending meetings in our house.

The level of excrement—as well as its odor—began to rise, as white, live wormy things took up residence there. Now being addressed as Padre Roberto, Bob McGlinn offered to burn it out with kerosene. The results worked: the level went down, the odor was less intense, and nothing appeared to be alive—until I pitched the ashes from my cigar into the hole.

In a fraction of a second, there was a mighty whoosh and tall flames burst out of the hole like a genie out of a bottle. Contrary to rumors which abound to this day that I was in the "shithouse" when it blew up, the outhouse was not destroyed but rather singed and blackened. So was I. I left the scene with no eyelashes, no eyebrows, and no hair on my head; my face was black from the soot and red from the burn. The cigar was stuck to my face, looking like a snake that has been stepped on by a heavy foot.

Stunned and shocked, I staggered to the house only to encounter McGlinn who was working to balance remorse with stupidity and to manage almost uncontrollable laughter; he admitted that he had used gasoline instead of kerosene, a decision he had failed to disclose to anyone. Having heard the commotion, Jack Greeley had rushed out of the house and gotten our VW Beetle geared and ready to go. "Leo, come on, I'll take you to the hospital," he shouted. So we set off.

"Hurry, Jack, hurry! Go faster!" I heard myself saying. "Hurry! Go faster!"

Although my physical recovery took but weeks, it took much longer to recover from the blow to my pride and the teasing that came with it.

In learning the ways of San Miguelito, we experienced other mistakes similar to being singed and blackened. In our village, thousands of people lived near to starvation. Catholic Relief Services (CRS) asked us if we would distribute grain and powdered milk. Eager to meet the basic needs of our people, it was not difficult to say yes. We didn't know that we were getting caught in a political trap.

When the U.S. government had a surplus, it could not give directly to a poor country without affecting the economy of nations that provided goods. It thus donated the food to a religious organization, such as CRS, which, in turn, distributed the food throughout the world. We became a conduit of that distribution. The leading Panamanians figured that they were queuing up for U.S. largesse and consequently looked on us as agents of the colossus from the North. They took the most needed goods, but resented the distributors—us.

It took us months to figure out that, through our misguided efforts, we were creating a greater chasm between us and the people we wished to serve. I had to ask "What master do I serve?"

We argued amongst ourselves. Couldn't we do both—remove ourselves from the givers, stay out of the politics and the emotional overtones that rippled through the community and built hatred for the U.S. government, *and* continue to supply food to those most in need? We resolved that we couldn't do both.

When we stopped distributing, those who came every week for food complained bitterly about our actions and raised their fists in anger. I faced sleeplessness, wondering how to deal with the fallout.

Fortunately, the people who were working most closely with us understood the tension and appreciated our courage.

It took us longer to recover from our second mistake. Food was not the only need in San Miguelito. The area also needed water, roads, schools, dispensaries, public transportation, sewers—all the basic necessities of urban life—as well as those things most of us expect in a civilized society—parks, playgrounds, recreational centers, a cinema, and a police station. We decided to identify ourselves with all those needs and began to organize the burgeoning population. We called the new organization "Los Hombres Cristianos de San Miguelito." We focused solely on the men of the village.

In the first few weeks of our residence in San Miguelito, a large delegation of women came to see us and offered their support and cooperation. Again, with the struggle of figuring out who we were there to serve and whether we truly were about a "revolution," we shared our thoughts with the women—there were no men there—and we asked if we might have a year to work with the men almost exclusively.

"*Padre*," said Adelina, a beautiful woman who served as a spokesperson for the women, "our men are not to be trusted. They booze and whore and sleep their days away. They do not respect themselves or us."

"That is the problem," I retorted. "Do you want them to continue in this way? Will they turn around and love you more if I work with you instead of them?"

"Ah, *Padre*, I see," she answered. Herself the mistress of a government official, she turned to the group of women who had gathered to discuss their conditions, got their approval, and graciously, but somewhat skeptically, granted our request.

We worked sector by sector, knocking on doors and asking to speak to the man of the house. It was easy to get the men to name their needs—they were as obvious as the fingernails on the men's hands as they pointed to the muddy ruts that served as roads. We explained that if we all got together and presented a united front, there might be a chance to pressure the government for help.

Most of those men had never spoken to a priest and not one of them had had any intimate contact with one. So while they were interested in organizing themselves, their reactions ranged from distrust to wonder. In Latin America, doubts about priestly masculinity hang in the air like the cotton-like tufts on dogwood trees. Eventually, they found us to be refreshingly human when we drank beer with them and traded off-color jokes, by custom two signs—though very superficial—of masculinity.

In a short period of time, we had some four hundred men organized and divided into working committees. Government authorities were impressed and the men themselves were pleased. We were
not. There was something all wrong. The meetings were full of dis-
putes and useless wrangling. On the outside a political movement
was building, possibly a big one. But our men were not about any
movement. Many of them were heavy drinkers, womanizers, or wife-
beaters; some were all three.

We had hoped to see some change of heart. In our attempts to
build a village, we had also hoped to build a church. It didn't seem
to be happening.

I was beginning to fear that a group as unprincipled as this
could do much damage in a small country; it might even catapult
an unscrupulous leader into power. After much discussion, my fellow priests and I stopped attending meetings. Little by little the
Hombres Cristianos de San Miguelito died of in-fighting and petti-
ness. We had been singed by misguidance again. We had plunged
into action out of a sense of rage and hurt, not love and commitment. I discovered that one doesn't organize church that way.

Saul Alinksy, the most famous community organizer of the day,
had taught us in Chicago to organize on the felt needs of the people. There were so many needs in San Miguelito; we had so much
to organize. Alinksy's tactics had worked somewhat in Puerto Rican
Chicago, but in San Miguelito the needs and deprivation were too
deep. The need to survive was too urgent, the desire to have fun
was too insistent, and the urge to get ahead was too powerful. Simply organizing wasn't enough.

Despite the debacle of failed attempts to build a sense of church,
Pinto and I became fast friends. And when a raging storm hit a
local town, we rallied to help. The river Pacora, which courses
through San Martin, is ordinarily a gentle stream of clear, clean
water. When the heavy rains come, however, it is transformed into a
raging torrent.

Sheets of water had been falling for three days and, during the
night, the Pacora had surged, overflowing its banks and overwhelming everything in its path with murderous violence. It was as though
a thoroughly inebriated man, after a monstrous three-day binge, let
out a gigantic belch which served to relieve his bloated belly but as-
phyxiated every living creature within range of his poisonous breath.

Scores of little houses built along the river's bank or on the adjacent lowlands were swept away. Some thirty corpses of adults and

children were found the next morning floating far downstream or hung on trees like ghoulish decorations. The stink of cattle, chickens, and dogs drowned by the flood began to intensify with the heat of day. In the space of a few hours, a hundred families were reduced from a state of poverty to one of misery—no homes, no livelihood, no food, no clothing.

The call went out to every city and province of Panama. No one is more generous to the destitute than the poor themselves. Money, food, medicines, clothing, housewares, and coffins poured in. At the very same time another river, the Po, rose up and inundated the history-laden, art-rich city of Florence, Italy. That city—up to its neck in mud and sewage—immediately got help from across the world, especially from the U.S. where collections were taken up in thousands of parishes and churches. I do not begrudge the Florentines the emergency aid that their city received, but books and paintings were at risk there, not, as in San Martin, human lives. No global appeal was made for San Martin. Before repairs could be made, many more lives were lost and many more hearts were broken.

We did not have much time to nurse our resentment, because shortly after the killer flood, Pinto and I were on our way to our first pastoral visit in San Martin. We started out in our VW Beetle and as we turned off the Panama highway onto the unpaved road toward San Martin, we found ourselves struggling to get through the muddy morass. Pinto, who knew the countryside, had anticipated the problem. Two men on horseback awaited us, holding the reins of two other horses, neither one looking eager to be ridden in the intense heat of the day.

Before I mounted, I asked the name of my horse, a short, unshod animal with a mangy coat that evidently had never felt a brush. It had no name, as was the case for the other three horses. Over thousands of years, ever since Adam, humans have been giving names to animals, particularly to those that served them. Yet these horses had no names! I wondered what that said about the state of culture in San Martin.

I found as I worked with the barren poor that giving a horse the dignity of a name wouldn't have crossed their minds. Functional objects, like an animal that moved one from Point A to Point B, had no identity for those seeking only to survive the daily stress of their lives.

Although at a slightly different level, I later saw that the relationship of the poor with priests was not much better. They saw us as functional objects, and when we worked to break centuries-old barriers, we were met with suspicion and distrust.

We picked our way across the river, which was no more than four feet deep at the time. I said a prayer that we wouldn't see an *aguacero* (a heavy rainstorm) that day, because if one came, the river would rise rapidly and we would be unable to ford the river on our return. I did not relish the prospect of spending a night in that desolate spot.

When my father immigrated to the United States, his first job was that of a cowboy in South Dakota. He later became a mounted policeman in Chicago and always was an excellent horseman. He taught my brothers and me to ride. So, while I could hardly ride a thoroughbred in the Santa Anita Handicap, I could still do fairly well on a horse. But not on this beast! I could not adjust to its gait, try as I might. After several miles, it dawned on me that my horse had neither shoes nor gait.

What difference did it make? I asked myself. At the end of our journey, two and a half hours later, I knew. I was writhing in pain. My spiritual duties took second place to my preoccupation with my body. How would I ever endure the ride back with a sore butt and a crotch rubbed red and raw?

On the way, we rode through several San Martin hamlets, clusters of small wooden houses with corrugated iron roofs and windows without glass. There were no shops, but occasionally there was a tiny tavern. The people came out of their homes and fields to watch us, but no one greeted us as we passed by. After we had gone a hundred yards down the road, the bystanders would shout out "*Adios, Padre!*"

"Why do they say good-bye and not hello?" I asked Pinto.

He laughed. "They regard you as superior. One doesn't speak first to a person of rank. You must greet them first and then they will have permission to speak."

I tried it in the next village and, sure enough, it worked.

This trip was the first of many visits to San Martin, a trip back to the eighteenth century. As I rode along on a horse, splattered with mud in the rainy season or eating fine white dust in the dry season, I could see the great jets, passenger planes descending to land at Tocumen airport, just ten miles away. But here people lived with wagons and horses, lanterns and charcoal fires.

I had never met poorer people, in the cultural sense of deprivation. I went out there once a month and on all the major feast days. Those days of rest and rejoicing were celebrated by heavy drinking and little else. In December I looked forward to seeing how Christmas would be celebrated. No carols, no candles, no Christmas trees, no candy, no decorations, no festive dinner, no crib. Another day of drinking for the men and working for the women!

On Holy Thursday, I did my best to try to explain the meaning of the Last Supper. A large crowd had gathered. The women stood passively near the table while the men stood warily behind them. I felt as though I was talking to a passel of Martians. No one received communion; they watched Pinto and me eat the bread and drink of the cup as one would stare at a pharmacist mixing chemicals with a pestle. No matter what approach I took, I couldn't seem to get the message of the Eucharist across to them.

"*Me rindo,*" "I give up," I vented to Pinto.

Pinto readily agreed that I had not moved one heart in San Martin, but I didn't know what to do differently. He said, "Let me have a year to see what I can do."

Pinto went to San Martin often. Being a stone mason and a *maestro de obras* (a master builder), he could do almost any construction task. The men of San Martin were almost devoid of skills, so Pinto taught them how to build. At the same time, he grew to be friends with them and finally got them talking. He gave me regular reports on his progress. One day I could tell by the grin on his face that he was very pleased.

"I found the clue to the mystery. Now I know why they have no appreciation of the Mass. They have no sense of table!" he exclaimed.

Not certain that I understood, I asked, "What do you mean they have no sense of table?"

"They don't sit down to eat dinner," Pinto said, with a ring of challenge in his voice. "They eat standing up if it's a large group or they sit on chairs, if there are a few, but they don't gather around a table."

It was like thunder and lightning crashing at the same moment. I knew he was right. Inviting people to a eucharistic table just didn't make any sense to them. No wonder my call to gathering was unheard and unappreciated.

Pinto formed a plan to introduce them to the world of sit-down dinners. He patiently explained the custom of the family meal and a fraternal banquet on a larger scale. Since there was no place to hold such a meal, he gathered the men of San Martin together to build a community house. It was, for that section of the country, a big structure, large enough to accommodate forty or fifty people seated at a table. The house had a sloping thatched roof set on pillars that were young trees cut and shorn of their bark. It also had a concrete floor, a rarity in San Martin. The centerpiece was a long rectangular table made of roughly hewn planes resting on trestles.

A year later, on the next Holy Thursday, they invited me to join them. The atmosphere at San Martin was different. The people were no longer shy, not nearly so passive. They smiled, joked, and talked with Pinto, yet were somewhat reserved with me. The men seated themselves at the table. The women did the serving and did not sit with the men. Having a table had moved the culture forward by centuries; it would take a bit longer for the women to be equal to the men.

I was asked to sit at the foot of the table on the left-hand side. Pinto sat at the head of the table, eyes embracing each and every one of the thirty men who flanked both sides. Pinto began by asking his companions what they had learned during the year and what they had reason to celebrate. A lively dialogue ensued. The men shared their feelings about becoming friends and about community.

Pinto summed up their thoughts by saying that, in his opinion, they had done what the Lord had commanded them to do, and, therefore, they had a right to be at this table. He opened the Bible to St. Luke's account of the Last Supper and read it slowly in its entirety. The men paid close attention and verbally nodded in agreement several times. There was a hush when he read those oft-repeated words: "Take and eat; this is my body." Breaking homemade bread, he passed the loaf to the men on his left and on his right. The last piece came to me. Then he took a beaten-metal cup that looked as though it had been fashioned from an old hubcap. He read, "Take this cup, all of you, and drink from it, for this is the cup of my blood. Now do this in memory of me." Pinto drank from the cup and gave it to the man on his right, saying, "Brother." The others followed and so did I. The word "brother" had never before sounded so sacred. Pinto then led the men in a prayer of thanksgiving. All answered with a loud "Amen."

I felt as if I was suspended in some unreal world, one that reached beyond my life experience, one of spiritual connectedness, one that had bonded these simple people in ways I couldn't have imagined.

The women, who had been tending their huge kettles of rice and soup, had also been watching and listening in wonder at the prayer of their men. This behavior hardly matched the whoring, drinking, and lazing they so often had seen.

At Pinto's gracious nod, they began to serve food. Everyone broke into noisy chatter and loud laughter. Everyone, that is, but me.

I remained numb. I was in awe at the presence of the Lord, a sacramental presence. I was the only one there who was authorized to celebrate the Eucharist and I hadn't done anything. Yet the Eucharist had been celebrated.

Pinto hadn't confected the Eucharist; he didn't seek that kind of authority; he didn't even claim to be pious. What he had done, in union with the men of San Martin, was bring about the Lord's presence in each heart. I felt it even deeper in my bones, and I was stunned by the overpowering epiphany: "He is here, as he promised."

In the humility of my failure was birthed a spirituality that I could not have formed. Pinto did what I couldn't have done. I learned, in real time, a theology that was emerging from Vatican II: the laity sharing in the priesthood of Christ. I hadn't been minimalized; I had been confirmed in ministry with those who serve their people with love and respect. I found that Jesus could be present, not only in the consecrated bread and wine, but in the sharing of life, love, and joy.

On that Holy Thursday afternoon, after many *abrazos,* the Latin bear-hug that says so much more than a handshake, Pinto and I mounted our horses for the journey home. As we rode away, I saw newness everywhere—in the newly built cement-block houses, in the recently opened grammar school, in fields that were far better cultivated, in the road that was carefully tended, in the smiling faces of the people who stood there together waving good-bye. Pinto had built a community and had celebrated it in the tradition of the Eucharist. In my euphoria, I gave my horse a name, Prince, and hoped he would continue to be called by name.

When we got to the Pacora and saw it flowing swiftly, but not dangerously, I said, "Just think, Pinto, this is the same river that brought death and sorrow just two years ago. And now it is so peaceful. And San Martin has come alive, more alive than ever."

Pinto answered matter-of-factly, "That's the way life is."

"Yes." In full accord and having no words to capture the moment any better, I simply repeated, "That's the way life is."

It was later, when I reflected with my friend, Don Headley, on the symbol of water, that I learned an even deeper truth. "It isn't the calm water that gives us symbolism for life, Leo," he said. "It is the flowing, coursing, sometimes raging water. When the rains finally come, after months of scorching drought, they come hard, filling the wadis and river beds. As they rage, they clear out what was dead or weak, even sometimes what was good, but always bringing new life and energy. That is the sign of life. Life is the pre-eminent gift from God. It's like a flowing river, sometimes peaceful, other times raging. It brings risk, adventure, sorrow, pain, but also new life and jobs. We have but two choices. For fear of losing our lives, we can remain on the bank and watch it go by, or we can trust in the gift and dive in, taking the risk of living or dying."

At the same time that I was experiencing Pinto's emerging leadership, I met another young man. He was a short man, about twenty-nine years of age. His muscles seemed to be trying to break through his skin while tightening to resist the pressure. His hair was close-cropped and his smile was a cross between that of an imp and that of a seducer.

He introduced himself as Severino Hernandez, a resident of Villa Guadalupe, a section of San Miguelito where the government housing authority had built lower-middle-class homes. Severino was a mechanic employed in the Canal Zone, a rare type of Panamanian worker, one with both means and security. He asked if I would help him put pressure on the Ministry of Education to build a new school in Paraiso, a poor, downtrodden neighboring community.

"Why me?" I asked him. "I am a newcomer. How can I be of help?" I didn't know where his trust in me had come from; perhaps word was getting around that I wasn't here to teach catechism and build churches. Perhaps stories about Pinto and my work in San Martin were spreading. Perhaps he believed that I knew how to gather people even though the Hombres Cristianos de San Miguelito had been a failure. I had no way of knowing.

I was curious and a bit skeptical about something else too. Why would a man of simple means want to help out another community? I said, "Tell me more."

His own children, he told me, were already enrolled in the brand new school in his own neighborhood. Oh, I see it coming, I thought. "Why are you working for a new school in another neighborhood? Is it because you don't want the children of the poor to go to the new school in your area?"

With an impish smile that I was to see over and over again as Severino and I worked together, he said, "You've got it right. Is there anything wrong with that?"

Wondering whether he might think I was moralizing, I said it anyway, "Yes, a lot."

So we talked. It was the first of many conversations between us. I learned much from him about life and love and the struggle to keep both in Panamanian life. I expressed my own observations of the world today and the world tomorrow. I could tell from his eyes, which both widened and blinked, that he had never before heard some of the ideas I was expressing about the nobility of man and life.

That day and many days to come Severino would echo the voice of the people: *Somos el pueblo humilde* (We are a humble people) or *Asi somos, asi seremos* (That's the way we are and that's how we shall always be).

I would curse those phrases and say angrily, "Whoever told you that you are less than the rich, less than the Americans? You are equal, in nobility and right, to me and to every single human being."

At first I had the feeling that Severino and others who came to listen would be looking over their shoulders to see who I was really talking to. No one had spoken to them that way and lived with them to prove it. Severino, however, was one of the first to believe solidly in himself and in his own. We became good friends and companions, so good that the night he severed our friendship, I felt that the rock of my ministry had just slid from its foundation.

He said, "Father, I've enjoyed being with you. But I am saying good-bye. We cannot be friends any longer. I am one of those men we've talked about. Besides my wife and children, I have another woman and children by her in another town."

He looked deflated, as though all the air had been sucked out of him with the confession. His eyes were dry, but there was despair, resignation, even a bit of anger.

My heart went racing and I offered the most comforting message I could. "Severino, I know." I had known for months that Severino's journey was one of many roads, each struggling to find identity.

He looked at me in surprise and said, "You knew all along. Why didn't you say something? Why didn't you bawl me out?"

"Would it have done any good?" I asked. I watched as he lowered his head, shook it, and reached for a cigarette.

"I want you to know, Severino," I continued, "that I see you as a fine man and a good friend. And more, I believe that somehow, someday, you're going to straighten out that situation and then you'll become the best that's been seen around here for years and years."

He sat quietly for a while and then squashed his cigarette in the ashtray, got up, shook my hand, and said, "I wish I could believe like you, Father." I watched him leave, feeling the helplessness of one trapped, one who wanted to change the situation but felt powerless to do so. I thought of Chu Rodriguez in Chicago and heard again the struggles of a man wrapped in his own misery, trapped by his own entangled web.

I didn't see Severino for a year, except for an occasional wave as he passed our house on his way to work in the Canal Zone. Then, one day in Lent, he arrived at our house.

Chuckling, clapping his hands as one with the weight of burden removed, he said, "Well, it's all done. I want to get married on Palm Sunday." My mind went racing: two women, children with both, and he comes back and wants to get married? He read my confused state quickly, almost apologetically, although the determinedness in his demeanor left no doubt that he had pulled something together.

"Father, I never was married to either of the women I slept with. I was like the woman in the Bible who claimed she had no husband and had many. I never committed my loyalty to either one. It's taken me a while, but I have accepted what it means to be a loyal and faithful husband. Guillermina and I want to be married in the church."

It was a glorious day of celebration. Under palm branches at least three feet taller than they, before a crowd of some two thousand people, they pronounced their vows. This sacramental act, so common in the U.S., was a prophetic act of community-in-the-making. Going public with their love and faithfulness, they vowed to share their love not only with each other but also with the community.

Severino and Guillermina's marriage marked a turning point in our relationship with the people. Those two respected community members stepping out and publicly admitting that they hadn't been and wanted to be married in the church gave others permission to do the same. We saw another ministry emerging: the preparation for the sacrament of marriage—not the ceremony, but the commitment.

Severino had felt a conversion, one that soared from the inner part of his being. Somehow those long nights of conversations we used to have about what it meant to own one's own life and build community among those who matter had reached his inner core. While many U.S. men in the 1960s were crossing the country in multicolored minivans, declaring one must be free—free of responsibility and burdens of government and tradition—Severino began visiting community after community, sharing what it means to live the gospel message. He showed that he believed in himself, and, with all the masculine fervor of one who had pent up the tenderness of love within, he invited others to rethink how they live. Several years later he quit his civil service job in the Canal Zone, renouncing both salary and security to devote himself full time to evangelizing and organizing communities.

Then something happened. It was as if his energy and enthusiasm left him. I suspected that he had finally run out of gas, both physically and spiritually. I couldn't have been more wrong. Severino died at the age of thirty-five.

On his deathbed he was able to tell me what he had concealed for months. He was dying of a virulent form of leukemia. When confined to his bed, he called us all in—his wife, his children, his friends and neighbors. His cheeks were sunken and his brown skin was graying, but his eyes burned brighter than ever. He joked about his sickness and, no matter how we wanted to resist, made us laugh. Beginning with his wife and children, he asked each of us for forgiveness. We stood enraptured by his courage and honesty. He shook the hand of each person, explaining that he wished to say good-bye while he still had the strength.

I anointed him that evening with the oil of the sick, hoping desperately that he would be cured. Then I left him, feeling the overwhelming anguish of having been in the presence of the holy and selfishly wanting to hold on.

Thousands of people attended his funeral. Most of them were accustomed to the old funeral rites with black vestments and the lugubrious *Dies Irae*, a terrifying picture of death and punishment. There was no dirge that day. We selected songs of brave joyousness and wore white vestments. The words of the Roman centurion on Calvary echoed: "He was truly a good man." The throng that accompanied the coffin to the cemetery on foot was larger than that of many presidential funerals in Panama. (And Panama had seen many presidents of late, some for only days or months in office.) Standing at the gravesite, filled with the pressure of conflicting emotions, his widow Guillermina took my arm and said, "Now I really do believe in the resurrection."

I, and just about everyone who walked the miles of dusty roads to the cemetery, knew we were burying a saint. As I look back, I only wish we had proclaimed that fact, whether or not our action had formal approval from the institutional church. Severino was a flawed human being who, unlike many of us, had come face-to-face with his demons and consciously worked at conquering them, becoming an advocate of all that was true.

I was fascinated with the man from the moment I first met him. He was all man. Some men have the gift of masculinity to an extraordinary degree; when Severino walked into a room, everyone knew, both men and women, that a man had entered. He never made excuses for himself. If he had done something wrong or if he realized that there was something he had not done right, he would do something about it and let his action speak. He was kind, tolerant, loyal and, above all, idealistic. In his mind there were two things that were far bigger and more important than himself—concern for others and dreams of the future. One could see it in his eyes. It is said that our eyes are the windows of the soul. They are that and even more; they can be glimpses into the future. Severino's eyes were wide open to life and love and adventure.

Severino could tell a marvelously funny dirty joke. Experience has taught me never to trust a man who cannot tell a good dirty story or at least laugh at one. If a man cannot do it, then either he is afraid of sex, and, therefore, of life itself, or he is too serious about it and, consequently, values pleasure and life more than honor. Severino could make himself and all the rest of us laugh at our own foibles, our ludicrous habit of putting second things first. My good friend George Kane used to say, "Watch out for the pious shits," those who can't face their humanity and enjoy it.

No matter how impoverished the people of San Miguelito were, they possessed, just as we do, a desire to put some sense into their lives, to taste the intoxicating nectar of greatness. Once they found it, then they could become heroic. Bob, Jack, and I abandoned our social service, external-focused ways and decided to start where the people were, with their own insights and wisdom, to proceed from the known to the unknown. Severino and Pinto were pioneers in walking with us on that journey. We had no idea what greatness would explode.

Report on the Parish of San Miguelito
To His Eminence, Albert Cardinal Meyer, S. T. D.
April 6, 1963

The following is a report of our progress during the first month of work, the month of March.

A. *Sunday Mass:* We are now saying four Masses on Sunday in our largest barrios (two each in Paraiso and Villa Guadalupe). The average total number assisting is 500. The number of men attending is slowly rising and now stands at 50. We are of the opinion that Sunday Mass will have to be said (because of distances) in six other barrios: Monte Oscuro, San Isidro, San José, Pan de Azucar, Cristo Rey and San Antonio. Because of lack of time and manpower we have not as yet begun to say Sunday Mass regularly in these places; once we do, the number of people assisting at Mass will be much greater. There may be another reason for not saying Mass elsewhere at present which we shall mention later (Section "H3").

B. *Sunday Collection:* The first Sunday collection amounted to a little over $5.00. It has increased gradually—the last Sunday was over $18. The entire income for the month was $61.

C. *Daily Mass:* We say Mass each morning (6:00 AM) in the "*barraca*" of San Miguelito. The number assisting has risen from 2 to 25, most of whom are daily communicants. The scriptural lessons are read in Spanish, a homily on the Gospel is given and the popular participation is excellent. We are of the opinion that a well-performed daily liturgy will be the most practical method of forming a spiritual elite in the parish and giving them adequate spiritual direction. Any attempt to guide this population spiritually on an individual basis seems to be clearly out of the question.

D. *Courses in Christianity for Men:* This phase of our work we consider the most vital. The course consists of a weekly 2–3 hour discussion based on the book *La Familia de Dios* and ending with a para-liturgical ceremony. The following are the locations of the courses presently started and the number of men assisting:

Cristo Rey	15
San Isidro	25
Pan de Azucar	35
San José	<u>50</u>
	125 Total

We plan to begin courses in the month of April in Pariso, Villa Guadalupe, and Monte Oscuro. Since these courses must be given at night, we are manifestly limited by the number of evenings in the week and the number of priests available to give the courses. However, they are clearly essential, the level of conscious faith being so abysmally low.

E. Organization: This we consider the second most important part of our present work. We must create a favorable atmosphere of acceptability within which we can identify with the problems of these men and through which we can train them to civic and religious responsibility. The work is difficult because of the almost complete lack of knowledge and experience of organization among the men and a significant lack of discipline which is most evident during the meetings. The organized men "Los Hombres Cristianos de San Miguelito" are divided into committees which work in the fields of Education, "Caritas," construction, Youth and Finance. We presently have organized the following chapters of the "Hombres Cristianos":

Paraiso	90 men
Cristo Rey	45 men
Villa Guadalupe	35 men

It will be necessary to set up chapters in San Isidro, Monte Oscuro, San José, San Antonio and Pan de Azucar. But since each of these organizational efforts demands a weekly general meeting and a host of smaller committee meetings (all at night) we are clearly limited by the number of nights in the week and by the number of trained organizers (at this moment, the priests).

F. Matrimonial Course: Although we have no statistics, we are almost certain that the vast majority of our marriages are not valid Catholic marriages (one estimate—80%) and that a big percentage of couples are living *amencebados,* i.e., with no legal status whatsoever. Each day more and more couples wish to get married "by the church" but we have resolved not to validate marriages "en masse" but rather to insist on a full understanding of Christianity and its attendant commitments before we proceed with the revalidation. We have begun a Sunday afternoon "marriage course" in which 8 couples are presently enrolled. Many more couples want to get married, which fact provides us with an excellent opportunity to prepare truly Christian families but also builds a heavy work load.

G. Baptisms: On Sunday, March 31, we performed our first two baptisms in the parish. The ceremony was done almost completely in Spanish according to the newly approved (and excellent) Latin American Ritual. Some 45 people watched the ceremony and were very impressed. There are hundreds of children to be baptized, but here again we wish to move a little slowly so as to make the sacrament meaningful and not just a near-superstitious continuation of an ancient tradition.

H. Observations:

1. We have encountered a "mountain" of good will among the people, but our general impression is that their cultural and religious level is far below that of either the Mexicans or Puerto Ricans with whom we have previously worked.

2. In each of these barrios that make up the parish of San Miguelito there is a desire and effort to unify and organize themselves. They seem to look to

us priests not only to give them knowledge but more importantly to serve as a center of unity, a rallying point. We seem to have an excellent opportunity to perform one of the most significant roles of the priest, that of "Christian Community polarizer."

3. All three of us are coming to the opinion that the present manner of saying Mass for the people may perhaps be doing more harm than good. Few, if any, of those who attend have a clue as to what the Eucharist truly means. Worse, the few who do go are almost all women and children— a phenomenon which badly impresses the male portion of the population. We are of the opinion that if we were to start again, it might be wise, from a strategic point of view, (if not for pastoral-theological reasons also) to declare a moratorium on Mass, say for a year. This first year would be spent in organizing the community so as to make it naturally "Christianable" and imparting the Word of God so as to challenge the people to a truly relevant form of Christianity. When formed and ready, the people would give their answer individually and collectively in the Great Act of Thanksgiving which is the Mass.

I. A Request: Your Eminence, it hardly seems appropriate to bring this matter up so early, but since you undoubtedly are beginning to plan the summer changes, may we be so bold as to broach the subject of the fourth man for the team? We would like very much to have him as soon as possible. One reason is so he could be in on the planning with us—almost from the very beginning. Second, it takes a good long time to develop adult male catechists, so the need for another priest is greater now than it would be in a few years. We would like to have John Enright who was one of the original volunteers and who is presently studying Spanish at home.

We put the matter in your hands, Your Eminence. We do realize that you have many needs to fill and already have been very generous to this project.

Rev. Leo T. Mahon
Rev. John H. Greeley
Rev. Robert J. McGlinn

3
BUILDING
THE UNBUILDABLE

Once the first rays of the sun opened the day, there were few options but to walk boldly into the light and feel the sting of burning skin. Daytime in Central America during the dry season is oppressively hot. I used to take morning walks around the community early in the morning, before the searing sun, beating down unmercifully, made the heat unbearable.

The original settlers lived near the Canal Zone in an area called San Miguel. After World War II, people who had worked for the U.S. armed forces were let go without jobs or money with which to pay high city rents. So they moved to the outskirts of the city and "invaded" private property on which they built shacks out of discarded lumber, cardboard cartons, and scraps of corrugated iron. The whole area had become a squatter's field filled with *casas brujas,* literally translated as "witches' houses." Tin, wood, straw, and cardboard were used as raw materials—families used any means they had to build some privacy and protection.

The rolling hills of the area were covered by these shacks. Remembering the city area from which they had come, they called their new neighborhood San Miguelito, little St. Michael or St. Mickey. They had no idea it would grow into the second largest city in the country.

As I walked down and around the unpaved roads, it was common to see new huts that had sprung up overnight. The people always did

46

their construction at night. If they started during the day, they would be stopped by the police. I can't count the times when we heard the clang of hammers on wood and tin ringing through the stillness of the night air.

I was dressed in the priest's white cassock, a Latin American church tradition that we were soon to abandon, since the cassocks not only added weight but *never* looked white. During the dry season the tropical winds coated them with the dust of the unpaved streets and during the wet season the winds kicked up enough mud to create zebra patterns on otherwise solid-white robes. I approached what looked like it was becoming another squatter's hut, a tiny 4' x 6' unit that hadn't been there the day before.

"*Hola*," I said to the man who was wrapping chicken wire around a rusty pole he must have found on the road and attaching the wire to the flimsy piece of tin that would be his new roof. "May I help?"

The man tried to ignore me, stepped back, shook his head vehemently, and appeared ready to use the pole on me if prompted. I stepped forward and grabbed one end of the pole so that he could angle the roof properly.

"I have helped others," I said in a tone I had used before. It usually melted defenses and led to people accepting my hand. My message was firm and suggested that I meant no harm, only human help.

"What brings you from the hills?" I asked.

"How do you know I am from the hills?" he asked suspiciously.

"Many have come before you," I replied. In the months I had been in San Miguelito, hundreds—maybe even thousands—continued to populate the already dense area, filling in the landscape with their simple habitats.

"The radio," he answered. "We heard about the changes on the radio." He offered a hopeful smile. The "radio" was the transistor radio now making its way into areas where no electricity flowed. This tiny invention opened up new worlds to those separated by hills and towns and rivers. People began to hear about the Alliance for Progress established by John F. Kennedy. This movement they called "the changes." Peasants were coming from the mountains and hills because there was promise of opportunity, of growth, of jobs, of better education, of provision of basic goods like their northern American neighbors had: *techo, trabajo y tierra, salud, y escuela.*

"We will sign up for the lottery tomorrow," he added. Winning the lottery in San Miguelito meant getting the materials needed to build one's own concrete house. His demeanor beamed with hope and expectation. He didn't know how long he'd wait or when his family would get the lucky draw. When it happened, his family would be part of the happy changes he had been hearing about on the transistor radio.

Pedro, once he allowed me to call him by name, seemed to have memorized part of Kennedy's commitment speech to Latin America:

> And so I say to the men and women of the Americas—to the peasant in the fields, to the *obrero* in the cities, to the *estudiante* in the schools—prepare your mind and heart for the task ahead, call forth your strength, and let each devote his energies to the betterment of all so that your children and our children in this hemisphere can find an ever richer and a freer life. (*Department of State Bulletin XLIV,* No. 1136 [April 3, 1961], p. 474)

Kennedy's promises were being fulfilled. But no one knew how many people would seek such aid. No services were fast enough to serve the multitudes. Without any defined disaster, like Hurricane Katrina, Central America's cities were swelling with displaced people, people who had no work, no decent living conditions, and increasingly no hope that help would reach their families. The onrush of new squatters was enormous, far outdistancing the government's ability to provide services.

The Alliance for Progress Act had built us decent housing— three concrete homes connected by a shared courtyard. Cement, concrete, and frames came four months after we arrived. Running water came six months later. Before that, the government trucked it in and several times each day we stood in line to get water for cooking and bathing.

It was a tricky thing, getting water from the government. I had to hope each day that the truck actually would come, that we had arranged our schedule so someone would be home when the truck arrived, and that there would be enough water for all who stood in line. None of those could ever be counted on.

As the population around the community grew, the lines for water got longer. We had to calculate what time would be exactly right so that when our turn came there still would be water on the truck and, while we waited, our sandals would be able to take the sun's roasting temperature on the mud-caked roads.

We had committed ourselves to living among the poor and we were doing so.

We had gotten to know Severino and Pinto well and they had invited the men of the area who were their friends. That circle was growing, but with the influx of more and more people, suspicion was our constant neighbor. People who chose fear as their protector remained in isolation. Those in the squatters' fields had little experience with priests and most who had dealt with priests before knew them to be money collectors, requesting fees for service. Help was not given to anyone without cost and the kind of "help" the native priests offered was intangible, rooted in centuries of superstitious practices and often without care or concern for the individual seeking the help. The few coins the poor had were highly cherished; they were not to be given to white cassocks that had power, arrogance and salvation—all in their hands. To top everything, we were *gringos*, so we evoked even more distrust.

Because, in those early days, many people would walk by our home, pause, and peer in, we wondered if they had organized an hourly watch to catch us doing something scandalous. Periodically we would open the door if we saw someone lingering for more than a minute.

"Do you want to come in?" we'd ask.

The immediate sheepish response, for the most part, was "No." As we got friendlier with the people from the hills, we heard that they couldn't believe a group of men could get along and have nothing else going on.

Trust is a rubbery creature. Just when you have it in your hands, it too easily can slip away. I debated and struggled and fought the demons of the needy after we removed ourselves from the Catholic Relief Services food distribution program. We had refused to continue handing out food since it represented a mighty power controlling the downtrodden. Emotions were high: one night a small group of people walked by our home shouting that we were nasty snake-like scoundrels, feeding off their young. They were gone by the time I opened the door, but I wondered with a weighted heart whether the larger good I was seeking might be lost. Those who had so little wanted everything they could get immediately, with no waiting, no concern for the consequences, no understanding that they were growing in greater dependence rather than independence. I could no longer link my ministry to that big brother, we-are-here-to-serve-you-poor-people mindset. I had abandoned that self-importance back in the Puerto Rican borough of Chicago where the people had taught me that the answers to their happiness lay within themselves and their experience and not in what I could give them.

In 1964, riots broke out in the Canal Zone, frightening people and sending most, including the Panamanian priests, to seek some kind of refuge. Our actions during these times helped solidify our presence.

We visited hospitals and attended to the victims. Since families were too afraid to come out of their homes, we visited them. We came to be seen as men of compassion, and when we began to formalize our efforts, we discovered that we had won friends.

One night while playing dominos, the apparent national sport— given the number of shouts, slams, and beer-clanking moves I could hear up and down the streets after the sun went down—I asked Pinto, "Do you think we could pull together a group of men for some discussion on life and God?" I was thinking of the groups we had formed in the States where men came together and talked, laughed, and reflected on the more serious and meaningful aspects of life. Perhaps we might have a chance of doing the same in San Miguelito.

Pinto helped me invite men we thought might be interested. We invited only the men to make certain they would come, but several curious wives as well as teenage boys and girls came.

That first night I knew would be important. I didn't want to repeat our earlier mistakes. This evening wasn't Saul Alinksy's night; it was God's. It was to be all about living well, but not about food, water, or sewage. I wanted to open the floodgates of self-reflection and self-discovery.

It was summertime, and as the sun went down I felt the trade winds flow over us. It was as though God was showing divine pleasure by turning on the world's finest air conditioner. The men sat in a circle of chairs, orange crates, and empty beer cases. The women and children stood behind them and some stayed outside.

I began that night with a question: What did they think about the war in Vietnam? Their response was swift and unequivocal: cruel and barbaric. I asked them why they thought war was so horrible. They turned that question over and over and came up with answers such as blood, mutilation, dying, waste of money.

One man said, "It's brother against brother. What could be more evil?" They all agreed that this was the essence of war's evil.

"Who's responsible for such evil?" I queried.

They became animated, "Why, you guys, you Americans!"

"No one else?" I asked.

"Well, perhaps the French," some said. Others added, "The Viet Cong."

Finally I asked, "How about yourselves?"

"Oh, no, that's your responsibility, not ours."

"Then you've never been engaged in war?"

"No, never," they said, but they were beginning to question the question.

"That's strange," I said. "I've walked these streets on Friday and Saturday nights. I hear shouting, dishes flying, cries of pain and cursing. What is all that?"

Silence draped the room. Soft murmurs began among the women. Those women who had remained outside were leaning through the windows, afraid they would miss the next words.

"Isn't that what you said was the horror of war—brother against brother—husband against wife, parent against children, neighbor against neighbor?"

Some began to nod and bow their heads. Neither angry nor offended, to a person, they agreed. "We, too, are war-mongers!"

We concluded that night with the biblical story of Cain and Abel. The response I was to hear not only that night but many times over was, "We never knew that book was so wise!" The participants asked whether they could do another evening. I replied that of course, if they wished we could meet every week. They clapped their hands with the joy of children discovering a new toy. They promised to invite their friends.

Sleep didn't come immediately that night. I was feeling excited that maybe, just maybe, we would be building church in Panama. I was wondering where my attitudes and thoughts about war had come from. How did I get to know the terror of war? What had brought me to ask such questions? My education had been narrow. I hadn't known war in my household. West-side Irish Chicago had its turf, but hardly its horror of war. The seminary back then didn't speak of social justice.

It was Lester Hunt, a pacifist studying at the University of Chicago, who educated me. I met him when I first began to work in the black parish. I was trying to find answers to explain why my beliefs and values weren't working. He introduced me to philosophers and sociologists Nick Von Hoffman, Lou Silverman, Sally Cassidy, and Polly

Verday who were asking the questions around issues I was living every day. Their ideas about life and social issues opened me to a new way of looking at the world.

During my early months at Holy Cross parish in Chicago, I sought understanding of differences. The people I encountered every day had a different focus on life, on church, and on everything else. I would spend my evenings with these bright people who were studying for their master's and doctoral degrees, each highly critical of the social injustices around us, highly sensitive to what wasn't working in the church and in society. We were just a think-tank at the time, debating the wrongs of the world, but the experience opened a world of passion in me to uncover, in real time, what the people I was serving thought and felt and believed. It was this experience that gave me the courage to organize the Chicago Puerto Rican community. Now I had accepted the same responsibility for San Miguelito, Panama. I was beginning a familiar exploration with others of their beliefs and values, needs and expectations.

W hen we met the following week, most had come back and had brought a friend. I was feeling encouraged. I began the dialogue. "A man has intercourse with a woman. Is it good or bad? What does it mean?"

The men seemed stunned. The faces of the women broke into broad smiles. Not only were the women not afraid of the question, they wanted it asked—and answered. The lack of marital fidelity, partnership, and companionship were a national phenomenon. The women complained that their men were abusers who used them as their in-house whores, their housemaids, and their caregivers.

"We are used as a parking lot," they would say. "They come in, take up space and don't leave until they want to. They do not understand our hurts, our needs, our pains."

One man snickered and made a crude remark. Another took on the challenge. "No, let's be serious. What does it mean?" Slowly at first, they began to answer.

"Sometimes it means I need to relieve myself."

"And really what does that mean?" I asked.

"I guess it's like using a woman as a toilet," he answered.

Another answered that it often was a game where a man worked to see how much he could get out of a woman for money or by charm or force.

"Control," someone echoed. "Yeah, sex is a powerful way to stay in control."

Then a man said quietly, "It could mean I love her—I wish it always did."

Every head turned to the speaker. I let the silence hang gently in the room. After a moment weighted with awe, there were whispers, "How beautiful," "Yes," "I wish."

Like a rushing breeze, it seemed that the Spirit was fully alive. It was such a moment that I would experience again and again—the moment of revelation. Mysteriously alive, the word of God was present. The power was with the group. I needed no voice. They went on to talk of true love, how one discovers not only another but also oneself. They explored how love is the best of all gifts both to receive and to give. They expressed their thoughts about what life would be like if giving love were a true exchange between man and woman. The stars shone that evening, not only in the skies, but more brightly in that circle of friends. I ended the night reading the Genesis account of the creation of human love and marriage. Once again came the refrain, truly liturgical, "What a wise book!"

Some of the most exciting dialogues centered on the personality of Jesus. "Did he cry? Did he relieve himself? Was he ever angry? Was he ever sexually aroused? Was he tempted? Did he ever fall in love?" These questions prompted many and varied responses. In the end, however, the common conclusion was, "Yes, yes, yes—it had to be yes, if he was truly human."

Then the wonder set in: "Why, he's one of us! What do you make of that?"

One time I asked whether or not Jesus was a leader, a popular leader. If so, what was his platform? What was his vision of the future? What promises did he make? The admiration for the figure of Jesus grew and grew until I could feel the presence of his spirit among those who talked about him so avidly.

We talked frequently about death. One night I asked them to put aside catechism answers and express their deepest, truest feelings about death. "Is it real? Is it permanent?"

The answers came, chilling in their honesty. "When you're dead, you're dead—stone-cold dead. That's the end!"

"What would the world be like if we could eliminate death?" I asked next.

"It would be wonderful," they gushed. "We would all have enough time to enjoy what we've worked for."

"Yes, but what would happen to the forest if nothing in it died?"

Slowly the question registered. The picture of that no-death forest began to appear. "Why everything would starve and suffocate. It
would be all death!"

"And if no human being were to die from this moment on?"

Again, a surprising but sober conclusion: "It would be a deadly
world—no hope for anyone. There would be no reason to bring a
child into such a world." An emerging sense of the Pascal Mystery
arose—that within the sacred cycle of life, death, and resurrection,
human beings can make sense of their lives.

The series of dialogues continued for twelve weeks—ending in
dialogues about God and community that resulted in new ways of
thinking about those realities. There were those who were scandalized by such questions—they fought valiantly to make Jesus out to
be God and, therefore, not like us. The effort served only to increase the powerful light growing in people's eyes.

At the same time we were working in Panama, the renowned
Paulo Freire was developing his program of *conscientização*
among the poor in Brazil. He searched for the key words in the lives
of the people and used those words to promote dialogue, making
the people conscious of themselves, their needs, and their dreams.
His ingenious method empowered the poor to meet the real person
within. Our approach did much the same, but we merged common
secular topics with religious ones. This helped people get in touch
with the profound, the noble in themselves and in their culture.
Their attitude toward themselves, toward their future, and toward
God began to change. Hope replaced cynicism, gentleness replaced
crudeness, community replaced the sense of isolation. The people
became aware of themselves, their own wisdom and insights.

With some, the change of heart was quick and dramatic, while with
others it was slow and subtle. A few, not wanting to change or fearful of being hurt, resisted stubbornly. But the communal friendship
emerging kept everyone inside the group. It was like a Panamanian
process—two steps forward and one step back—which set the pace
so that even the crippled and the elderly could march together with
the young and able.

The book I held in my hand at each gathering gradually became
their book. Catholics in San Miguelito, not unlike 1960s Cath-

olics in the States, knew almost nothing of the Bible. At first we quoted scripture only as a way to confirm the people's life experience. As time went on, the Bible acquired enormous authority. We could open the book and read a passage whereupon the people would listen carefully and then look for a parallel experience in their own lives in order to understand the biblical message.

It was during such a set of dialogues that Modesto Contreras stopped coming. He appeared several months later. Although I didn't know what he would say, I shouldn't have been surprised when he shared his story.

"Modesto," I said giving him a warm embrace, "it is so good to see you again."

Smiling as though he had eaten a whole iguana, his words rushed with pride, "I can read."

Then he went on. "I never had reason enough to read before. My wife took care of those needs. But when you began reading passages from the Bible, I had to be able to read them myself."

He explained that during the past three months, his wife had spent each evening teaching him to read. Painstakingly he mastered the words, the context of a sentence, and eventually the art of understanding how ideas were put together. He and his wife used the Bible whenever they could to build his knowledge. He was rarely seen after that without a copy of the *Good News* in his hand.

This spiritual awakening was no revolution. It was an evolution. Little by little, beliefs and values began to change. When a Panamanian man said he was a "Catholic," it meant he was devoted to some saint and celebrated with a day of drunken binging. Being Catholic was devoid of the messages of Christ and meant being totally dependent on external religious practices. The kind of Christianity we were instilling was different. It invited a daily review of how one treated oneself and others.

Through the sharing of faith, through communal seeking of the truth, the people of the barrio began to take on a new relationship with one another. They were learning to understand, accept, respect, and even love one another, to dream and work together. It did not take us long to recognize and name the phenomenon—church in its original meaning—the faithful ones gathered around the personality of Jesus, asking the same questions, healing and forgiving one another, dreaming with him a new vision, willing by his grace to be the sign of a new world.

We called these groups *igesiolas,* little churches. And they evolved into twelve-week programs, La Familia de Dios.

We had approached our mission to Panama with three basic principles and they were beginning to form. There was the need to create a living Christian community—the family of God, the kingdom of God. Our forming of twelve-week courses in small groups was accomplishing just that. We needed to form the community in and through the scriptures. We had introduced the Bible and it was thriving in the hands of the people. We were to be prophets. We, the priests and the sisters and the laymen who had joined us, were to become sensitive to the Word of God and sensitive to the people seeking the Word. Through the animation of the Holy Spirit, we were building a church—something that had seemed only months ago to be unbuildable.

It was at one of our team's morning prayer and planning meetings that we decided it was time to recruit and train lay leaders. Such men had already begun to emerge: Pinto and Severino and Fidel Gonzalez, a growing enthusiast of our mission and work. These men had been trained "on the job." They watched us, learned from us, applied their wisdom and understanding, and expanded their giftedness and, in turn, ours. But training had been informal, and now, it appeared, incomplete for what we saw the future holding.

"How will we get them trained?" Jack asked. "Work and family fill their lives."

"The burning desire for more is there," I said.

"We need a motivator, an instigator, one who inspires with the tongue of the Holy Spirit," declared Bob.

In a rolling minute, Chu Rodriguez came flashing through my mind. The fervor of the first Cursillo at that rustic Chicago farmhouse re-entered my gut and I felt the same flush of being alive rise within.

Enthusiastically, Chu, formally known as Don Jesus Rodriguez, came to San Miguelito. We held a mission for three Sundays, 7:00 AM to 7:00 PM. We advertised—newspapers, radio, and television all announced the event. More than a thousand people came.

He began with, "Please do not be shocked to see a layman speaking to you this morning. Back in Chicago, I have a wife and eight children. I come to you because I love like you do, I believe like you do, and I am like you are."

Chu's grasp of sacred scripture, his ability to use his life experience in storytelling, and his great oratorical skill, as I knew, were quick to move the people. The Spirit of God truly worked through him, like a forest flame reaching across the tops of tall trees and touching each in turn with its burning brand.

After Chu's work, it was not difficult to recruit candidates for lay leadership. We invited thirty men to join us to be adult catechists, Christian community organizers. We called them lay deacons. Their training involved more than three intensive months teaching them the Familia de Dios program so they could run the program; it meant preparing them to minister among their people and to be visibly engaged as parish lectors and commentators, something that was unusual in the 1960s.

The sheer number of people wanting to get involved in little church communities would soon outnumber our ability to serve them. From my work in Chicago, I had learned that the human capability to sustain essential connectedness peaks at about four hundred people per leader. The timing of our decision to develop lay deacons was good. We had already hosted six hundred in small groups within the past year and the number of those interested continued to grow.

These lay deacons became our brothers—Pablo and Rafael and Fidel and Ernesto among them. Their families became our families. We journeyed together through this faith-enlightening, faith-sharing experience.

Wednesday night in San Miguelito became "deacon night," not just a mandatory night, but a night when all else was suspended. We were together—brothers in faith, building faith, building community. Toni and Marcelino would tell of their travels to Pan de Azucar and joke in graphic detail about how Toni had conquered the foot-long scorpion that almost bit him as he stepped out of the car. Eugenio and Julio would talk about their visit to Apartment #9 and how they overheard a couple arguing about what it was *he* did between the hours of work and his return home.

Somebody would tease Pablo, who used to be called the "playboy" of San Miguelito, and question what his collection agency was collecting. Pablo, in addition to his small group ministry, was committed to making the mission of San Miguelito financially independent of Chicago. He initiated a system of "head tax" and once a month collected one or two dollars from each family actively involved in the community.

Rafael, bitterly anti-gringo and anti-clerical one year before, would speak with the poetry of a newly converted disciple. He was alive with the spirit of building community and came up with the idea of establishing a parish cooperative supermarket. He traveled to the States to learn what it would take to build a cooperative in San Miguelito.

No evening would go by without a particularly poignant story being told. One time Fidel Gonzalez told of how a member of his *iglesiola* resolved an ugly situation.

One man in his community of twenty families returned to his previous ways, spending his wages on drink, carousing with his beer buddies, and sleeping with women other than his wife. The electricity in his house had been cut off because he hadn't paid the bill in over a year. His behavior degenerated to the point of striking his wife during a violent argument.

Two men from the *iglesiola* approached him as he was racing out of the house for another night of rendezvous. They promised him moral and financial help if he would reform, but warned him that if he continued, he would be cut off from all contact, friendship, and fiestas, all of which were increasingly meaningful for the community of San Miguelito.

Fidel described how the man broke into tears, deeply touching the emotions of all who were present. He begged for their forgiveness and help.

"Yes," added Jack. "He approached me last Sunday and said, 'I thought I knew who my friends were' (referring to his drinking buddies), "but now I know who my real friends are. I promise you, *Padre*, as I promised the men, that with their help, I won't get into trouble again."

Fidel's story took on even more meaning when we could celebrate that it wasn't the priest, it wasn't even the lay deacon, it was the members of the community who approached each other and called forth the conversion. They converted themselves, aware of their call to help those in need.

It was often that I would hear Jack say, "I don't want to be anywhere but here tonight. You are the heart of all we do. You are the heart of all we are."

Report to
His Eminence, Albert Cardinal Meyer, S.T.D.
On the Parish of San Miguelito

Your Eminence,

Much has happened since we sent you our last report on July 9, 1963. Please allow us to summarize under four headings the more significant events:

I. The Mission
Our people need and will need for a long time concentrated preaching of the Word of God. What they know is very limited and that, many times, way off the center of Catholic Faith, A good mission was clearly in order but first we had to clear many obstacles:

> *Where*—the *barraca* we use for a church has a 200 person capacity: not enough.

> *When*—the distances are great in our parish and when it rains, the roads are almost impassable: an evening mission would be unfeasible.

> *What*—the traditional mission concentrates on the four last things: good doctrine but usually far too individualistic.

> *Who*—to preach the Word of God—essentially the call of God to unity in Christ by sacrificial love. Few, if any, priests down here have broken out of the mold of preaching individual salvation and moved on to the Word of God and the Pascal Mystery. Not one of them could do the latter in a simple enough but profound manner.

We attempted to solve our problems by arranging to use the lovely campus of Colegio Belen about five miles away from us; the sisters loaned us their school buses for transport; we held the mission on three successive Sundays from 7:00 AM to 7:00 PM. For a speaker we brought in a layman, Don Jesus Rodriguez, the chief catechist for the Cardinal's Committee for the Spanish Speaking in Chicago, Don Jesus is one of the finest preachers (lay or cleric) we have ever heard. He has had plenty of experience and an intuitive bent for good theology.

To sum it all up, the mission was highly successful: the first Sunday for young people 15–21, 350 attended; the second Sunday 215 men came; at the last mission 350 women assisted. We worked hard with Don Jesus preparing the material for the talks and the paraliturgy or liturgy after each talk. The effect was little short of spectacular. He held all three audiences in his hand for hours on end with the most solid of doctrine, mostly by talking their language and using their thought patterns, For instance, his talk on Christ was a classic (we really should print it up). Instead of using meaningless (to them) forms like shepherd or king, he presented Christ as the great revolutionary leader (a concept fascinating to these people who are so interested in revolution).

Results:
- – Sunday Mass attendance soared. The number of men going to Mass went up to 150—a true phenomenon in Panama,
- – Many couples came to us to have their marriages revalidated,
- – Many young men came to us asking: "Father, what must I do to be like Don Jesus and do the kind of work he does?" We believe no cleric, be he a Bossuet or a Sheen, could have had that particular effect on our men: it gives one an idea of the possibilities of using laymen in this apostolate.

II. Intensive Course for Lay Catechists

While Don Jesus was still with us, we invited thirty men from all the various sectors of the parish to begin an intensive course in Christian doctrine with an eye to forming them into adult catechists, Christian Community organizers, "lay deacons"—if such be the will of the bishops and the supreme bishop.

Twenty-six men came and have been coming ever since—five hours a week. The course is almost over now and we happily can report that we have formed a solid nucleus of trained laymen and that we learned a great deal from them of the Panamanian mentality. In a few weeks they will go out to begin their own adult discussion groups in the various sectors of the parish. One man is already teaching a class of twelve adults; many are also our lectors and commentarists for the Divine Liturgy.

We believe we have gotten a good start on one of the principal facets of our experimental plan. Virtually every soul (all 25,000) in our parish needs a solid ground in the faith; unless we train literally hundreds to do this work, we cannot hope to accomplish our mission here.

Interesting sidelight: three young unmarried men in college, all participants in the course, have indicated their desire to enter the seminary.

III. The Fiestas Patronales

The biggest occasion each year in a Latin American community is the Patronal Feast Day—in our case, that of St. Michael on September 29. There is usually lots of dancing, games, climaxed by the big procession (carrying the statue of the saint) and Mass on the feast day itself.

For several years, a few "enterprising" people in the area have put on the Fiestas—i.e., built the temporary *toldos* (dance pavilions), paid the priest to come for the Mass, bought the fireworks, etc.—all for the "community" benefit but each year, strangely enough, they "broke even."

Many of the people wanted the Fiestas Patronales used this year to raise funds for our building project. So a Junta de Festejas of some sixty people, most of them men, was organized with Father Mahon serving as treasurer, The Junta worked very hard and managed to put up two large (one 60' x 130', the other 60' x 100') toldos. The "enterprisers" entered the field by building still two more *toldos*. By custom, only the Junta de Festejas can get permission for dances or games and we tried to prevent this commercial competition but got nowhere principally because this is election-campaign time in Panama in which the politicians will do almost anything to win even a few votes. So the stage was set for the big test.

How important was this Fiesta to us in our work? Besides making some money, there was a lot of prestige on the line. The average Panamanian strives desperately for community and prestige, but fear and a strong sense of inferiority usually combine to make the first two impossible. Sure enough, halfway through the preparatory stages, as the debts began to pile up, the men had fallen into a state of bickering, carping and disunity. We called them all together and told them that our unity and faith in ourselves were far more important than money: "So, if we're going to fail, let's go down together and like men; if we succeed, let's also do it together." The medicine worked and there was very little disharmony after that.

Well, the Fiestas Patronales were celebrated from September 26 to the 30th. They were in every sense a success:

> **Financially:** Our expenses ran almost to $10,000 and we got exactly that much back so we, too, "broke even." But we really did make money. You see, we built one large building which will stand as our church and center until we can build others. When we demolish it, we can get about $3,000 from salvageable materials. Meanwhile, we can put on more activities to raise money.

> **Religiously:** Six hundred people (our largest single Mass attendance so far) attended the Community Mass. Everybody sang the Mass and dialogued with the celebrant (about 25 men communicated). In the afternoon (Sunday 29th) we had the procession. It was one of the finest ever seen in Panama and in a country so devoted to processions, that's saying something.

> **Socially:** The men found out they could succeed by hard work and faith and discipline. They are delighted. Besides, they won a great deal of badly-needed prestige—every newspaper and both television channels gave wide coverage to the Fiestas.

Politically: The local "enterprisers" had a political as well as a financial stake in the Fiestas. They suffered severely in both. It may be that their back is broken. On the other hand, the politicians are getting very friendly to us as they see signs of growing organization.

IV. The Local Panamanian Clergy

We were privileged to meet all the native secular Panamanian clergy at the recent annual retreat. They impress us as being mostly young, intelligent, pious and open. They are not well molded as a group and like most Panamanians feel inferior and are fearful. They seem to like us as well as we do them and they are fascinated by our new ideas and methods. We meet every Wednesday—all of us together—to discuss pastoral problems. This work may easily be one of the most important we do here in Panama.

Leo T. Mahon
John H. Greeley
Robert J. McGlinn

San Miguelito, October 9, 1963

4
QUESTIONING
THE UNQUESTIONABLE

Where did you say you were going to work? San Miguelito? Good luck. You are going to need it." Those were the first and almost only words of welcome from the priests of Panama. Even though we were staying in the bishop's house when we first arrived and there was the constant activity of priests coming and going, we engaged with them very little. They would look at us curiously, drop their eyes, and scurry off. It was hard at first to decipher their behavior.

I would joke with Jack and Bob that the Panamanian priests maintained the best "custody of the eyes" that I had ever seen. Custody of the eyes was an antiquated practice where seminarians learned to keep their eyes cast down so that they would not be distracted by the world, especially the lure of the opposite sex, and so they could stay focused on communing with God. We hardly qualified as tempting goddesses, but it was amazing how engaged they could be with each other until one of us would approach and they would turn silent and begin studying the bumps on the concrete floor.

Sometimes, to make sense out of their distance, we'd concoct some dialogue. We would imagine them saying:

> *Padres*, we are so pleased you are here. You American priests have a population of 800 Catholics to one priest. Our ratio is 10,000 to every one priest. We need your help.

The poor, we cannot reach.

The rich have turned to lusting for the pleasure, money, and things your television is showing them. We cannot bring them salvation with this pagan mindset.

We are tired, *hermanos*. Our work is without pleasure. We have exhausted our abilities ... and our understanding.

But know, dear *amigos*, you are most welcome to try. Don't expect much.

We met one priest who encouraged us, Monseñor Felix Alvarado, a native Panamanian, former secretary to the archbishop, and presently the pastor of Santa Ana, the busiest and the most prestigious of Panama's churches. Alvarado sought us out and listened to our dreams and expectations. He visited us several times once we moved to a simple home.

Our dialogue was a genuine give-and-take of pastorally focused theology. We felt in alignment with his vision, his beliefs, and his expectations of church, especially in contrast to the others we had met.

"What if I joined you? I will be seeing the archbishop next week. I would resign from my parish and ask permission to join your team," he added hopefully.

I felt a rush of excitement. He was respected by his peers; I was already sensing that we were going to need some connecting point with the local church. What a bonus it would be to have him on board! We shook hands in agreement. "Hurry back with good news," I responded.

That week he was stricken with a massive heart attack and died instantly. He was in his thirties. Rumors were that he was slated to become a bishop. I often wondered what would have happened had he lived. With his death, we lost what could have been our best channel of communication with the native clergy. None better ever came along.

Deterioration of priests' relations continued the more we got to know the practices of the local church. One of the cultural practices that set us apart was how the priests got their financial support. The United States had almost completely abandoned a centuries-old practice of Catholic priests accepting donations for services rendered. Not so in Panama. The practice thrived.

One day, while walking in the city, I saw a line of people standing on the steps of the church. The priest was sitting near the entrance and the line seemed to get longer as I watched. I asked a woman descending from the church what was going on. She carried the burden of the poor, a child at her hips, barely clothed, and there were two others with little expression in their eyes close in age trailing behind her.

"Today is the anniversary of *mi madre's* death," she said. "I asked the *padre* to say a prayer for her."

I looked over the crowd and saw the raggedness of the poor in each of these people. "And what are the others asking for?"

"I do not know," she answered, "but at 10:00 every day, until the last person leaves, the holy priest is at the church to offer prayers to God."

Sensing there was more than service involved, I asked, "And how much does Father charge for his prayers?"

"Oh, it is not a *charge*," she answered defensively. "It is an offering. He asks 25 cents for each prayer. He is a *holy* man; God will hear his words."

I was to learn that other such "offerings" were expected. On All Souls Day, the priests spent the entire day in a cemetery saying prayers for grieving people. Another custom was that they would "accept" $1.00 for giving a dispensation from the Lenten fast.

It was common to require that $5.00 be paid before a baptism, thus, in effect, creating a charge for the sacrament.

It is somewhat unfair to blame the priests in Panama for these questionable practices because they inherited a system from the Middle Ages and hadn't yet let it go. For some, abandonment of the practices would have meant starvation; the hierarchical church did not support their basic needs.

We refused to accept money for our services and this threatened the livelihood of the native priests.

It wasn't only the financial practices that separated us from the Panamanian priests. It was our theology. One disquieting skirmish occurred during the annual catechetical competition. Children from all the parishes competed against one another answering questions from a panel, much like a spelling bee.

Two children from San Miguelito had arrived at the finals. When they were asked, "If a priest is coming to administer the sacrament of extreme unction, what is the most important thing to have ready?" the little boy and the even smaller girl paled, both faces completely blank.

The panel was about to ask them to sit down when one of its members, a young Jesuit, said, "Hold on. Maybe they know the sacrament by its new name, the anointing of the sick."

The children's eyes lit up immediately. They put their heads together and answered, "The most important thing is to gather the community."

Silence ensued.

The members of the panel looked down at their notes where the answers were printed and saw the correct answer: "*Cotton,* so the priest can wipe his fingers."

Our children did not win the contest, but the panel created a special award and gave it to them—for creative imagination. To have argued that they had a better answer than the "correct" answer would have been like pointing out that a worm was eating through a cherished Bible.

Eventually the competition was cancelled, since more children each year, most from the missions we were serving, were coming up with answers that weren't in the "answer book."

Much of our theology grew out of our sense of liturgy, and that quickly evolved into a point of contention between us and the local priests.

As we got to know the people, we saw that their life was one of deprivation, an utter poverty not only of material but also of spiritual resources. They had little understanding of their faith, and the use of Latin, the language of the church, hadn't helped.

Knowing that permission to use Spanish instead of Latin was soon about to be given, we anticipated the change and began to use the language of the people before it was "licit" to do so. The local clergy were upset and complained—some because they wanted to keep Latin and others because we were doing things *without* authorization.

As we got to know the women of the area, many of them superb seamstresses, we invited them to make vestments, altar cloths, and banners using native cloth and folkloric designs.

And music, ah, that is how our liturgies came alive. At one Easter Vigil liturgy, I was playing the organ and José Nelson Rios, or

Pepe, as he liked to be called, was improvising verses to the slow and stately music. At the end of communion, Pepe asked me with a wink if he could do a song the way it should be done. I gave him the nod and he swung into a lively rhythm that soon had the people dancing and singing. I realized once again how much I had to learn about where the spirit of real ministry lies.

Not long after that, Pepe made a Cursillo and I suggested that he express his new-found fascination with his faith by composing a folk Mass. Pepe was a clerk in a government agency and had no formal training in music. He looked at me with both doubt and expectation and said shyly, "Do you really think I could?"

"Yes, I do."

It took him over a year. *Misa Tipica de San Miguelito* became one of the first to come out of an indigenous culture in Latin America; it was the first in Central America. This was the music of the people and they embraced it as they would have welcomed a fresh fountain of cold running water on a hot day.

Dancing during liturgy was a natural next. The native rhythm was so moving that spontaneous dancing couldn't be contained. We encouraged dance, especially during the great liturgies of the year: Christmas and Easter.

The papal nuncio, whom I was to encounter in many uncomfortable ways during my years in Panama, when asked if he had ever attended a liturgy in San Miguelito, was heard to say, "those people have vulgarized the sacred liturgy."

The principal reason for the mounting tension that grew between the local priests and us became the changing "attitude" of the people of San Miguelito.

Many people had begun to experience church as Christ in community and were defining themselves as church, not as its subjects, but more as its owners. They were enthusiastic about this and quite negative about what they considered to be non-authentic Christianity.

They were critical of the clergy who had not explained that Christianity was a call to freedom. They also blamed them for their not "being allowed to read the Bible."

"The church is emerging from the embers of an old system," I would say. "Vatican II has opened our eyes to a new church."

I saw Vatican II also as history's longest, grandest, and most expensive wake. Being Irish, I knew wakes and loved a good wake. Wakes were times to sing of the glories of the past, to renew friendships, and to start all over again. Vatican II seemed to be such a wake. And as I viewed the "corpse," the ways of the church being challenged and set aside, I realized that there were a lot of cosmetics superficially helping make things look good. We had a long road ahead, one filled with the beliefs of a resurrection people, one willing to work at building a new way of being.

It was hard to dampen the fires of evangelical fervor, especially when the gasoline of anticlericalism was poured on those fires. In every town in Panama, Christendom can be seen in the central plaza: a green space faced by the imposing structures of the tri-partite system—the church, the city hall, and the Army headquarters. Not only is the church seen as part of the establishment, but the clergy is viewed as no different from other men when it comes to their sexual appetites. So many Panamanian jokes are directed at the avarice or lust of the men of the cloth.

One day, Adelina de Duarte, who had helped the women understand that we must work first with the men and had been responsible for getting several of the men to come to the church, approached me.

"*Padre*," she said, "do you know Maria Garcia?"

"No," I answered.

"She lives close to the parish," she explained.

"Adelina, I don't know her," I repeated, now wondering why she was continuing this line of questioning. "Why do you ask?"

"She is going around saying she is your mistress," she answered.

I had wondered how long it would be before such accusations would take place. Womanizing was a practice not uncommon among the powerful, clergy included. We were watched at every turn to see if we would engage in the same activities.

"Do you believe I have a mistress? Any mistress?" I asked, looking at her directly.

Her long black eyelashes fluttered as she worked to maintain her composure.

"A group of us were talking the other day," she began. "It is difficult to understand how single, virile men are not sexually involved. You are handsome. You are bright. You are caring. Every woman in Panama loves you. Why wouldn't you choose a woman to be with you?"

As I listened, I wondered if her compliments were their own come-on and she herself had intentions, since she, too, had been a mistress, or whether she was just talking out loud about a phenomenon she couldn't understand. While I trusted Adelina, I kept my guard up. I let her continue, feeling a little uncomfortable.

"So, Adelina," I asked, "Why are you telling me all this?"

"Well, we *hermanas* came to a conclusion. There are three kinds of priests: those who should get married, those who shouldn't get married, and those who could get married and won't."

Now she had my curiosity, "Where do I fit in?"

"We all agreed. You are one of those who could get married, but you won't. We couldn't imagine you even having a mistress. You believe too much in the sacredness of a promise. I'm glad you don't know Maria. *Padre*, have a good day."

She walked away, leaving me to think. Perhaps I was modeling what I believed.

O ur first church, Cristo Redentor in San Miguelito, caused irreconcilable tension with the native priests. Its exterior was inviting: a circular structure built like a huge tent with no pillars and with open sides to catch the cooling breezes. It was the interior that was controversial.

We had asked Lillian Brule, an artist from Joliet, Illinois, who had solid scriptural grounding and who had painted the murals at the Cursillo center in Chicago, to paint our murals. She accepted the commission for a pittance, but insisted on two conditions: that she would have artistic freedom and that she be allowed to live among the people for a time long enough to get to know them.

After two years, Lillian produced the preliminary sketches for three large murals. When I first saw them, I saw the people's experiences coming alive and I also caught the tinge of anti-clericalism. I thought about asking her to tone down one of the images, but I wanted to respect her artistic freedom and couldn't help acknowledging that she had captured the sentiment of the world in which the people lived.

The mural behind the main altar was dedicated to liberation: the poor were gathered around a lantern discussing their life experience in the light of scripture. The rays of light showed that they were inspired to challenge the domination of the establishment, the politicians, the military, and the clergy.

The clergy were depicted as tall, severe figures garbed in black, holding a cross above their heads in their right hand while grasping money with their left.

Once the wall was painted and opened for viewing, priests and bishops visiting the church saw only its offensive message. They would shake their heads and point their fingers in angry objection.

After a while, I began to like the strong message depicted in the mural. Why can we not learn to accept criticism, even harsh criticism? If we had learned, we might never have lost Martin Luther, James Joyce may not have left the church, and both Oroczco and Rivera might well have made their powerful statements within the church and not outside of it.

Later a Belgian welder, Victor van de Broeck, came to visit our church and offered to add ironwork to the exterior fencing of the church as a memento to his companions who had suffered in concentration camps. This ironwork became more symbolic when, in 1975, I left Panama and political leaders ordered the tarring of his work, filling every lattice with blackness.

A ll the criticism and attacks seemed to coalesce and form one swift, pointed arrow—at me, and secondarily, at my team. The charge? Arrogance.

I had heard snatches, hints, and rumors. They would generally come in a "*se dice*" manner: "It is being said, by others, of course . . ."

The first time it was spoken openly it was said by the papal nuncio, in front of a group of priest consulters. "You know you people are arrogant."

I looked around the room as silence held like a thick curtain.

"What do you mean?" I asked. A flood of responses came back from every direction. I listened and nodded, demonstrating that I was hearing what they were saying. I decided not to respond just then.

"You act like you are better educated."

"Nothing good seems to have happened before you came."

"You have taken away our income."

"You treat us as if we were ignorant of our own people and our own culture."

The list of accusations went on for longer than I could ever watch minutes on the clock. By the time they were suggesting that we were ignoring Panamanian ways, my anger rose and I finally spoke.

"That's where you are arrogant. You presume you know how the people think and feel because you were born here. I challenge that presumption. We are strangers to this land and we have to question and to listen. But you do not!"

Even though the room contained more than native priests, I chose not to address the other arrogance. Some of the priests were Spanish and they exhibited a *colonial* arrogance. They, conscious of the "mother" culture from Spain, looked down on the people in the colonies such as Panama. The reality that Panamanian culture was a mixture of influences—from Spain, France, the West Indies, and the United States—all superimposed on indigenous Indian culture seemed beyond their comprehension.

I figured that if a group of priests from Bolivia were to work in the poorest slums of Chicago and achieve success, then surely we would be chagrined by that success. I hoped, however, that we would have the grace to ask them what they were doing and why. The priests of Panama didn't seem to seek those answers, nor ask the questions. Their accusations felt more like efforts to discredit our work.

Among the few who had begun to take interest in our work was one Panamanian church dignitary, Archbishop Clavel. He had been out to visit us in San Miguelito several times. He had seen the disputed mural at Cristo Redentor and was able to translate it as a message for reform. He showed interest in our work and the apparent engagement of our people.

At a gathering of the priests of Panama, ourselves included, several heated exchanges had taken place between Clavel and the priests who disliked his apparent interest in our work.

"Monseñor, what you really want is for us to be like the priests of San Miguelito?" The glove had been flung to the floor.

Clavel responded, "I guess you might put it that way. Yes, that's what I want."

The priests went away bitter and irreconciled. Clavel had signed his own "death warrant." In a few years the dissatisfaction would be so great that he would be forced to resign.

The accusation that I was arrogant rankled. Do I feel special? Am I different? My answers were *yes*. If that is what arrogance means, then I am arrogant.

I learned it from my parents. I was never allowed, after having done something unworthy, to excuse myself by claiming that others were doing the same thing. I was taught that I came from people who were downright special, with a high sense of morality and nobility. My mother used to say, "No one is better than we are. We're not any better than anyone else, but there's nobody better than we are."

And, having been raised in the United States of America, I was indoctrinated in the land of "manifest destiny" in the "freest, greatest nation on earth." I accepted those self-serving beliefs without doubt, until much later in life. I noticed how widespread that attitude was when people visited us from the States. Somehow the people always knew which visitors were *gringos*, no matter their race, color, or dress. One day a parishioner asked about a particular visitor, correctly identifying him as coming from the States.

"What makes you think that?" I asked. Looking at the visitor's simple dress, hair tone, and skin color, I myself believed he looked more Panamanian that the parishioner did.

"Oh, it's easy," she said. "You can always tell a *gringo* from the States. He stands as though he owns the land he's standing on."

Perhaps it was my stance, I mused, that added to my arrogance. I made a note to monitor my gait.

Another charge was leveled at a public meeting. This time it felt personal, really personal. I was receiving invitations to talk about San Miguelito in many places, such as El Salvador, Costa Rica, Guatemala, Nicaragua, Peru, and Brazil.

I had been invited to speak in Chile at the annual South American Catholic Church conference. A large crowd of lay people, priests, and bishops had gathered to hear my talk. When I finished, one of the bishops present rose to ask me a question.

"Leo, did it ever occur to you that it all happened because of you? That it is your gift, your charisma, that makes the story of San Miguelito, and that without you there would be very little to talk about?"

It wasn't the first time I had heard such a remark, but usually it was uttered by a sycophant or an unperceptive observer. Now I felt the sting because it came from a distinguished source in a public forum. The question hurt and upset me.

It insulted the dedicated and gifted members of the team: Jack Greeley, Bob McGlinn, and those who were to follow, like John Enright and Don Headley. It offended the remarkable lay leaders such as Octavio Pinto, Severino Hernandez, and Adelina de Duarte. It insulted the Maryknoll sisters who had begun to work with us. None were being slavish imitators and unthinking water carriers. It was as a group that we thought, dreamed, and worked. The Mahon of my early priesthood had learned that the superman, the solo traveler, the one who knew the answers while others were just to follow, had disappeared. At Holy Cross in Chicago, for a short period the

African Americans with whom I had worked in the early 1950s had allowed me to direct while they followed. The Puerto Ricans of the late 1950s hadn't.

My friends at the University of Chicago, too, had opened my eyes to how narrow my understanding of life was and how dependent I had to be on others if I was to be successful. My mission friends kept me aware daily that it was the team that was the dynamic.

"Bishop," I responded, "you meant those words as a compliment, I believe. I cannot say thank you. The work and the success of San Miguelito is due fully to the team.

"From the description I just gave you of what is happening in Panama and how it is happening, can you truly attribute this work to one man? I am a gifted man and I am well aware of those gifts. Yet, everyone on the team has gifts that are essential to our mission's well-being. It is in our unity, our working together, that our success lies."

Report to
His Eminence Albert Cardinal Meyer, S.T.D.
On the Parish of San Miguelito

I. Ecclesiastical Appointments

The Archdiocese of Panama has been without an Ordinary since the death of Archbishop Francis Beckmann last October in Rome Bishop McGrath, auxiliary to the Archbishop, was elected Vicar Capitular for the inter-regum.

Two weeks ago the Papal Nuncio announced two important changes in the hierarchy of Panama. The province of Veraguas was cut off from the Archdiocese of Panama and formed into a new diocese with Santiago as its See City. The first Ordinary is to be Bishop Mark McGrath. The new diocese has a population of 120,000 people with 10 priests, 6 sisters and 4 brothers. The province is one of the most backward in Panama: 70 percent of the population is illiterate, 20 percent are aboriginal Indians. The area is a center of unrest both among the "campesinos" and among the students in the normal school at Santiago where Communist influence is formidable. Bishop McGrath is young and energetic with a sound pastoral-theological vision. We wish him well in his new and difficult post and clearly we shall miss him in Panama.

The Holy See two days later announced that Bishop Tomas Clavel, presently ordinary of David, had been promoted to the metropolitan See of Panama. Panama has over 400,000 Catholics and 90 priests. There are serious problems in Panama also, such as the uneven distribution of priests and an over-identification with the rich.

Bishop Clavel is young (42), personable and astute. He becomes the first native Panamanian to succeed to the archbishopric in 150 years. We wish him well in these critical years ahead and we promise him our full cooperation and loyalty.

II. Holy Week

There remains in the Catholic Faith of the Panamanian people a deep sense of the sacredness of Holy Week. Immense numbers of people who rarely, if ever, attend Mass throughout the year, try to be faithful to the ancient tradition of Holy Week. Many journey to the interior where the traditions are preserved more faithfully.

In what do these observances consist? Principally in the great processions of Holy Week. These derive from the Spanish extra-liturgical traditions. Evidently the Spanish clergy found the Latin liturgy almost completely useless for the instruction and edification of their people. Afortiori it did not suit the needs of a missionary apostolate in Latin America. The clergy then performed the liturgy almost privately in the church and took the popular devotion out to the streets where they organized processions in the Spanish tradition of living tableaus depicting various events in the life and passion of the Lord.

These processions have the advantage of being very popular (they draw thousands) and somewhat instructive. They fail to give, however, a sense of living mystery and of the necessity for interior conversion. In planning our Holy Week in San Miguelito we were thus blessed by the desire of the people to sanctify the great week and their willingness to spend long hours in the ceremonies. At the same time we were hampered by the procession tradition (wherein the procession is the great act, not the liturgy) and also by the Roman Liturgy, which, although greatly simplified, is still ill-suited, both in language and form, to popular, intelligent participation.

We decided to build our Holy Week Liturgy on the following principles:

1. a liberal use of processions to *collect* the people for the liturgy.

2. use of para-liturgy in Spanish to complete the sense and form of the liturgy itself.

The week worked out as follows:

Palm Sunday

We held processions and "solemn"services in five different areas of the parish. Approximately 2,100 people came. Only adults were allowed to march in the procession—the priests and officials of the liturgy (all men) went first, followed by the men and then the women. Palms were given only to those who marched in the procession so that throughout the year God would bless the homes of those who had publicly proclaimed Christ king on Palm Sunday. Three men read the Passion in Spanish. (There was demonstrated all through Holy Week an intense interest on the part of the people in the reading of Sacred Scripture in a language they can understand.)

Holy Thursday

We held five Masses in various parts of the parish. In the big ceremony, twelve men dressed in white albs (to represent the apostles) carrying the implements of the liturgy (wine, bread, basin, water, towels, etc.) marched in procession along with the celebrant. The para-liturgy followed the scriptural account of the Last Supper. The Lord and His twelve disciples seated at a banquet table reenacted the Last Supper, which included the washing of the feet, the betrayal and the Last Discourse. About 1,200 people assisted and were truly fascinated.

Good Friday

Two big ceremonies were held and approximately 3,000 people attended. Along a mile route, the procession wended its way, Fourteen large crosses had been erected. At each cross a man read a station of the Cross. At the words "If a man wishes to be my disciple, let him take up his cross," the man pulled his cross out of the ground and carrying it on his shoulder joined the procession of crosses. The immense crowd sang over and over again *"Perdona tu pueblo, Señor"* in response to the Improperia sung by the chanter in Spanish.

Because we have no place to reserve the Blessed Sacrament, Communion was not included in the liturgy. All the other ceremonies (lessons, passion, orations and veneration) were done as para-liturgy in Spanish and concluded by the beginning of the *velorio* (wake) which lasted until midnight Saturday. The people were very impressed and seemed to benefit from a new (for them) sense of the Pascal Mystery. For example, the explanation of the unveiling and veneration of the Cross: that the cross is now a symbol of victory, success and glory; thus even Good Friday is a day of glory despite its note of mourning.

Holy Saturday
In various far-flung communities of the parish we held the vigil ceremonies from 3:00 PM on. The big ceremony was held at midnight and attended by a very large crowd. The new fire, the pascal candle, the blessing of the water, the renovation of baptismal vows, the litanies, the great alleluias all made a great impression on our people, once the people understood and participated. Some two thousand people attended.

An interesting note: *Pascua* in Spanish has become synonymous with fiesta, especially that of Christmas. Thus *"Felices Pascuas"* is "Merry Christmas." Our people had no idea until now that *Felices Pascuas* literally means "Happy Easter"—that Easter is the *great* Christian feast, from which all the rest derive their glory. We have found that, without doubt, the liturgy simply done and explained is a "master teacher."

III. Construction

You will remember that the big dance pavilion we had built for the "Fiestas Patronales" in September of 1963 we converted into a large (capacity: 1500) provisional church. Because there is soon to be an inspection of the area by BID (the International Development Bank) the government asked us to remove the church. In return, the government has built a chapel for us on the ground floor of a multi-family dwelling which will seat about 300 people. With the materials from the demolished "church" we are building six more small chapels in the parish and also starting a cooperative factory building. Thus we will soon have ten chapels built in the parish and shall be well advanced on our plan of decentralizing the parish. These chapels are very simple, roomy and serve as community centers also. All the work on these chapels is being done by the people themselves, supervised by superintendent Father Bob McGlinn and because we already had most of the construction materials, the cost will be minimal.

In the center of the parish, we are constructing a chapel "del Santisimo" and a large parish center to accommodate 1,000 people. The construction at a cost of approximately $85,000, will be financed by a loan from the Archdiocese of Chicago which is to be repaid by the people of San Miguelito. This central building will be the home of the Lord and a center of solemn ceremonies, activities, and training for the entire parish.

Leo T. Mahon
John H. Greeley
Robert J. McGlinn
April 10, 1964

5
LIBERATING THE UNLIBERATED

*P*anama City was squeezed between the Canal Zone on one side and the Pacific Ocean on another; the only large area for expansion was ours. The community of San Miguelito was growing like Illinois corn on a hot night in late July, beginning in 1963 with a population of twenty-five thousand. When I left in 1975 it was more than two hundred thousand.

The twelve-week course and the lay deacon program, though both had been well received, were not enough to sustain transformational change. For most, habits, beliefs, and values aren't shed forever with one life-turning event. Besides, the political scene as well as an ever-changing mix of people tested their faith every day. San Miguelito became a turnstile where the pass codes got changed every week. Other community- and faith-developing programs were needed.

We decided to initiate the Cursillo as a follow-up for those who had completed the Familia de Dios program.

A Cursillo, a weekend encounter, or any such gathering under one roof, where people eat, sleep, converse, share sorrow and pain, joy and laughter, where they forgive and console, plan and dream together—all in the name of the God-with-us and in the style of Jesus—is a grounding experience.

The Cursillo had preceded our arrival in Panama by several years. It had achieved considerable success, especially among the upper and upper-middle classes. The lay directors of the movement, upon hearing that we were interested, invited us to send some of our people. We decided that it would be wise to join an accepted movement outside of San Miguelito. Cooperation with a successful and trusted organization would gain us some points with those in the church who criticized our every step and followed our shadows. We were offered two places at each Cursillo and began by sending Pepe Rios and Fidel Gonzalez and a few others, but this would not last.

"*Padre*, it was an inspiring experience," Pepe was to say. "We talked into the night. I was moved by the dedication of the people, by their faith, by their love. I have grown. I feel that my faith could move mountains."

"Just think of it," Fidel added. "Here we were on an unbelievable high and we've had no whiskey to drink or women to screw."

"Ah, yes," I responded, thinking of the many times I had heard the same from the Puerto Ricans in Chicago.

"But, *Padre*," both added. "We were the poor. They treated us nicely, but we were different from them."

They experienced what I had feared. With two places out of twenty-four, we would effectively be integrating the poor into the rich. Jesus did exactly the opposite; he invited the rich and powerful, the few that come, to walk among the poor. To mix a paltry number of common people with a large group of wealthy is to overwhelm, intimidate, and defeat the poor. The proper Christian dynamic, we felt, would be to invite a small number of *rabiblancos*, the Panamanian colloquial term for the rich, and thus encourage some powerful people to listen to the wisdom, the self-reliance, and the goodness of the lower classes. We had no rich people in San Miguelito.

"And *Padre*," Fidel added, "How will we ever send all our people? It will take us more years than we have lives."

If making a Cursillo was going to be an important element in the formation of lay leaders, then we needed more slots. One drop of rain after a long drought would not help parched land at all; it would serve only to frustrate the people.

We asked for a minimum of twelve places in each Cursillo. They offered us five. We insisted on at least half the slots. We felt that we were dealing with an important principle. We believed that we should not give crumbs to the poor, nor should we do more things to increase their sense of inferiority. It was to no avail.

Consequently, we launched a movement on our own. We called it the Cursillo de Inciacion Cristiana, the Little Course of Christian

Initiation, in order not to confuse it with the established Cursillo. Fidel Gonzalez took the lead. At the end of each three-month dialogue in the barrios, we invited participants to make a weekend encounter. The response was enormous. At times we needed space for seventy or eighty people.

We faced a housing problem. We had no facility that could accommodate large numbers of overnight guests and then we remembered the many times individuals had said to us, "Hey, Father, anytime you want to use our house in Chepo, or Pacora, or El Valle, just let us know." It was customary for the upper class in Panama to offer the use of their getaway places to priests, so we decided to test their hospitality by asking for the house in order to conduct a retreat for a few parishioners.

The "few" turned out to be fifty to eighty people. We slept several in a bed; we lay on the floors. One time Bob McGlinn emptied the pool and he and several others slept there. Most of the owners were surprised; some were shocked by the outpouring of people, but, to give them credit, they did not withdraw the invitation.

After a year of our depending, and imposing, on the kindness of the wealthy, Archbishop Tomas Clavel offered us the use of the empty seminary building, a fine three-storied facility perched like a beacon on top of a hill that caught the breezes, a wisely structured edifice that rose above the suffocating heat in the hollows of Panama.

The Cursillo became a symbol of all that is good in life and love. When I gave talks I was frequently asked why the Cursillo was so meaningful to the people of Panama. My description usually started with a metaphor:

> Have you ever spent a weekend with friends at a summer cottage? To smell the coffee brewing and the bacon frying in the morning, to stand in line in your skivvies waiting to use the only WC, to play ball on the lawn, to broil over charcoal the fish you caught, to play charades in the evening, to end the night with a brandy, a roaring fire, and a good conversation—that's an experience that turns acquaintances into friends, friends into close friends, and good friends into lifetime partners.

The weekend encounters were very much like that—sharing food, conversation, stories, and games and putting on humorous skits. It captured the Upper Room experience that Jesus must have had with the apostles. It created an intimate and safe community that the people of San Miguelito hadn't experienced before.

Some of us were raised in families that shared a loving, faith-filled, freedom-loving environment. I was one. My family did not know cruelty or intimidation. I never saw my parents fighting with each other, or, for that matter, with the members of our extended family, their brothers and sisters, my uncles and aunts. I am fairly certain that our team of priests and sisters came from the same kind of families.

Most of the people we served came from homes that mixed hurt, fear, and disloyalty with love and concern. Worse, many people in our world and in our church have suffered a horrendous experience of family—abuse, incest, arbitrary punishment, abandonment, in experiences that have left them scarred, resentful, and cynical.

Vital to the development of building a weekend of a safe and intimate world were the faith talks and the dialogues that followed. The talks, initially given by the priests and sisters and later offered by lay leaders, were on the challenge of Jesus; the question of God; the dream of Jesus; love, sex, and marriage; forgiveness and reconciliation; and the second coming.

It was in the dialogue that followed that people heard themselves express their own faith and be amazed by their own insights when they listened to others and marveled at their wisdom. The event climaxed on Sunday afternoon with everyone sitting around a table, celebrating the Lord's Supper. This Mass gave people a heightened awareness of what it means to have a fraternal meal, a love feast.

The process of conversion was multiform, depending on the individual. In some cases, it created new strife and discord.

During one Cursillo, one woman approached me and asked if she could see me privately. Disconsolately she told me she had a problem with her husband. I remembered her husband from an earlier Cursillo. He had seemed to be a man of integrity so I geared myself up, not wanting an affirmative answer, "You mean he has another woman?"

"Oh no," she replied. "He's so kind, so helpful, so understanding. He doesn't criticize me and never gets angry at me. It's like living with a saint."

While I was breathing a sign of relief, she was smiling ruefully. "I guess the problem is really me," she added. "Do you know what I do? The only thing he doesn't like to eat is celery. Sometimes I find myself putting celery in the salad just to see whether I can get him mad."

The conversion process in the women was often considerably different from that of the men. The men could make a major decision in their lives, like abandoning a mistress or stopping drinking. It was as if they could stand up, make a 180-degree turn, and walk away from their former way of life without so much as a glance over their shoulder. The women, on the other hand, had deep within them the feeling that they were the object of hurt and the victim of sin. It took them longer to forgive and to conquer their resentments. Their conversion generally meant not turning away from sin and turning to goodness, but rather renouncing the posture and habit of being an object, a half person, and becoming a full person with the right and responsibility to make decisions and to demand equality and respect.

The slower part of healing and change for the men was sharing their feelings out in the open—with men or with women. Consequently, their only form of intercourse was genital. It was rewarding to see them hurrying off after a Cursillo to test a new desire—to share the *good news* with their wives.

Within a few years thousands of people made the Cursillo de Iniciacion Cristiana. We were exhilarated by this success. Selfish people became generous; good people were turned into service-oriented leaders. At the same time, we were painfully aware that we were touching, in a significant way, only a small minority.

A Protestant minister, as he observed our ministry, said to me, "Perhaps we Protestants ought to leave Latin America and let you Catholics deal with it. And maybe we shall one day, if we can be convinced that you are serious about converting the people you have baptized." He issued a mandate; we had yet to fully follow it.

There were two distinct Catholicisms in Latin America when we arrived: the organized church of the middle and upper class, the one that bound people to the controls of the hierarchy, and a second, the church of the people with its own laws and deviated doctrines, the one that contained rituals stemming from pagan rites and full of self-serving, superstitious practices. Both churches had one thing in common—corruption and manipulation of the people. The *faithful* were used and abused by those in charge.

We were introducing a third church: one that spoke to community and gospel living, one where people were freeing themselves to live as Christ taught us to live within His kingdom.

The people moving into San Miguelito had little respect for the institutional church and used it only as a sacrament station, paying for service. That was fine by us and we stayed as far away from the hierarchical church as we could. The dictate from Chicago to create an *experimental* church freed us from the rubrics of common practice. On the other hand, the people were rooted in ancient traditions and for a while we priests tried to serve in this system.

Each little barrio was named for a saint—Santa Librada, Santa Rosa. Every year the *cacique*, the barrio's petty chief, allied with one of the political parties, along with his committee, organized the *fiesta patronal*, the saint's feast day celebration. We priests were invited to walk in the procession with the statue of the saint and then formally begin the festivities by celebrating Mass in honor of the saint.

I detested walking in those processions more than anything else I was asked to do in the whole of my experience in Panama. I felt foolish and so used, walking behind the statue, accompanied by a few women and children. Four little girls held a bed sheet by the corners into which bystanders threw coins and bills—money traditionally given to the priests.

Men were conspicuously absent. They had already begun the drinking, the games of chance, the dancing, all of which were the *real* celebration and out of which the cacique and his cohorts made plenty of money. Major politicians were invited by the *padrinos*, the godfathers of the whole affair, often donating the beer and liquor for the three-day event. The *fiestas patronales* were pagan festivals covered by a layer of Christianity so thin as to be transparent.

I had running battles with the organizers of such events. Often I offered to do the religious services a week before or after the "pagan" rites so as to give some seriousness to the religious aspect. But my offer in no way pleased the *Juntas Catolicas*, the Catholic Committees, responsible for such events. They went screaming to both ecclesiastical and civil authorities complaining of how the *gringo* priests were destroying Catholic tradition.

One year I invited myself to a meeting in the sector of Santa Rosa at which the inhabitants were organizing the festival in the saint's honor. The people there watched me with suspicious eyes; few had accepted the work we were doing.

I asserted, "I am a *fanatico de Santa Rosa.*"

The crowd cheered.

"Do you know who Saint Rose was?" I asked.

The crowd fell silent.

I began telling the history of Rose who, as a young and beautiful maiden of Lima, Peru, disfigured her face to make herself less attractive to those who lusted after her.

"To be devoted to St. Rose," I went on to say, "means to have respect for one's own body, but, above all, for the integrity of women."

Some rumbling began in the crowd. I ignored it, braced myself, and continued, "Rose is a symbol of chastity and purity. To honor her as the patroness of the community without resolving to stop the whoring, to put away your concubines, to offer your hand in marriage to the woman with whom you are living not only does not make sense, but rather is the same as dishonoring the saint."

There were a few side glances of the women to their men. The rumbling became shouts. Several leapt to their feet all at one time.

One pointed to the statue that had been placed in the corner of the room and shouted, "That's our Santa Rosa. She it is who protects us and brings us luck."

I was not invited again to march in their procession.

The political system was based on much the same kind of patronage. There were many newer sectors being organized, not around religious symbols, but rather around the principle of mutual help. These were the *Sociedaeds de Ayuda Matura,* in which the inhabitants pledged themselves to help one another build little concrete-block houses.

The same phenomenon of dependency showed itself in the newly developed groups. Here, though, the dependency was political. The groups exerted strong pressures on the government to give them both the land and the building materials for free. When the people were charged a minimal amount, they often refused and provoked sit-ins, hoarding, stealing, and any creative means to get what they felt was justly due them. They reasoned that the government was rich and they were poor, so the government owed them.

I felt helpless to reframe their view. "If no one pays," I would say, "the money will run out and other poor families will get no help." As with their idolatry of Santa Rosa, the demagogic leaders would accept no argument. So ingrained was this attitude of subservience and dependence that it was close to impossible to get beyond their myopic vision or change their beggarly stance.

Involvement in politics remained an issue, not an urgent one, but rather a vague ideal, for the men and women who were becoming the Christian leaders of San Miguelito. They were so busy with the task of evangelizing the burgeoning population that they scarcely had the time to consider what loomed before their eyes as an even more arduous and gargantuan work of reforming the political mentality of their people. They had no notion whatsoever of where to begin or how to do it.

The corrupted political power of Panama remained irksome for me. Here I sat with thirty dedicated lay deacons, three priests, and five religious women who had recently arrived. We were making a significant difference in the personal lives of the men, women, and children of San Miguelito, but encircling us every day was the heavy arm of dictatorship and corruption.

Months after we began our ministry I had abandoned organizing for political power and gain because there was no sense of community, no respect for self or for others. I had learned that organizing without a community and faith foundation was like sowing weeds—they were fast to grow and wickedly hard to manage. We were at a different point now. A community had been founded and it was growing. It might be time to look at the health and well-being of the political world.

"Jesus didn't die for theological reasons," I said one day after realizing that I couldn't hold in my feelings any longer. "He died for political reasons. He claimed he was divine. What did that do to the established authority?"

"Threatened them," said several. With that, the topic took over. It launched us into a denunciation of politics and politicians, a trite, unholy litany I was to hear repeatedly and persistently when people talked about their view of the essential corruption of politics.

"Politics," I interjected, "is the means by which people direct, govern, and discipline themselves for the common good. Politics protects especially the poor and defenseless." I quoted Senator Paul Douglas, a great man from my home state of Illinois: "Politics is the noblest of all professions." I quoted the Hebrew prophets who strongly criticized the shepherds of Israel, the politicians, and who predicted that one day God himself would come to shepherd his people, and thereby forever make politics sacred.

I challenged them, "Who rules Panama—the people?"

They answered, "Of course not."

"Then your claim to be a democratic republic is a sham," I said. "And who must bear the blame, just the big shots?"

As in our earlier discussion on war, the challenge of the question startled them and encouraged dialogue about what role they played in their own politics.

The dialogue, which went on for weeks, served to exorcise them of their dangerous and paralyzing obsession with the evil of politics. The question then arose: how were they to rid themselves of their false belief that they were helpless? They turned their focus to arriving at a new and deeper understanding of the significance of the passion and death of Jesus.

The word "passion" sparked an idea. Why not present the message in a theater piece? A play? Passion plays were common in Panama, but there were none that were set within a contemporary Panamanian context.

We conceived of the play as a drama with an interlocutor, much like the evangelist narrating the gospels. Panama has an exquisite poetic form called the Decima, ten rhyming lines. It is customary among the rural people for a singer to choose a theme, such as the treachery of women, and then extemporize a ten-line poem on the subject to a guitar accompaniment. The Decima serves as a challenge to another songster who takes the opposite view, that women are our salvation. The answer is called the Contra-Decima. Often these musicians are unable to read or write, but they can compose and sing.

We agreed that each scene of the play would begin from a corner of the stage with a Decima announcing the theme sung by Pepe Rios. Then there would be significant scenes from the life of Jesus and his community, all in Panamanian dress, context, and language.

One of the Maryknoll nuns and a native of Argentina, Madre Cecilia, took charge of the project. She spoke flawless Spanish and equally impeccable English without a trace of an accent in either tongue. For months she prodded a group of us to reflect on the story of Jesus and to act it out in a Panamanian context. She took notes on the dialogue and action and translated them into dramatic scenes. At last it was ready—the life, death, and rising of Jesus—Panameno. The solders were not Roman, but Guardia Nacional. The opposition to Jesus came from the autocratic and powerful of the country who used fanatical religionists, status-conscious clergy, and venal politicians to do their will.

Jesus was a *campesino*, a peasant, clad in native dress, *gutarras*, sandals, and *capotillo*. He did not die on a cross. Instead he was shot to death by two bullets fired by a hired assassin. His friends and followers, ordinary Panamanian poor, followed him enthusiastically, but in the crucial moments largely deserted him.

The result was a dramatic success, an evangelical tour de force. Thousands upon thousands came to see it. Their reactions varied. Accustomed to Roman soldiers and Jewish priests and lawyers, most were at first mystified. They understood every word and gesture, but only a few got the point the first time. Many returned to watch several times. They were to discover that the play was their story. It was the human story. It was also God's story. The play itself was called *De las Tinieblas Hacia la Luz* (*From Darkness to Light*).

There were those who were shocked by its "irreverence" and its lack of "historical" accuracy and they proclaimed it blasphemous. Because of the play, many others became friends and supporters of our work. Others grew more persistent in their distaste for and even hatred of what we were about in San Miguelito.

Word of the play spread far beyond San Miguelito and many came to see it from all parts of Panama. Their reactions were like those of our own people. Some understood it, some questioned it, and some detested it. One night the president of the Republic, accompanied by several cabinet ministers and flanked by bodyguards of the Guardia Nacional came to see the play. They left stunned, the expressions on their faces indicating that they were not at all pleased. Looking more deeply, one might even have sensed that they had felt abased and dishonored.

The play was performed many times during that Lenten season in San Miguelito. It was repeated for several years between Ash Wednesday and Easter.

Then we decided to write and produce another "mystery play," this one depicting the dreams and methods of the Christian movement in San Miguelito. It was titled *El Despertar de un Pueblo* (*The Awakening of a People*).

This play was extraordinarily successful, once again largely due to the formidable talents and persistence of Madre Cecilia. The leadership team called the first play, the passion play, the Gospel according to San Miguelito; *El Despertar de un Pueblo* was its companion piece, its Acts of the Apostles.

The next step was an easy one and moved us further into an analysis of the politics of power in Panama. Good Friday had traditionally been the most sacred day in Panama. On that day people were fitted out as historical personages: Roman soldiers stiff and impersonal, Pharisees dark and foreboding, scribes cautious and officious, Mary and her companions weeping, disciples cowering, Judas slinking, and the bearded Jesus crowned with thorns and carrying a heavy cross. Hating Judas and pitying Jesus, the spectators looked on, naming the good guys and the bad guys.

The problem, as we saw it, was that these processions enabled the spectators to view the event as outsiders and judges and not as participants in the perennial, universal struggle between the good and the evil, the courageous and the cowardly in all of us.

We decided to present the Via Crucis, the Stations of the Cross, in contemporary Panamanian style. The men of San Miguelito were invited to volunteer for a station. Each made a personal meditation on that particular moment in the Via Crucis. Each also constructed, together with his family and neighbors, a large wooden cross. A week before Holy Week, fourteen large crosses lined the principal avenue of the community. One by one the men delivered their meditations on suffering and evil in their own lives and in their society while the people listened and then prayed. The man then lifted his cross out of the ground and carried it. The next man did the same at the second station. The process was repeated fourteen times. Hundreds walked along reverently and prayerfully with the cross-bearers. The procession took place in silence—the only sound heard was that of the heavy wooden crosses being dragged along the pavement.

As San Miguelito grew, so did these annual processions until there were five of them. Seventy crosses rose above the streets, paths, and hills of San Miguelito. The crowd grew to as many as five thousand. The processions all terminated in one central plaza in front of the largest church in the area, Cristo Redentor. There the men deposited their crosses in one huge pile to symbolize the enormity of suffering and injustice in the world. Finally, and all together, we prayed the fifteenth station, the rising of the Lord from the dead, expressing our faith that life can conquer death, that love can overcome evil, that courage can be born from the womb of fear.

I could hear in the rhythm of art the truths of the faith, the song of life, and the emotions of love—all expressed in a series of songs, in the poetry and music of Panama. It was a new creed in words that breathed life, in songs that touched the heart. And its visual vibrancy sent a message, creating a sense of awareness that Panamanians had not faced before.

It is one thing to mock the political system in plays and music; it's another to organize for reform.

The discussion of political reform never seemed far off. How could it, when people were talking and dreaming of becoming a people of God—a sign of the future? Often at night when the work was done we would gather to discuss the successes and failures of the day over a glass of chichi or a stein of beer. All of us knew that someday we would have to face the political challenge squarely. By an unspoken consensus, we agreed that, as with many of the great issues in life, we would wait for it to come to us.

It was not long in coming. One day Arquitecto Jorge Riba walked into my study. Riba, at that time the minister of housing, was a tall, handsome, dedicated man married to one of the most beautiful women in all of Panama. His was the unenviable job of building new housing for the poor and the working class in Panama. Even more, his was the responsibility of urbanizing the immense squattersvilles, which meant putting sewage pipes, water conduits, and roads into areas already densely populated. Nowhere was his concern greater than in San Miguelito.

Riba opened up. "My problem is the poor living in the *barriadas de emergencia*, slum towns. Unless the political attitudes of the people change, my efforts are doomed to failure."

I appreciated the man and his efforts and felt sympathy for him.

"I admire the Christian movement in San Miguelito," he went on to say. "You are educating and inspiring the people. Perhaps you could help me begin a similar effort to educate the people politically."

However strong my feeling for his plight, I was not eager to double or triple our educational efforts. Besides, right off I could sense the danger of the church mixing in politics.

"Jorge," I answered, "the decision is not fully mine to make. I will gather a group of our leaders and present the situation to them."

Jorge joined us for the first meeting. I had called José Arrocha, Vicente Mosquera, Octavio Pinto, and Severino Hernandez. No one there doubted the necessity of political education. We knew that if we really believed in the kingdom of God, then we had to so something besides talk to help bring it to pass.

"Are we the ones to do it?" Severino asked.

Riba riposted, "Who else? No one else has the will to do it or the necessary authority with the people."

"But it has to be separate from the church movement," asserted Pinto and José simultaneously. All agreed. They feared the repercussions if political organizing were to be linked to their community and faith development.

"We will create mixed messages. Our people's growth in Christianity is about understanding their inner strength one with one another and with God. To mix that with politics is to mix oil and water," continued Pinto.

"Where will funds come from?" asked Severino.

Riba answered that he knew several wealthy people who would put up money. "If Father Mahon meets with them and says the word, they will give."

"What kind of educational materials do you have?" asked Pinto.

"We shall have to write our own," said Riba.

Over several months of planning, Riba and I met with prominent Panamanians blessed with a finely honed social sense and an almost desperate wish to get their country out of its political morass. These men volunteered their financial backing so the work could be done. A central committee was set up and others were contacted. Each sponsor would give $50 a month for a period of no less than two years. Soon there was enough money to support four full-time staff members.

Once we were ready to begin, the serious question of who would man the office had to be decided. Jobs were not easy to come by in Panama. To give up a job, along with the security that went with it, for such a risky undertaking would take a lot of courage. Severino Hernandez who, as a master mechanic in the Canal Zone, had the best job and security, made the sacrifice. He quit his job. As long as he lived, he was the heart of the movement. He was followed by José Arrocha, Vicente Mosquera, and Ramon Hernandez.

Always careful to separate the political movement from the church, these men looked for a place that could serve as headquarters. Jorge Riba gave them an empty lot and Dana Rosa de Martinez, the widow of one of Panama's wealthiest men, donated a two-story prefabricated building.

Albeit on the sidelines, I stayed involved. I would be neglectful if I didn't admit to the ambiguous feelings I had. Could I serve two masters—my faith and politics?

Members of my team would challenge me. "Leo, if you divide your time, won't your ministry suffer?"

I was determined and—probably more than ever—the name Leon, which I had taken when I had come to Panama, was serving me well; I was a lion with a new adventure, territory to cover and conquer. The rational side of me argued: "How can one live one side of himself in peace and harmony, and the other in strife with his country and his future?" I reasoned that our mission was about education, providing deeper understanding of the person within, the one who can make choices not only for his own well-being but also for that of others. Its focus, I felt, was broadening the kingdom of God.

We prepared a series of dialogues, much like the Familia de Dios program. Our discussion topics included the duties and rights of citizens, the political parties and what they do, and the meaning of a nation.

The staff people went out every night to conduct the dialogues. The first people to attend were those who had already gone through the Christian dialogues. Soon it became evident that others were becoming interested, men and women who had little connection with religion.

Some were disillusioned with the church; others were downright hostile. Having participated in the political dialogues, a good many got interested in the faith and became active in church. I felt my efforts had been justified. I was advancing our primary mission. Others kept their distance, but found a new respect for the church they had formerly ignored or disdained and were eager to work with this new kind of movement.

One propitious day a young man, Eric De Leon, arrived at the headquarters of MUNDO, the National Movement for Democracy and Unity, the name we had given the movement. Eric was an eccentric genius. He had recently returned from Belgium where he had acquired a doctorate in industrial psychology as well as a striking blond wife. Slim, soft-spoken, and wearing thick glasses, he was as serious and nervous as an expectant father pacing a maternity waiting room.

He wouldn't go near a church, maintaining with a wry smile that he was an atheist, but he was fascinated by the vision and goals of MUNDO. At first he worked as a volunteer, but then he quit his position in the Planning Department of the government to take a full-time job with the movement. The pay and the security were so meager that Eric's wife accused him of losing his mind.

On the contrary, once Eric had made up his mind, nothing could deter him. It was Eric De Leon who was to put all our ideals on paper in logical fashion. He began working on the Plan of San Miguelito which was destined to startle Panama and interest political circles in places as far away as Europe.

For those who wished more than an introduction to political theory, the team organized weekend seminars featuring lectures by some of the most prominent Panamanian professionals and intellectuals, who shared their knowledge of political science, anthropology, law, and labor relations. Almost all of the lecturers held doctorates and were greatly in demand. They gladly volunteered to spend weekends with the men and women of the working class without ever asking for or receiving a fee.

Dr. Carlos Lopes Guevara, an eminent jurist and statesman, summed it up when he said, "The important thing about the experience was not so much the high quality of the lectures, but rather the opportunity to prove that it was possible to bring together two elements of our society which had historically been always very much apart—the intellectual or the professional and the simple man of the people."

One night as I was returning from a political discussion I saw two men illuminated by the headlights of my car, waving me down. Braking the auto, I stuck my head out the window to see what they wanted.

When they recognized me, they said excitedly, "Oh, it's a good thing you came along, Father. There's a man in the grass raping a woman. You've got to do something."

I briefly wondered why *they* weren't doing something about it, but there was no time to consider the question. I could hear a woman's piercing cries coming from the direction they had pointed out.

It was a hillside covered with grass taller than myself. I lunged into the dense vegetation and very soon came upon a clearing where I spied a woman on her back with her dress pulled up to her waist and a man with his cotton pants and shorts down at his ankles stretched out over her and pumping away vigorously.

Grabbing him by the collar of his shirt, I pulled him off the woman and to his feet. I told him to pull up his pants and button his fly. He did so rather meekly, muttering some incoherent sounds.

The woman rose, stopped screaming, and pulled down her dress in a gesture designed to regain as much dignity as possible.

Despite the womanizing behavior throughout the nation, women rarely were raped. Now that I had had to stop a rape I had no notion of what to do next. So I announced that I was going to take them to the police station. When the three of us emerged from the tall grass, a small crowd had assembled.

The two men who had "reported" the rape threatened to beat up the rapist.

"Leave him alone," I said, as I directed the man to the back seat of my Volkswagen Beetle and the woman to the front. Off we went down the road to the barracks at Panama Viejo.

The man leaned over the front seat and spoke to me, but he was still incoherent. Then it was that I realized he was a deaf mute and was trying to tell me something with guttural sounds and hand signals. He put his index and second finger in the air, pointed them at his private parts, and then pointed at the woman's crotch. I knew he wasn't making a V for victory sign, but his message escaped me.

Then it came to me. He was claiming that he had paid two dollars and it was no rape at all. The woman apparently felt shamed and held her silence. Now what?

I stopped the car and let them both out. He took hold of the woman's hand and they proceeded to walk down the road as if they were two lovers on a stroll.

I was speechless.

A foolish hero!

Years afterwards I could honestly say the same about my political involvement in San Miguelito. I did what I thought was right at the moment. I didn't know then that the forces against our success were much more powerful than our own.

Someone once said that education is a dangerous thing. Our people were building a sense of self-confidence and a commitment to what was right for themselves, for their families, for their community, and for their country. Political unrest was beginning to mount.

One of the threats that encouraged me to get involved in politics was the fear of Communism taking over the country.

Both the Communist Party and Communist propaganda were outlawed in the Republic of Panama. Merely passing laws *against* them, however, didn't diminish the attractiveness of the Marxist solution to the problem. Rather, the contrary might be true.

The situation was so ripe with the lack of jobs, poor distribution of wealth, and an ineffective and often corrupt government that we were of the opinion that one good, well-trained Communist worker could organize all of San Miguelito in a relatively short space of time.

We wondered why a full-time Communist organizer wasn't in San Miguelito. We suspected that the Communists must have had an even greater shortage than we priests had.

There were some Communists working near us who periodically tried to infiltrate and influence local organizations and leaders. One day a few men came to the barrio of San José where Bob McGlinn was working. Padre Roberto, as he was called, had become aware of outside Communist influence and discovered contraband Communist propaganda on a table in the community center when he went to say Mass one Sunday morning.

He waited for an opportunity to do something about it. One day he was invited to a town meeting, called to discuss the problem of building a school in San José. All the men of the town were present as were ten outsiders—some of whom were representatives of the University Student Federation (Communist-dominated) and others who were leaders of a squatters' *syndicato* (union), also reported to be Communist-infested.

He described how for two and a half hours the visitors held the floor using the school question to hurl vicious attacks on the government and to repeat all the usual Marxist slogans.

Finally, Bob told us later, he rose to speak. He explained why he was there—to help solve the school problem. He then went on to comment on the remarks of the outsiders.

"Our distinguished visitors have spoken much about solidarity with the workers of Panama in the struggle to uplift the poor class. I am for all of that, if we mean a solidarity based on Jesus Christ's teaching of love of neighbor and on Christian social justice.

"This is why I am here. You all know what and who I am. I am a priest pledged to work to build a Christian community here. But there may be others here who do not want a Christian community at all—what they want is a Marxist community.

"In my opinion they have a right to work for what they think is right and I am willing to work with them as far as I can.

"But let us have no deception. The people in this community want a Christian community and they are working under the impression that our visitors want the same.

"And so I would like to ask one simple question: Visitors, do you accept or reject the Marxist-Leninist ideology of social reform?"

Predictably, the dam broke and out came a torrent of vicious anti-clerical, anti-Catholic, anti-Yankee accusations, all coming from the visitors.

The local leaders whom Bob knew and worked with sat silent, shocked, and shame-faced during all the abuse. One young rabble-rouser shouted at Bob: "If you were in any other place but this, you would never get out of here alive."

The next week Bob was invited to another meeting of the town leaders. This time the "visitors" were conspicuously absent. The men apologized to him and reiterated their support of Christian principles and action.

In the light of this experience and several of a similar nature, I became convinced that it may be that the Communists are successful not so much because they are so many or so well-formed or so intelligent but more because they have a marvelous vacuum to work in—a lack of clearly enunciated Christian "revolutionary" principles and a shortage of trained Christian organizers, both lay and clerical.

The movement to "politicize" the people of San Miguelito along intelligent, self-determining lines had begun and was progressing swiftly. Those of us who participated in it thought we had considerable time before the new awareness would be tested. We never dreamt that very soon indeed San Miguelito would be at the heart of swirling controversy. Nor did we ever imagine that the area would be the site of the beginning of a new experiment in popular democracy. Some have accused us of going too quickly without adequate preparation. But how were we to know that the political system of the country was about to fall to pieces like an overripe avocado that plummets to the ground, breaks open, spills its guts, and stinks to high heaven?

San Miguelito was being watched. We were becoming an embarrassment to the government. We were increasingly an annoyance to the native church.

Report to
His Eminence Albert Cardinal Meyer
On the Parish of Cristo Redentor en San Miguelito

November 28, 1964

Your Eminence:

In the last report we attempted to explain the urgency and the methodology of the preaching of the Word of God in San Miguelito. Now that we have worked here for 21 months, we would like to comment on the effect of the Word on our people.

We believe we began at what must have been almost point zero. Ours was truly an abandoned people—uninstructed and uninformed. Various factors contributed to this abandonment: lack of priests, the population explosion, great distances between settlements in the interior of Panama whence most of our people come. We found the vast majority of our people not only ignorant of the basic truths and central mysteries of Christianity, but also of what most of us take for granted is natural law. We have discovered that many of the truths (such as monogamy) which were taught to be primary principles and immediately self-evident to all men are in reality no such thing, at least here in San Miguelito.

To make things worse, we found that whatever faith and piety our people had was seriously disoriented. For a long time we were accused of being Protestants (and still are in some quarters). Why? Because we speak of the Word of God; we preach the Gospel; we point to the Second Coming; we sing Alleluia in the Mass— And, of course, only Protestants speak and act in such a manner! We do not wish to imply that this condition is universal in Latin America or even in Panama because the middle and upper classes have not been so abandoned...

We have been privileged to be present for the springtime of the faith in our parish—a time when the first fruits are appearing in San Miguelito...

Rather than describe all this in glowing but over-general terms, bet us present some case histories of conversion—conversion in the original sense of the Word—of turning away from one type of life to another, nobler life with others—the conversion seen in the River Jordan—in the Pascal Vigil in the days of old.

Carlos C. — Age 36:

Carlos C. is the son of a Chinese immigrant and a Panamanian woman. It took him eight years of night school to earn his law degree at the University of Panama. Intelligent and hard working, still Carlos fell victim to two of the besetting sins of his environment: adultery (he had another woman besides his wife) and cynicism about democracy (in fact eighteen months ago, Carlos was on the verge of becoming a dedicated Marxist).

When he became acquainted with the priests of his parish, San Miguelito, he was fascinated by their revolutionary social doctrine and talked at first about organizing a new revolutionary Christian party with the priests as leaders. But as the months went by, he gradually realized that Christian revolution means much more than reforming the "other guy." It means a basic reformation of self, of family and of community long before a change in political structures. Carlos finished his course on the Family of God and then made his Cursillo whereupon he made his big decision to become a true Christian. Away went the other woman and his cynicism—in their place came a truly faithful love of his wife and children and a joyful, confident attitude toward making the kingdom of God come alive in San Miguelito. His family life is now a startling example for his neighbors and friends. He has organized all his immediate neighbors into a discussion course on the Word of God. His oldest boy wants to enter the seminary. Is he still a revolutionary? Yes, more than ever, but now he realized that unless we transform the masses into a people of God, radical change will mean but another change of masters.

Evaristo S. — Age 31

Evaristo S., a butcher, is married and the father of four children. In his own immediate neighborhood he had quite a reputation: aloof and discourteous to his neighbors, at home unfaithful and a wife beater besides.

The newly trained men of his sector never gave up on Evaristo. They invited him to play dominoes, to drink beer, etc.—but never a word of religion. One night he went to the discussion group of couples in his area. His attitude to the priest was plainly hostile. He stayed away for several weeks, but then for some unaccountable reason (except for the manly kindness of his neighbors) he returned to the classes and kept coming. He never really participated much in the conversation until the group hit on the subject of Christian marriage. The dam of hostility seemed to break for Evaristo when he discovered that sex is not merely for pleasure—that if men want to be human and not mere animals then the marriage act must be a symbolic expression of love, a giving of self to one's wife. Evaristo's reaction was a mixture of surprise, delight and anger. He blurted out, "That's the most beautiful thing I've ever heard! Why haven't we been told this before?"

Such was the beginning of Evaristo's conversion—a man who never in his adult life had put a foot inside a church. He finished his course and made a Cursillo. All his friends and neighbors were invited to his Catholic wedding. All were amazed by the change in this man but no one more than his boss, an Austrian businessman who came to the wedding to see what could possibly account for such a dramatic change in a man who formerly was so surly and bitter and now was so warm, open and friendly. Evaristo and his wife are presently daily communicants. When Evaristo meets one of the priests he never fails to shake hands with both hands and say with tears of gratitude and gladness in his eyes, "Thank you, Father."

Pedro A. — Age 33

Pedro A. is married and the father of five children. Startling handsome, he possesses a superbly engaging personality. He sings and plays the guitar beautifully and is in constant demand at all the social gatherings of the neighborhood. Many of Pedro's friends began to attend the discussion courses and Cursillos, but Pedro always hung back, much to the disappointment of his good friends and wife. But you see, Pedro had serious problems: two other women and children with each besides his own wife and family. Ever so slowly he was brought into the new "church" in San Miguelito—mostly through the Sunday afternoon dinners organized by the Catholic families. Pedro made his Cursillo and soon afterwards made his break with the past (and no one but God and Pedro himself know how hard it was). The day he first stood up to receive communion, to be "one" with all the other men in Christ, was truly a day of rejoicing for our community. Pedro is now one of the great apostles of San Miguelito—a leader of one of the discussion groups, a lector for the liturgy and a professor in the Cursillo movement.

Juan M. — Age 29

Juan is married, the father of two, and has almost completed his university education in accounting. He was working for the government housing agency when a scandal was uncovered regarding misuse of funds. He never denied his part in the affair but the big shots who were involved and actually got the money got off scot-free and Juan went to jail for a year.

When he was released, he was a shamed and almost broken man. But the priests of the parish and the young Catholic couples began to visit him and gradually he responded. He entered one of the courses, made a Cursillo and is now one of the leaders of the parish. Last week Juan was assigned to give one of the homilies at Mass. The passage was from one of St. Paul's prison letters. Juan gave a beautiful explanation of how St. Paul must have felt when he was in prison. When he finished the homily, there wasn't a dry eye in the church.

Maria A. — Age 41

Maria was a practicing Catholic before we ever came to San Miguelito inasmuch as she went to Mass as often as she could and was married by the church. Yet she was the type that dominated her husband and three grown sons (19, 20, and 21) if not by sheer force then by feminine hysterics. The home was an unhappy one and the oldest boy began to drink a lot and finally left the house. The husband took to drinking and gambling a great deal. Then the other boys were threatening to leave. Each time a crisis grew in the house Maria had an asthmatic attack that left her near death. These attacks, whether real or imaginary or both, had enslaved the whole family. The second-oldest boy, the finest of the three, was supporting the family alone. Finally, upon advice from one of the priests, he left the house. Gone was her support, both financial and moral and Maria was helpless. She had been highly critical of this newfangled religion, but now she begged for help. She and her husband entered one of the courses for couples. Eventually Maria, her husband

and all three boys made a Cursillo. What a difference it has made—the family is reunited now and happy. But the biggest change is in Maria. She had come to know that true love does not rest on fear or force but rather on trust and service. She no longer suffers attacks—in fact, she works harder than ever and has no ill effects now that she realizes that she must give rather than demand. One would never know that she had been sick or that the family was once near disaster as one watches them taking the long walk up the hill for daily mass and communion.

Isabel S. — Age 35

Isabel is a good-looking woman with two children—known in her sector as a good mother, a hard worker and a wife with a marriage problem. Isabel one day came to the rectory for help in obtaining the bishop's permission for a divorce and the legal aid for the same. She told her sad story of her husband's infidelity and lack of responsibility, and seemed to have every reason for a separation. While the matter was pending she accepted an invitation to participate in her area in the couples' discussion on the Word of God. She came alone because her husband had long since left the house. At first, she poured out her bitterness in front of the other couples but as she began to listen to the other couples discuss their love and their problems, she became more and more silent. Finally with the other women of her area she made the Cursillo. When it was over, she had but one sentence to say to the priest, "Father, I'm going to save my marriage." However she did it, her husband returned to the house and was soon participating with the other couples in their discussion course. Finally he made his own Cursillo and they received communion together at the Mass of the Clausura (closing of the Cursillo). Now they are the talk of the neighborhood as they walk together holding hands like sweethearts. Isabel recently told one of the priests "Now I see that much of the problem was of my own making—I learned what love is: true love forgives all, is patient and tolerant and is not demanding but giving."

Author's note: This report was not signed.

Fr. Leo Mahon, a Chicago priest who had a vision
of building the kingdom of God, led the missionary
team in San Miguelito from 1963 to 1975.

Roadless rows of family homes, often built overnight by peasants seeking a better life.

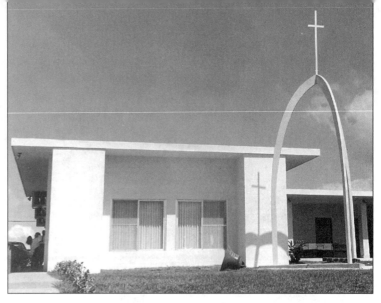

San Cristo Redentor, primary worship and gathering center of the Panamanian mission, built by the Archdiocese of Chicago.

Tiny church in the village of Pacora.

A statue of the risen Christ high on a hill in San Migueltio, overlooking the countryside.

Dust, intense heat, and the lack of accessible water didn't stop the devoted from participating in Holy Week processions.

Panamanians performed modern day passion plays written and directed by Madre Cecilia and local musician Pepe Rios.

Mass being conducted by Cardinal Cody, the morning after Leo Mahon (second to left of Cody) was accused of heresy.

Lillian Brule, an artist from Joliet, Illinois, spent two years getting to know the people before depicting them in this controversial painting. Found in San Cristo Redentor.

Families leaving their huts to join a Holy Week procession.

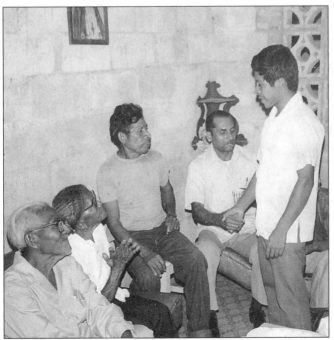

The Familia de Dios program, a twelve-week course held in homes where the faithful came not only to learn the gospel but to live it.

The faithful listening to Leo Mahon in an open prayer center. Churches were built with no walls to send the message that all were welcome and to catch the cooling trade winds.

Blending pagan and Christian traditions, each Panamanian sector honors its own saint in festive day and night activities.

The missionary team on the right being honored by church and political dignitaries, two days before Leo Mahon (center priest in white) was accused of heresy.

Three of the five sisters who served on the missionary team. The sisters complemented every aspect of the priests' work, enhancing community and family life.

Homes were built from straw, tin, wood, and any scraps families could find for shelter.

6

TENSING WITHIN TENSION

Within a year of our request to Cardinal Meyer, John Enright joined the team. He came with a fair mastery of Spanish which helped in his assimilation. I had vowed to recruit only individuals who knew Spanish, since there were many adjustments and lack of fluency in the language frustrated the individual and stifled his ministry. Jack Greeley had experienced what a limping knowledge of Spanish could do to his daily living; I didn't want to put anyone else through that.

John came bearing gifts—peanut butter and gin, the staples we expected of our most intimate visitors. The biggest gift was John himself.

John had been born and raised a block from my home, and we had built-in rapport. When you grow up with someone—throwing rocks at a tree to see who can make the biggest mark, competing in bike contests, and later monitoring whose voice drops the lowest and who has to shave first—there is a bond that only life-long friends can have.

John fit in. He was unassuming and a bit halting in language, both English and Spanish, and his even temper, blended with his smile and friendly demeanor, made it easy for people to be around him. He had a habit of leaning forward when speaking and that pulled the other person naturally into the conversation.

John was named "Padre Juan Segundo," Father John the Second, to differentiate him from Jack Greeley, who was given the name "Padre Juan Primero," John the First. Just weeks after John's arrival, one of the team leaders said, "Padre Juan Segundo knows how to sit with us; he is a priest for our people." John quickly became a steady anchor who could take a team vision and make it come alive in his own work.

I had been sending frequent reports to Cardinal Meyer and they were received with much enthusiasm and support. Meyer remained a stalwart champion. The building of Cristo Redentor was almost complete and a date was set for him to come to Panama to dedicate it. He wrote a letter saying that his ill health had forced him to postpone the visit and he would set another date as soon as he felt better.

Then one day he called long distance and asked me to come to Chicago, "I want to talk to you." The suddenness of the request made me move quickly.

I caught a plane and drove directly to the Cardinal's residence, an old red-brick Victorian mansion with lots of chimneys, a building that would look more at home on Knightsbridge Road overlooking Hyde Park in the West End of London than on North Avenue overlooking Lincoln Park in Chicago's Gold Coast. A somber butler opened the door and ushered me upstairs.

As I entered his study, the Cardinal was seated in an armchair, with a dressing gown over his white collarless shirt and black trousers. I was unprepared when I saw his ashen face and looked into his sunken eyes. He was holding his hand to the side of his head.

"Does it hurt much?" I asked.

"Oh yeah! I'm going in tomorrow," he said.

"Do you know what it is?"

"No, but whatever it is, it's bad!" he whispered. Then, with a little more strength in his voice, he continued. "I wanted to speak to you before I go into the hospital. I want you to know how important I regard your work down there as being.

"I have this feeling, Leo, that the bottom is about to fall out of the American church. We're in for some very rough times, but there seems to be a new way, a new church coming out of communities like San Miguelito. So please keep going."

I scarcely had time to digest the compliment and absorb the encouragement when the Cardinal added, "We don't have the nerve to do what you're doing down there, but we've got to get it. I have a desire. I want our young priests to catch that spirit. How would you like to have one-half the ordination class every year? Keep them in Panama for one year. That would be twenty guys each year."

I felt the same skip of glee I had known three years earlier when he had checked to see if I was still interested in doing "mission work." The Cardinal of Chicago was asking us to train future priests.

"If you give me a couple of more priests to help," I responded. He winced through his pain as if to say, "Leo, you always know how to set me up to get what you want."

"Would three extra priests on your staff be enough?" he asked.

I said yes, still not certain I wasn't imagining all this. We got into the subject of the education of priests. I proffered the opinion that priests my age and older were all trained to be doers of sacraments and communicators of the Word, and that they should have the opportunity to re-tool themselves in scripture and homiletics. I added that I thought if they weren't given that chance, they would be so dissatisfied with themselves that many would leave the priesthood.

"But they can't do that," Meyer protested. "They made a promise." I'm glad he didn't live to see the mass exodus that occurred a few years later.

There was no small talk, as there never was. I noticed how tired he seemed and how much pain he was in. So I made a move to get out of my chair, saying that I thought it was time to be on my way. He readily agreed. I wished him well and left. I walked down the stairs and out the door underneath the porte cochere.

Cardinal Albert Meyer never left the hospital; a major brain tumor took his life. I returned for his funeral. Stunned and grieving, I stood in the second row of mourners at the unpretentious gravesite in the seminary graveyard at Mundelein, Illinois, and watched my friend and patron's corpse being lowered into the ground.

Did you get anything in writing?" more people asked than I would ever want to remember. Bishop Cletus O'Donnell, Meyer's close friend and confidante who had been elected interim administrator of the archdiocese, listened intently to my retelling of my final conversation with Meyer. Besides having no record of our plan, O'Donnell, as an interim administrator, was not allowed to make important decisions or significant moves. Nothing could come of the discussion. All waited for the naming of the new archbishop. Meanwhile, O'Donnell and I and many others mourned the passing of a good, courageous man who had grown mightily in the last and most important job of his life. With Meyer's death went a church legend of greatness—and any dreams he had had for the Chicago church.

The first clue about our new episcopal leader came when we heard that the priests of New Orleans were throwing gala parties all over their archdiocese. Their archbishop, John Patrick Cody, was leaving and they were not shy about celebrating. That was not a good sign. Cody, with no known intellectual or pastoral leadership skills, was to be the head of the country's premier see—Chicago. Word was out that Cody was no Meyer, that Vatican II hadn't touched his heart, and that he remained a traditional Prince of the Church, one who took his office seriously, thriving on its power and dignity. He was to be my boss.

I put extra effort into our first report to him, sending a nine-page document outlining not only the theology behind our work but also its results. It was August 12, 1965, when we wrote:

Your Excellency:

Within a fortnight, you will be installed as the sixth Archbishop of Chicago. We welcome you into our midst as our pastor, shepherd and guide. We send you this report #13 on the work in San Miguelito as our own message of congratulation and as a sign of our loyalty, for it is an account of our work, of our problems and of our dreams. Conscious of our privilege of sharing in your apostolate, we greet you with the ancient words: "How beautiful are the feet of those who preach the good news" (Is 52-7).

Your priests, sisters,
and lay apostles in Panama

No answer came. No invitation to confer came.

I wrote to him several times and sent many memos. San Miguelito was growing rapidly and I felt some decisions had to be made and some initiatives either confirmed or abandoned.

Then finally it came, a summons to meet with him in Chicago. I went directly to his office.

He sat behind his desk in a robust wide brown leather chair that had lost any competition against his large overflowing frame. Without a greeting, he waved a thick file in his hands and said right off, "Meyer ran your whole operation out of his back pocket! That is no way to run anything."

He complained about the way the finances had been handled until I interrupted him. I had little patience. "Why are you yelling at me? I had nothing to do with the administrative procedure from this end. That's a matter between you and your dead predecessor and not between us."

He stopped in mid-air, as it were, and, looking at me intently, said, "You know you have quite a reputation for being controversial."

I answered, "And so do you, Your Excellency."

At that he smiled, not so much at the cleverness of my riposte, but rather with self-satisfaction in being controversial. Thus began a long, stormy relationship with John Cody. Interestingly, I was to discover that, after having complained about Meyer's administrative style, Cody proceeded to operate the Chicago mission at San Miguelito out of *his own* back pocket for the ensuing years.

On Chicago's West Side growing up, I used to play King of the Hill. It was a simple game. The one who claimed the hill got to make all the rules and everyone had to follow. Once I caught on that Cody intended to play that game and be the winner every time, I learned to play with him.

Each time I met with him, I would begin the conversation by bringing up one of his current problems or quarrels. That would get him off his attack on me and take up thirty to forty-five minutes of our meeting time. He got, though, his share of time.

Once he began by saying that he had received a complaint from Rome—that I had allowed lay people to distribute communion, a practice forbidden at the time.

"It happened without plan, Your Eminence," I began. "Greeley and I were concelebrating in the presence of some two thousand people. We knew most would be planning to go to communion. The sun was heavy in the sky."

I continued, "If just the two us had distributed communion, we would have been doing nothing else for an hour. Heat would have taken our people. So we gave the ciboria to some laymen who had been trained in our classes.

"And, since then, we have continued the practice," I added.

I expected that he thought I would deny the accusations, something he faced frequently when he confronted others. "Oh well," he muttered, "why do these things have to get to Rome?"

Cody had trouble praising anyone. He would use what I'd call a punch-and-pull method. He would punch out an idea and pull out information from another person, trying to gain ammunition for further discrediting others.

"Do you know this fellow Andrew Greeley?" he asked one day.

Greeley hadn't yet begun writing fiction, but was gaining a reputation for his insightful sociological analysis of the present-day church.

"Sure," I responded. "He's a good friend."

"Is he really smart?" Cody asked.

"Smart?" I exclaimed. "He's one of the most intelligent people I've ever met."

"Oh, I don't know about that. He can't be so smart. He'll never get anywhere in the church, saying the kinds of things he does."

Just as swiftly as it began, that part of the conversation ended.

During another conversation, Cody asked if I knew Father Ted Hesburgh, then president of Notre Dame. Once again I replied that he was a friend of mine. I had learned that if I didn't identify the person in question as a friend, the remarks were liable to be much more degrading.

"I just don't understand," he said, "People pay much more attention to what Hesburgh says than to me and he's a simple priest. I'm a cardinal archbishop."

It did not take long for the clergy of Chicago to understand that Cody was playing King of the Hill and in a deadly serious way. They responded to Cody's erratic and authoritarian style by organizing. In a matter of months they had formed the Association of Chicago Priests, ACP, an organization that still exists. It was designed to be a full-scale union to counteract the Cardinal as well as to protect the church they loved and served.

The leaders of the movement were, for the most part, contemporaries and friends of mine. At one point they invited me to speak to the organizers. I came up one day and went back to Panama the next. Cody, however, found out and never forgave me.

"What if you win? What if your demands get met?" I asked my peers.

Hopeful and somewhat desperate, they answered that everything then would turn out well.

"I don't think so," I replied. "You're fighting about structures, not about real church, which is deeper and far more peopled than that. We simply must come up with a more profound and authentic sense of church and begin to work together so that it can emerge under the guidance of the Spirit."

They were so outraged and eager for battle they could not catch what I was trying to say. Besides, I was suffering their pain. It was hard for me to fully put my experience of church into words.

The priests won many battles. Some might even say their struggle ended in a draw. But it didn't really, because they were fighting on Cody's own ground—structures and power. Whenever the last shot in a battle had been fired and the smoke had cleared, Cody was still standing on the hill.

One day, after another series of months with no acknowledgement of our notes and ministry reports, we received a cable saying that Cody would be arriving later that day and would spend several days visiting San Miguelito. We decided to rally the people. After all, he represented to the people of Panama the powerful one, the *dignatario de la iglesia* of Chicago, and the one who sustained us in San Miguelito.

When Cody arrived, he couldn't have been prepared for the welcome he received. Stepping down from the airplane onto a broad field, he was greeted by thousands shouting "*Bienvenido!*" His robust three-hundred-plus pounds seemed to float and he grinned broadly, catching the air of excitement. As the airplane engines let go their final breath, his purple and gold robes billowed in the breeze, adding to his grandeur, so that he seemed to rival in glory even the mighty sun ablaze in the cloudless sky. No one seemed to notice the heat.

Handcrafted signs of welcome waved as far as the eye could see. He was presented with gifts of serapes, rosaries, and statues. In an enthusiastic outpouring of feeling worthy of a homecoming champion, the crowd cheered:

"*Principe de la iglesia!*" "Prince of the church!"

"*Nosotros te amanos!*" "We love you!"

The strings of Panamanian guitars filled the air and accompanied Cody to the waiting black limousine, a car used only for the highest dignitaries of Panama.

The next couple of days were filled with the same excitement. As Cody went from mission to mission, streets overflowed with people welcoming him. Guitars serenaded. Groups pulled together spontaneous concerts.

And through it all, Cody felt not only the warmth of the people but also their poverty. While we were saying Mass in one of our open-area chapels, a rooster jumped on the altar and walked around the table gallantly as if saying that even a bird could claim territory over an archbishop of the church if he was bold enough to do it. Cody, perhaps concerned about what the people might say if he brushed him off, allowed the haughty bird to take his time.

That same evening the lights didn't work and Cody caught Jack engaged in a ritual that we had faced before: lighting the gasoline lamp. This time it didn't work as well. While Jack was attempting to siphon the gas, he swallowed some of it, gagged, and then spent the evening with a stomach that didn't want to settle down. Perhaps this exercise helped "ignite" the generousness Cody offered before he left.

The air was calm and the excitement had settled for the first time in two days, as Cody and I drove together down from the mission where we had said goodnight after an evening Mass and spontaneous festivities. He was dressed in the black robes of a bishop with the stole of his office draped across his broad body. The moon's light, seeping through our VW Beetle's window, seemed to rest on the stole's purple massiveness.

He began to muse on the future of the mission we had just left. "We'll build a big church atop the hill. We'll make a large and comfortable residence for the priests on that same hill."

My thoughts struggled to keep pace with his words and my mouth was silent. I heard the King of the Hill building a kingdom, setting the rules, and establishing turf.

"We'll put an extra suite in it, so I can come here when I retire." He paused. "But I'll never make it up that hill. We'll have to put in an elevator."

I laughed.

"You're not taking me seriously. I'm not kidding. Get some plans for it," he added.

It wasn't the only time he brought up the idea of an elevator, even after I explained that the hill was solid rock, the construction feat would be major and costly, and the scandal caused by such a monument would be even more costly.

"They are poor," he said, pointing to the squatters' fields still stretching across the hills. I held my tongue, remembering his earlier request for an ice-making machine. I thought of accepting that one as a compromise substitute for the elevator, but fortunately we ended up with neither.

The end of our visit felt bitter, since that very day I learned that he had come to San Miguelito to escape Martin Luther King's visit to Soldier Field. He, along with all religious leaders, were to assemble in a massive show of strength, but he announced that he had urgent commitments in Panama. The poor come in many shapes, I thought.

"They are needy, but they appreciate the church." He smiled. I am sure he was wondering how he would carry back the boxes of treasures they had given him.

I was ready to offer to ship his gifts, perhaps him, too, in a wooden crate, when he blurted, "Leo, we will give you what you need. Build what you have to build—these people need churches. Send me a proposal; Chicago will make it happen."

As our efforts toward building community with the people grew, our needs as a team grew. Two more priests joined us, Fred Mc-Ternan and Mark Sheehan.

Fred had been serving in Panama as a military chaplain. He had visited San Miguelito several times and had been instrumental in getting us acquainted with the area and the needs of the people. He was influential in connecting us with some of the right people and was a positive promoter of our efforts and our mission in Panama.

Fred had spirit and energy. He would frequently bring us to song, echoing the spirit of work, "Hey, ho hey ho . . ."

Adjusting to civilian life wasn't as easy for him as he or I would have liked. It was hard for him to assimilate the culture and he'd mock his own Spanish, sometimes offending the natives. Once in a while he used a biting tone that didn't sit well with the women. He liked to sing, "Why can't a woman act like a man?" When Fred left us, he returned to his family home in Jersey.

Mark Sheehan, a Benedictine priest from Newark who had been studying what we were doing, asked if he could join us. Mark came at a time when we were in the greatest need to expand and to provide more autonomy to pastoral leadership.

Five Maryknoll sisters had been working with the women and children of the community and we began to see the strength of their efforts. Modeling the sisters' sincerity of focus, dedicated spirit, and unrelenting ways of living out their work, the Panamanian women were gaining voice and power.

I had worked with Madre Maria de la Cruz in Chicago and, in consultation with her, asked the Maryknoll sisters if they would send her to San Miguelito. They sent her as the superior of the convent and, under her gentle leadership, two sisters who had struggled like Fred to identify with the people were replaced. Three new ones arrived. The new team of sisters thrived and so did their work. The superior would describe the sisters, each with her own spirit: Maura, a flower child, intelligent, inspiring, and creative; Cecilia, fondly called Che, a get-it-done woman with musical and writing talent that could transform traditional, ritualistic, practices to contemporary, relevant ceremonies; Beatriz, a determined woman from an elite Nicaraguan family; and Graciela, a gentle and giving woman.

By 1966, with Cody making good on his promise, we had five parish church structures, each costing $85,000. They were designed simply and practically, with much of the gathering space left open to send the message that more were always welcome and to catch the trade winds when they deigned to grace us with their presence.

It was time, we all agreed, to redefine our roles.

The talent within our team was boundless. It was time to rethink how we worked together and I was the first to admit our efforts would be limited if I was to remain the primary and only head of our efforts.

It was no longer fitting for me to be the sole lead of the "experimental church" of San Miguelito. There were multiple structures across San Miguelito, multiple activities and multiple ministries. The 1963 population of twenty-five thousand had almost doubled and there was no sign of the growth stopping.

We assigned a priest and a sister to each parish and named them co-pastors. It wasn't an easy decision. My dedication and work was with men, empowering them and ensuring that the community would thrive because of them. Yet, I couldn't deny that the sisters had brought a dynamism that we men would never have generated. A lot of discussion went into this decision.

"We want to model how men and women can work together— in Christ."

"Do we have enough credibility to live out our celibate lives?"

"We want a work where each of us is co-equal, one with the other."

"Who will have the last word?"

"We teach the principles of collaboration. Can we not live them?"

"How will Chicago take to this design? Rome?"

"It is within the gifts of both men and women that the church will thrive."

Officially, taking on Hispanic derivatives of our names, we became the co-pastors of each parish. I, as Padre Leon, remained at Cristo Redentor, the first and central parish on the hill. Madre Cecilia joined me at Cristo Redentor as co-pastor.

Jack Greeley (Padre Juan Primero) and Madre Maria de la Cruz established El Cristo Hijo del Hombre. Around the corner, Padre Federico, Fred McTernan, and Madre Beatriz co-pastored at Cristo Luz del Mundo. Padre Marco Sheehan and Madre Graciela became co-pastors of Cristo Resucitado; and Madre Maura and John Enright (Padre Juan Segundo) worked together at the parish of San Isidro.

We agreed that we would begin each morning together, praying, reflecting on our ministries, and making plans. The lay leaders joined us and we became a force that many wanted to join, emulate, and model.

T he core of activities that was so much part of the church of San Miguelito—that of building community—was happening in Chicago and in other parts of the United States. Springing up all over were similar movements designed to form the laity in new and creative ways. In the States such movements as the Christian Family Movement (CFM), Young Christian Workers (YCW), Young Christian Students (YCS), and the Cana Conference as well as major liturgical changes with lay involvement were breathing life into the church. What was different was that the hierarchy and the average parish priest were not recognizing what the impact of all this could be. The hierarchical church in the United States gave cursory acknowledgment to these movements, tolerating and sometimes touting their activities. And especially with the war going on between Cody and the parish priests, my peers, who were some of the brightest, most dedicated men of Chicago's church, had little energy to experience the movements' depth and meaning.

As the years of struggle went on, priests began to leave the ranks of the priesthood—fine, competent men—in one of the saddest emigrations I have ever witnessed. Some left out of sheer anger, others because they were disillusioned. Not a few, in their hurt and discouragement, turned for solace and affection to the women near them, not because they intended to violate their vow of celibacy, but because who is better at counseling a deeply hurt and frustrated man than a good and understanding woman?

Many people were hurt and many lives destroyed. Some of this would have happened anyway because of the radical changes in both society and in the church, so I cannot lay all the blame on Cardinal Cody. But there is no doubt in my mind that he was a major contributing factor to the debacle facing the Chicago church of the late 1960s.

The decade of the sixties was an era of tension within tension. I was fortunate to be living in Panama, working to build church while others were watching it tumble. I shudder to think how I might have dealt with the Chicago turbulence.

Our primary work of building *iglesiolas*, small communities, continued. Trained laity, priests, and sisters visited the homes in the area. New huts and sometimes a whole new sector would sprout up overnight.

We would try to wait until the late afternoon before setting out for our visits so that we could capture the time between dusk and dark, often the most pleasant time of the day. The trade winds would pick up and at that time of day we had to cope only with the dry dust in the hot season and the muddy puddles in the wet season. The unpaved roads made the going rough as we worked for balance, making our way up and down the hills and in and through the tall grass where the hint of house could be seen.

Waiting too long in the day when vision might be impaired could be disastrous, since poisonous snakes made their livelihood in the grass unless they were visiting a cold damp place like our shower stalls. Jumping cockroaches were frequent visitors on our shoulders. And we were ever watchful of the scorpions that seemed to like toes. Fortunately, the one blessing the area had inherited was a mosquito-free environment—thanks to the U.S. Army, which had sprayed the entire Canal Zone.

The visits were an essential part of our evangelizing. We walked among the people, conversing casually with them, showing interest in their interests, discussing the state of the Alliance of Progress efforts, and asking about their needs. In our visits we would invite them to take the Familia de Dios course. The families told us again and again how much they appreciated the visits. When, as a result of word of mouth, people approached us, we made sure that we visited their homes before they took the course.

Following the course, people attended the Cursillo, with the men and women attending on different weekends. After completing the Cursillo, each participant was invited to become a member of his or her local church.

This formal step of becoming a parishioner usually started with a man marrying his wife. One-third of the existing "marriages" were by common law; and 80 percent of the people had not been married in the church. The restlessness to resolve their situation began during the course and often peaked during the Cursillo.

Some men would leave the Cursillo, "fix" their problem, and return to take a second Cursillo, commenting on how new and improved the Cursillo was. The Cursillo hadn't changed. I figured that these men, once they became aware of their present state, were so absorbed in themselves, unable to focus on anything but their present state that they experienced only a cursory level of the Cursillo and, once freed of their burden, they would return, open to a fuller experience.

The conversion of individuals wasn't individualistic. It was a commitment to live no longer for oneself, but for the community. For individuals coming from the hills, with no trust of their neighbor or of authority, this was truly a radical conversion.

Word of our work spread across Latin America, Europe, and the United States. In addition to the fact that several of our lay deacons and I were giving talks in different parts of the world, visitors began to pour into San Miguelito. Forty to eighty visitors would visit us monthly.

When our friends from the States asked us what they could bring, we would say peanut butter and gin. Gin and tonics were a favorite after-hours drink. Peanut butter was a comfort food from home, not sold in Latin America and thus all the more desired.

A euphoria took over San Miguelito. The people knew they were about something special. They were feeling blessed and they were experiencing a deep sense of joy.

Our pastoral teams were being stretched in every direction. The priests and sisters often together were on call to greet visitors as well as to care for the growing needs of the people. I was glad that we had had the foresight to divide up the work, that Chicago had provided us with five parish churches, and that the co-pastorship appeared to be working well. One day I gained insight into a new reality.

"Have you noticed the way that Madre Graciela looks at Padre Marco?" one of my lay deacons asked.

I hadn't noticed. Graciela and Mark were co-pastors and had, like the rest of us, been paired off for a little over a year.

I had always trusted my instincts and felt I had a pulse on the mood and tone of our activities. Perhaps my work with the political movement was taking its toll and I was missing something.

Before I had a chance to notice any special looks between them, Madre Maria de la Cruz approached me. Graciela had told her, "Maria, I am in love with Mark."

It was like a thunderclap splitting the sky over my head. I felt betrayed. We were celibate people, committed to the church. I didn't quite like the rule of celibacy—still don't today, but it was our promise and it was the expectation of the people that we live it. Celibacy was what differentiated us; we lived out our promises, an important image to the people.

Everyone knew about the exodus of priests and nuns in the States leaving and many marrying each other. I had attributed it to the restless state of the 1960s church there. I didn't expect it here. We were doing such fulfilling work, work that answered every dream of a minister—to reap the fruit of our labors. Every day was a generative process: working together made it happen. I trusted that the vitality of our work would sustain our relationships. I didn't expect romance. I didn't want it on my team.

Madre Cecilia, my co-pastor, and I were doing fine. She was an independent woman and I was an independent man. We argued and agreed. We respected each other and resolved issues decently. She and I worked together and we worked alone. Our parish, the largest and most established, was flourishing.

I remembered Adelina, one of the first women I had met in San Miguelito, telling me that I was one of the priests who, according to the women of the community, could get married but wouldn't.

Opportunities were ever present to get involved with women. We priests were the gentle, caring, altruistic men that few men of their community represented. It was common for the local priests to have a mistress.

One time an American woman living with her husband on duty in the Canal Zone called me. "Father Leo, I am very sick and very alone. My husband is away and I have a problem. Could you please help me?" she asked.

I drove to her home.

She greeted me at the door, dressed in a robe that covered her body but not much of her intention. "Come in, come in," she said as she closed the door quickly behind her. "Please sit down, Father. I have a problem. It has been with me for a long time," she began in a contrite and coquettish way.

I nodded, but I sensed something like a snake beginning to coil around me.

"I am in love with another man," she said.

I paused. The snake tightened and I said, "You mean me, don't you?"

Her head nodded in silence; her eyes were now downcast in a way untypical of her usual demeanor.

"It cannot be," I said, attempting to get myself out of the chair that seemed to have more cotton than bounce. Why had I picked this chair, I thought to myself. I couldn't get out of it fast enough.

I dropped my keys as I headed for the door. Picking them up I muttered again, "It cannot be," and left the woman lingering sheepishly behind me.

I was a foolish hero—again!

Concern for Mark and Graciela heightened. When I found out the feelings were mutual, I asked them to leave. It was a difficult and painful decision. The work of our ministry could not continue with co-pastors in love. Our work was controversial enough, being watched by the world. Celibacy was not an issue the church was ready to address; in fact it still isn't today.

The mood and tone of our pastoral team changed. We were divided in thought and the tension was like that in a smoldering volcano. One day it would seem that we had a relatively peaceful mountain and the next an unstoppable torrent of frustrations, accusations, and complaints about unmet needs would flow forth. Mark and Graciela's departure had unleashed an effusion of issues, not many related to them, but all now seemingly incapable of containment. The pressure of our work had been mounting, gradually but inexorably increasing the stress; their leaving prompted the eruption.

I had heard of a movement coming out of the National Training Laboratory Institute in the United States called T-groups or "sensitivity groups." Religious and lay leaders struggling with unsettling times were participating in these groups across the States. A session consisted of five-day encounters led by a trained facilitator. The intergroup dynamics focused on the present and immediate environment and were designed to address and resolve interpersonal problems.

I chewed on more cigars those days than I smoked. Was our team falling apart? Was our team too threatened to rebuild? Did we care enough for our work, for ourselves, and for the future of the church to continue? I didn't want a fire fountain and decided to seek help. Several of our lay deacons, fully aware of our situation and our plan to address it, asked to participate in the sessions.

Jack Gorman, a priest psychologist from Chicago, came to facilitate. During one "trust" exercise, Jack asked the team to lift me in the air. I was struggling with my own vulnerability and didn't know if I wanted to let go that fully. Before I knew it, I was being held in the air by my team. Jack was asking us to close our eyes, to be fully present, feeling our emotions and letting ourselves sense the moment. Then he said, "Let him go."

In a quick flood of fear, my thoughts began to spin. Visions of tumbling, falling, and being abandoned welled up inside me. I was torn between hope and despair, trust and fear.

The team, all but Jack Greeley, did as they were told. They let me go. Jack held on just long enough so that I could gain my composure. I looked around at everyone in the room.

Most eyes were downcast. It was a moment of release—the rushing out of anxiety, of anger, of pent-up feelings. The intensity of our life, far from home and heavy with demands, had climaxed in that moment. Letting me go had freed people of those feelings and they didn't know what to do next.

Gorman looked at Greeley and asked, "Why didn't you let Leo go?"

"We can't let *him* go," answered Greeley. I looked at him and didn't know what to say.

Tears, honesty, apologies, and recommitment filled the days. My trust of and respect for our team grew as we talked through our concerns and expectations. We were a church-people, yes, but we were also human, filled with the desire of all humans—to love and be loved in return.

Later, after we were back in the States and Jack Greeley told me that he had left the priesthood and was to marry Madre Maria de la Cruz who had left Maryknoll, I celebrated with genuine joy. I had gained a new respect for the wholeness of our being. Their work in San Miguelito had created a lasting union of two hearts. How could that be so wrong?

As a result of our sensitivity session, we established a Tuesday through Friday hour's meditation to start the day. For the first fifteen minutes, the pastoral team and lay deacons would read in silence a chosen text from the Bible. Then a discussion would open during which we would explore the meaning and application of that text in the community. The daily drama of San Miguelito became more intimately shared.

It was like the early days of our work together, and from these sessions many new and exciting programs evolved.

We had already added the Cursillo to follow the twelve-week course and still found that these programs were only the initial phase of a lifelong development process. As fast as we invited and brought new people into the community of the faithful, others fell back to their own ways. It was unrealistic and dangerously unsettling to evangelize men and women outside their natural family and work environment.

There wasn't yet a Christian sense of family and it was a growing social problem. We initiated the Christian Family Movement (CFM), taking on and adding to the basic principles that churches in the States were using: a model that was called See-Judge-Act. To *see*, or to become aware, couples would gather in groups of about ten and discuss family-related issues. Discussion would move to *judge*, to evaluate what changes needed to be made. Some choices would be personal, where each family would make choices as to how they would improve their relationships; other choices would be community-based, where families working with families would define how to build parish life. Finally, they would *act* on their decisions. Families organized themselves and were soon engaged in all aspects of community and parish life.

During all the years I spent in San Miguelito, I never stopped celebrating the hunger and spontaneity with which our people sought their own development and well-being. Once the faucet was open, eagerness flowed smoothly and continuously. In each of our five parishes, there could be as many as twenty CFM groups meeting in their groups of eight to ten. Activities began to need organization and each parish established a leader-couples coordinating group that soon became the hub of planning for the parish.

In tandem with CFM we instituted a program for young unmarried workers, Young Christian Workers, a methodology developed by Canon Cardijn in Belgium. This, too, took on life within each parish.

Our team had rallied once more, strengthening not only our mission but also the ministries with which we were building and creating church in Panama.

The floodgates of ministerial success were shadowed by the growing political unrest in the country. Our people were torn and so was I. In the name of good, we were to face a danger we had never faced before.

7
CHALLENGING THE UNCHALLENGEABLE

*E*mpty soda bottles stood on the table next to a crumb-sprinkled plate, one that an hour earlier had held freshly baked bread. A few women were fanning themselves through the heavy breath of summer. We were almost knee-to-knee, sitting in a small living space typical of San Miguelito homes. Those present, nine men and women, were engaged in their third dialogue of the Familia de Dios program. I had just asked the question, "Why should we show respect to those who do us wrong?"

The phone rang and, like a child wanting attention, it wouldn't stop until it was answered. The owner of the house grabbed the receiver, listened, shook his head rapidly up and down, and hung up with an "OK."

"That was my brother-in-law," he said excitedly. "He told me to turn on the TV. There is a coup in progress."

"For the good of the country," a spokesperson for military was speaking. "We have overthrown the government. Dr. Arnulfo Arias is no longer president of Panama."

For many years the *enfant terrible* of Panamanian politics had been Arias, a member of a prominent family, once a medical doctor, later a wealthy coffee plantation owner. Dr. Arias, a strong authoritarian, often rumored to be a Fascist, refused to share power with the other members of his class. He had his own party, the Panamenistas, which had wide support among the populace. Twice before he had been elected to the presidency and each time he was deposed for being high-handed.

In 1968, when Dr. Arias again ran for the presidency, the ruling coalition pulled out all the stops to defeat him; they used government money and personnel, even officers of the Guardia Nacional to persuade and intimidate voters, to buy and steal votes. Arnulfo Arias, despite being a member himself of the ruling class, had become for the people a symbol of the drive to break the stranglehold of the rich on the country. Our own area, San Miguelito, was heavily Panamenista. We knew weeks ahead of time that he would sweep San Miguelito.

With partial intervention from Archbishop Clavel who had organized a civic committee to monitor the counting of the election votes and despite all the forces and illegal actions of the opposition, Dr. Arias won the election and was sworn in as president on October 1, 1968.

Many believed that the closer Arnulfo Arias got to the presidential chair the more eccentric he became. That was borne out in 1968 when the new president began to make his appointments, giving high posts to party hacks out of a conviction that he could rule the country himself.

What put him deeply in trouble was his intention to punish the officers of the Guardia Nacional who had worked to defeat him in the elections. He sent them out of the country as military attachés in various embassies. Major Boris Martinez called a secret meeting of younger officers at the Tocumen Camp. Originally, Colonel Omar Torrijos had not been invited, but he managed to get in anyway. The officers decided to engineer a coup to depose Dr. Arias and thus save their positions and rank.

"For public safety, we ask you to stay in your homes." The spokesperson punched his words. "Stay calm. There are to be no public meetings. No more than three people are to gather at any time."

One reason for the coup's surprising success was that Arias fled to the Canal Zone, under U.S. protection and, perfectly safe himself, he took to the radio and exhorted his followers to rise and fight off the National Guard. It was a serious mistake to call people to risk their freedom and, perhaps, their lives when he was clearly unwilling to risk his own. If, for instance, he had hidden in San Miguelito, the people, largely his devoted followers, would have defended him and the rest of the country might well have given him the support he needed. It would have been a long shot, but one that could have paid off handsomely. He chose not to make the bet.

There was silence in this little house that six months ago hadn't existed. These people who had lived in isolation high in the hills had come to San Miguelito for a new start and had begun the journey to building their faith and their sense of community. They sat there stunned. There was little sorrow or outrage—just curiosity and fear.

"My goodness," the owner of the house said, "what will happen to us?"

They were concerned, but reacted mostly as spectators. I could not find in them any sense of being involved directly as responsible, active agents of democracy. I was burning to speak but, for several reasons, principally because I was not a Panamanian citizen, I managed to muzzle my words.

When I got back to the rectory I found the leaders of MUNDO, our newly founded organization working for democracy, waiting for me. They had been scheduled to begin a political education seminar for seventy-five men at the seminary building in Las Cumbres. When they received the news of the military coup, they decided it would be wiser to cancel the weekend seminar and get the participants home safely. Afterwards the leaders returned to our house and we sat around a table and talked until three in the morning. What a difference grounding in democratic principles makes. They were serious about their responsibilities in the face of this threat to the freedom and peace of San Miguelito as well as that of the whole of Panama.

They resolved to convoke a meeting of citizens from every sector of San Miguelito in order to determine what answer was to be given to the military usurpers. Sectors, like Chicago's wards, were areas divided according to demographic boundaries. These meetings would have to be held in secret and would have to circumvent the appointed politician who oversaw each sector.

Streets were blocked off to prevent bus and taxi drivers from getting through. The military was sent to prevent people from traveling anywhere, especially to points where they could organize.

We knew that a large gathering could not be held at the parish center. The rectory was located on a hill and we could see that the Guardia had already placed an observation post on the area's highest hill, which looked directly down on us. I wondered what they thought at seeing the leaders of MUNDO leave the rectory two by two as the false dawn grayed the tropical sky. The leaders had agreed to invite two representatives from every sector to a meeting at the seminary in Las Cumbres on the following Monday evening.

Violence in the neighborhood came with the real dawn. The Ministry of Housing office was sacked and burned to the ground. Every government vehicle in the area was stoned and destroyed. The Army responded quickly with troops outfitted in battle uniforms and carrying rifles and machine guns.

Most of the residents of San Miguelito, including ourselves, stayed within the safety of our homes. Peering out our windows we watched teenagers darting in and out of cover given by houses and trees, throwing stones at the soldiers, who were young and visibly nervous. It must have been a frightening experience for them— their first taste of battle. Once they opened fire, the bullets flew everywhere. The youngsters tormenting the soldiers shrieked with laughter and danced with glee like Davids confronting the hated Goliaths.

Suddenly a woman standing in her doorway across the road from our house fell to the ground. We could see that she had been hit by a ricocheting bullet. We stared in horror at the bleeding, prostrate woman. No one came from inside her house or from the adjoining houses to pull her to safety.

In haste, I donned the white cassock that I had years earlier stuffed in the back of my closet. I figured the soldiers would not shoot at a priest. I asked a young man in the rectory to accompany me. Dashing across the road we picked up the bleeding woman and carried her down the hill to the command jeep. No one stopped us.

We deposited her in the vehicle and ordered the startled officer to take her to the hospital as quickly as possible. "Can't you see we are at war?" he mouthed back.

I screamed. "Against whom, women and children?"

He hesitated, then let out a long sigh of exasperation, climbed into the jeep and, surprisingly, as I found out later, actually took her to the hospital. The woman was not seriously injured. Once I crawled back to the rectory, it was a long time before the lump left my throat and the palsy my fingers. We had been saved from attack.

In utmost secrecy the word went out to all the sectors. Monday evening ninety-four persons were recognized as official representatives of forty-nine sectors. The meeting was long but orderly. Finally they decided, almost unanimously, to send a Manifesto to the Military Junta demanding a guarantee of civil rights, free elections, a prompt return to civilian rule, and, above all, fair and adequate representation from and by the people of San Miguelito.

Aware that the Junta might well ignore the Manifesto, the group passed a motion to mention that if the military did not answer within one week's time, then the signers would organize a protest march against the "temporary" government. An executive committee composed of ten members was elected and instructed to draft the Manifesto and deliver it to the Junta. The assembled delegates knew they had involved themselves in a dangerous undertaking. Indeed, they adverted to the possibility of spies being present.

One delegate warned the potential Judas: "If you cannot agree with the policy of this assembly, we respect your freedom, but those who are tempted to betray us should beware."

The delegates dispersed and the designated committee returned to the rectory to construct the document. It was a frank, lengthy, and bold piece of writing put in excellent Spanish prose largely by Ramon "Chacho" Hernandez. Pride and fear pulsed my being when I read:

> We do not want promises without deeds. Convinced that what we seek is just, we shall not tolerate any more deceptions. We declare to the nation and to the world that if this document is not answered affirmatively within the stipulated period, we shall make a massive non-violent demonstration. We shall send into the streets men, women and children and perhaps you will slaughter us but many more men, women and children will take to the streets to cry out our opposition to and displeasure with the death of our freedom.

The document was completed and mimeographed by dawn of the next morning.

Now it was up to us to deliver to the various sectors copies of the document along with an outline of how to carry out a non-violent march plus instructions on how to rehearse one.

We put the fat bundle of papers in the trunk of my car and proceeded to begin the early morning deliveries. Accompanying me were Chacho Hernandez and Orlando Wynter, a native Panamanian who could speak neither Spanish nor English well, but a gentle man blessed with the kind of courage one sees only in older men.

We were aware that the whole area was under martial law and that we were almost certainly being watched by the soldiers manning the observation post on the tallest hill in San Miguelito—the one we called "El Cielo."

I watched nervously through the rear mirror for signs of trouble and it didn't take long for my fears to be justified. A military jeep roared up behind us, pulled abreast of my car, and ordered us to stop. They were searching every car on the road.

I felt my hands gripping the steering wheel as though we were about to go off the road and over a cliff. I identified myself as a priest and explained that we were out on a "pastoral" mission. The soldier eyed me suspiciously, looked into the back seat and then said, "All right, Father, you can go on. But you shouldn't be out here at all. These are very dangerous times."

As I drove away slowly, no one spoke. I thought to myself, "*You're* telling *me* they're dangerous!" If he had searched the trunk, he would have found the Manifesto—hundreds of copies! Finally someone muttered a prayer of thanksgiving.

We managed to distribute all the copies that morning. Through the offices of Jorge Riba, the Manifesto was delivered to the new government.

That evening the whole nation heard some sensational news on TV: "The Catholic church of San Miguelito and the community it represents has given its *support* to the ruling Junta." The papers the next morning carried the same concocted story.

Fury filled the home of every representative who had worked on the Manifesto. The priests and sisters, all of us, were frozen in indignation. Phone calls came all day, burning and spewing anger and disgust.

"How can they distort our message?"

"What outrageous lies!"

"Looks like they want war right out of San Miguelito!"

"They must be desperate to make up such stories."

"Let's hit the streets and show them we mean business!"

Others advised that we wait for the seven days we had stipulated in the Manifesto. We were almost certain that the government was not taking us seriously and there probably would be no answer, but we wanted to honor our own request.

The community used the time to prepare itself along the principles of non-violent action. The Maryknoll sisters Cecilia, Maria de la Cruz, and Maura maintained a word-of-mouth network with the women in all the sectors. Non-violent instructions were reinforced

and peaceful actions rehearsed. These women worked so successfully that the ever-present Guardia never suspected what the *Madrecitas*
were doing.

When seven days had passed and no response had come from
the government, on the morning of October 23, 1968, we
moved. At the appointed hour there were only fifty of us. Panamanians have a habit of arriving late to almost any function, but we felt
that that alone did not explain the paucity of participants.

One of a group that had successfully arrived told us breath-
lessly, "It looks as though the whole army is waiting for us at the entrance to Paraiso."

We figured that many had not come because they had seen the
troops and thought the march would be forcibly suspended.

We started down the hill—some fifty strong. As people (those
who weren't hiding under beds) saw us from their houses, many
joined and soon we were five hundred strong.

We marched six abreast, with arms locked with those on either
side. At each street crossing we stopped to pray silently and then re-
cited the *Padre Nuestro* together. We carried a large wooden cross,
the one we used for the Good Friday procession.

Flashes of my Chicago youth shot through me: an adventurous boy
roaming the city streets, playfully trying to find any bit of excitement that would fill a day. "This isn't play." I shuddered. "What
made me think that this was my business? Will it be a day of defeat
and death?"

I wasn't particularly frightened of the violence that might come
to me. I felt the burden of men lost, women injured, and children
homeless. I questioned whether the "experimental" church had
anything to do with exposing Panamanians to this level of harm. I
was fearful of my own aggression.

And hounding me more furiously than the thought of gaining
nothing from this march was the thought of gaining something.
"What if we win?" I asked myself, "What then? What are we getting
ourselves into?"

Marching slowly, in deafening silence, we passed over the last little rise in the street and then we saw the troops stretched out
before us, blocking our way. They stood ready for combat with tear

gas canisters and machine guns. *Multi-familiares,* high-rise, low-cost housing, had been constructed on both sides of the intersection. The balconies and stairwells were packed with spectators. Other people lined the streets, careful not to get too close to the soldiers.

We drew up to the front line of the soldiers and stopped. Once again we prayed silently and then said the Our Father out loud. We could hear the people on the sidelines joining in. Several moments passed when no one moved or spoke.

The officer in command, Major Ramiro Silvera, strode up to Chacho and me, I dressed again in my white cassock, and from not more than two feet away he shouted, "Go back! You will not pass!"

With a dramatic gesture of pointing to the direction whence we had come, he again shouted "Go back where you came from!"

Chacho stepped forward even closer and answered with an equally dramatic gesture of pointing forward, "We are a free people with the dignity of free people. We are going that way!"

Cheers and whistles rose from the bystanders. The captain turned to me and menacingly said through gritted teeth, "Father, you had better stop this right now. If you don't, women and children will be hurt and it will be your fault."

I replied, "Major, we are not armed and we are pledged to non-violence. You are the ones with the clubs and the guns, so, if anyone is hurt, you will be responsible."

Flustered and frustrated, the captain stared at us for several moments. Then he said, "Stay right where you are. I'm going to call in for further instructions."

Walking over to the command jeep, he picked up the telephone and talked to his boss, Omar Torrijos. We could hear a heated discussion between the two—even strong obscenities coming out of the radio receiver. Not one of us moved, but I could feel the need to find a water closet coming on me soon.

The captain put the mouthpiece down and returned to us. "Colonel Torrijos says that you have permission to continue the march under one condition—that you allow us to escort you in order to prevent any violence."

Chacho replied sardonically, "That would be very good of you."

Someone behind us began singing the national anthem. The cross was raised high: the signal to continue the march. The crowds roared their approval and many more joined us.

What a strange procession—with the troops marching and riding on both sides of us. By the time we arrived at the church in Villa Guadalupe, we numbered five thousand.

Chacho addressed us all, the Guardia still with us: "We believe in our freedom and in our dignity. We have asked the Junta for an answer to our Manifesto. They chose not to respond. Once again we demand an answer. If it doesn't come during this week, we shall march again next Sunday and we shall have ten thousand people with us."

The crowds dispersed and the troops returned to their barracks. Many of us went back to the rectory for a post-mortem and a cold beer. A beer never tasted so good.

The same evening, feeling bolder and more determined, the MUNDO leaders held a meeting at the parish center. Most of the leadership of San Miguelito attended and plans were made for the next march.

Almost at the stroke of midnight there was a commotion outside. Looking out the windows we saw flashing red lights and heard men shouting orders and troops running to take positions.

In strode Major Natera, dressed in a camouflage battle uniform, wearing a metal helmet, and brandishing an evil-looking machine gun: GI Joe, Panamanian style.

"How dare you gather like this! The High Commander is very angry with you."

We remained silent.

"You will have no more protest marches. If you do, there will be immediate repression! Who are your leaders?"

Chacho stepped forth, gesturing with his hand to signal me to stay right where I was.

"You and this Father Mahon," Natera said, pointing to me. "You are to come to Army headquarters. Colonel Omar Torrijos will be waiting."

"If you fail to come," Natera was looking at Chacho, "we will take direct action against Father Mahon."

There wasn't much sleep that night. A group chose to accompany Chacho and me. They assembled at the rectory in early morning. Among them were Adelina de Duarte, José Arrocha, and Madre Cecilia. We prayed and began our trip to Army headquarters. It took less than an hour and felt as if we were walking into a distant land, separate from anything we had known before. Torrijos made us wait. We looked at each other but remained silent and docile, the very behaviors his lateness was imposing on us.

On his own time and at his own moment, Torrijos burst into the room with the fury of a bull ready for the matador. He looked around the room and his blood-shot eyes found mine. "You—come with me," he barked and I followed him out to another chamber. Chacho rose to support me and I motioned him to wait. I'd faced Cody alone; I guessed I could face a dictator.

"You won yesterday," he began, "but you'll never make fools of us again." Barely able to articulate clearly, his face flushed with fury, he went on. "We have risked our lives, our careers, and our families on the coup and we're not going to let someone like you take it all away. Your life right now is not worth one cent. We're not afraid to kill if we have to. Do you understand that?"

"Yes," I answered, knowing that his rage had not yet subsided.

"I could have you put on a plane and flown to the States tonight," he barked.

I replied, "I know that, and I could do nothing to prevent it. If you think that will solve your problem, then do it."

He continued to pour out a torrent of words describing the dangerousness of our actions and the precariousness of his regime. He exclaimed that apparently we didn't understand how few men he had for controlling pillaging and riots. Finally he said, "Do you know that if every part of Panama did what you people have done, we could not control this country?"

I nodded: "Yes, that's just the point of it all."

He grunted and began to tell me of his plan to proscribe the corrupt politicians and then present a slate of "acceptable" candidates for elections, thereby returning the country to civilian rule. I had no idea whether he was sincere, but I must have looked skeptical because he ended the interview by saying, "I warn you and all your people that we will not tolerate any further action against us."

He then returned to the other room, anticipating that I would follow him. I figured I'd better.

Immediately Torrijos began tearing into the others who had traveled with me, issuing threats and complaints: "It seems you want the rich to continue to rule you. Where did you get the idea we would kill women and children?" Evidently he had gotten around to reading the Manifesto.

In the midst of frightful tension, Chacho interrupted Torrijos and said calmly, "I don't believe we can really dialogue if you continue to use that tone of voice, Colonel."

Torrijos glared at him and sputtered, "*Tu eres cura?*" He used the word *cura* (priest) with consummate disdain, "Are you a priest?"

Panama's future dictator wasn't accustomed to being answered directly and boldly. Chacho explained what the people of San Miguelito wanted and ended by saying that they were willing to suffer to protect their rights. There was no doubt that the Colonel was impressed by the words and courage of the young man before him.

One woman who had supported us since we had arrived, and who was known in military circles because of her earlier relationships with some of the men, Adelina de Duarte, spoke. She spoke with the authority of her ancestry as a direct descendant of Indian royalty and thus a princess in her own San Blas tribe, calling forth the respect she had long commanded from those who knew her.

Adelina spoke of the good that we had brought to Panama, of the good that we could continue to do, if only Torrijos would work with us. She had a knack of moving her body with the rhythm of her words so that most men found themselves shaking their heads in agreement with her before they even knew what she was saying. Torrijos listened.

Torrijos protested that the Guardia's role was only a temporary one, to last a short period during which they would cleanse the nation of its corrupt politicos. He suggested that we meet with several of the civilians whom the Junta had appointed to ministerial posts. He specifically mentioned two, Dr. Carlos Lopez Guevara and Juan Materno Vasquez.

I remained silent. Chacho agreed to the proposed meeting under the condition that the two ministers of state not be accompanied by any Guardia.

"They'll get killed by those ruffians in San Miguelito," stormed Torrijos. Oh, I thought, we really had made an impact. He's scared.

Others spoke in rapid succession. Guevara and Vasquez, they guaranteed, would be safe. We were not a violent group. It worked.

San Miguelito and the government had agreed, under a temporary truce, to negotiate. I had remained silent. I was delighted at how the lay leaders had taken charge and was in awe of what our dialogues in political awareness had created.

I woke up early Sunday morning to see the parish church surrounded by armed troops. I looked out my window right into the muzzle of a long gun mounted on a mobile carrier pointed at my window. I could see the label on it that said "Gift of the U.S.A." The second protest march scheduled for that day had been publicly cancelled. The military, apparently, wasn't taking any chances.

There was no choice. With the presence of the Occupation, we cancelled all Masses.

During the day, because of the scorching heat, we sent out sandwiches and cold Cokes to the young soldiers "guarding" us. They refused at first, as if to say, "But you're supposed to be the enemy." After a few hours, the heat as well as our smiles and white cassocks convinced them we meant no harm and they gladly accepted our hospitality.

I thought back to our first months of wearing those cassocks and how I had shoved them far back in my closet as soon as I could. Now they were a symbol of a difference that I wanted to maintain— a symbol of peace. It was my uniform and it offset the camouflage of the Junta. My "uniform" stood defiantly in the heavy sun, pronouncing its defense against the shadowed green and black. I appreciated it for the first time.

D uring the week the two ministers, Lopez Guevara, who was the foreign minister, and Vasquez, who was the minister of justice, met with a large crowd of delegates from every sector of San Miguelito. Chacho chaired the meeting that took place in our parish center. At times there was restrained listening and at other times there were explosive accusations. There was no physical violence but there were plenty of verbal fireworks. The people spoke boldly and asked some very hard questions. Juan Materno Vasquez, a brilliant, black Panamanian, who himself had come from the lower classes, took umbrage at accusations that he had sold his soul to the military in order to get the position of minister. At one point he was about to leave in a huff, but Lopez Guevara constrained him.

The ministers asked for a little more time to organize themselves and start moving toward a restoration of civil rights and a renewal of free elections. The MUNDO leaders responded with a stern and clear message that the people of San Miguelito were strongly opposed to the new government and were prepared to act against it.

The military coup had prompted a general strike called by the labor unions and by the university students. There was scattered violence throughout Panama, fortunately not involving any who had joined with us, but the Guardia managed to quell the uprisings. There remained some intermittent guerilla warfare in the Chiriqui province near the border with Costa Rica. That ended and the whole country was quiet—resentful but quiet.

The Guardia used that period of calm to consolidate its power and establish its leadership. Older officers were pensioned off; dissident officers went into exile. The "Indian chiefs" were down to two: Colonel Boris Martinez and Colonel Omar Torrijos. But that too changed when one day Martinez was arrested, gagged, handcuffed, and flown off to Miami.

Torrijos assumed the rank of general and became the chief of the Army and ruler of the nation. Messages carried to us in San Miguelito were that the *Jefe Supremo* was impressed with the movement in San Miguelito and would be in contact with us in the near future.

The phone rang jarringly. I did not feel like answering it. I was putting the finishing touches on my sermon for the big Mass of the day—the Misa Tipica, which was scheduled to begin in fifteen minutes.

The ringing continued. Sighing, I picked up the phone and heard a voice ask, "What time is the Mass, Father?" Stories of people calling to ask the time of Mass are legendary in Catholic life. The most famous is: "What time does the Midnight Mass begin, Father?"

Irritated by the interruption, but controlling my annoyance, I told the caller that Mass was to begin at nine o'clock. The voice said cheerily, "Could you wait until I get there?"

I had long been a stickler for promptness, a trait I inherited from my father, so I answered, "No, it will start at nine." I wondered who could be so bold.

"Say, who is this anyway?"

The man behind the voice laughed. "The General. I'll see you there," he said, and hung up. It was Torrijos; I now recognized the voice.

While walking down the steps to the church I made up my mind to begin the liturgy precisely at nine, General or no General.

The General arrived at the very moment I began the procession. The wild noise of the helicopter descending upon us made the church bell, which ordinarily boomed its message as far away as a mile, sound like a dining room bell tinkling in a hurricane.

The people assembled for Mass were distracted. Some were terrified. The altar servers and the musicians abandoned their posts and ran out to see the huge helicopter landing on the rectory lawn.

There was no way to begin the liturgy, so I waited for our guest to arrive. The door of the helicopter opened and out jumped General Omar Torrijos and his bodyguards.

I wanted to be upset about starting late but I, like everyone else, was astonished by his grand entrance. All we needed were the elephants for a full entourage!

The drama was not yet complete. Instead of taking his place among the worshipers, Torrijos walked directly up to me. I was vested and ready to begin the entrance procession. Grinning, he stuck out his hand in greeting and said, "Hello, Father, thanks for waiting for me." He was of medium height, in his late thirties, and not at all unhandsome. He continued, "Father, it's been a long time since I've been to Mass. Will you hear my confession?"

It was neither the time nor the place, but how to say no? I knew I had been upstaged and outmaneuvered. I looked around for a more private place, but the General said: "It's all right, we can do it right here."

So we sat down on the nearest bench. Torrijos whispered his sins and I gave him absolution while hundreds of eyes looked on in amazement. Mass began. The people sang lustily and so, I noticed, did Torrijos. He received communion from my hands. After Mass, he stayed around to talk with many of the people and then he came to our residence for coffee and rolls.

Was this real or was I in a wonderland? Would I wake up to discover that I had been in some fatigue-induced fantasy? Here was the man who had detained me, threatened me with expulsion or worse, and now we were eating breakfast after having shared the Eucharist together.

This was the beginning of the strangest relationship and the most intriguing friendship of my life.

In our conversation Torrijos immediately made it clear to those gathered how much he admired our protest action, our standing up to force. "That's the kind of spirit," he said, "that could make a new nation."

He asked all sorts of questions about our activities, our plans and our dreams. We explained that San Miguelito had been set up as an "experimental" community to find new ways to teach people about their faith, to devise methods to train the laity for an active role in the church rather than relying as in the past on ordained clergy, especially foreign clergy. He listened avidly and appeared to be absorbing everything he was hearing. Subsequently Pinto and the other lay Panamanians peppered him with questions, such as, "When are you going to relinquish power? When will you restore our rights? When do you plan to hold elections?"

He answered that he did not think the country as a whole was ready for civilian rule, that it would only sink back into its previous corruption. "If the rest of common people of the country were as politically conscious and responsible as the people of San Miguelito, then we could move much more swiftly."

He had left an opening, perhaps deliberately, perhaps not. Taking advantage of that opening, I asked him, "Then why not start here? Why not make San Miguelito a laboratory experiment in democracy?"

Like a wave suddenly rising and ready to flip in the glistening sun, all the leaders concurred.

He answered, "Let me talk it over with my people." It was evident that he was interested, even enthusiastic. This visit was the prelude to the creation of San Miguelito as the "model city" of Panama.

8

ESTABLISHING
THE UNESTABLISHABLE

*I*n the center of our parish lawn stood an eight-foot cactus—the kind that sprouts a huge beautiful white flower every ten years. I saw that cactus bloom but once; the blossom appeared at sunset and stood tall and proud all through the moonlit night. By dawn it had wilted and died as though its heart had been broken by the disappearance of its lover, the moon.

Whenever Torrijos's helicopter landed on the same lawn—and it did frequently—the pilot had to avoid the outsized cactus. Because it looked like a phallus in a state of mammoth erection, several of the earthy Panamanians close to me remarked on the sexual symbolism of the government descending on the church. I enjoyed the metaphor and envisioned it as a creative symbol of union, one that brought dignity to government and church working together. I dared think nothing else.

The General returned within a week to announce that his government looked favorably on making San Miguelito a model autonomous city. "Not everyone was for it," he told us ruefully, "so you had better make it work."

Immediately the staff of MUNDO began their work with an enthusiasm that was then and always will be to me a sign of the Spirit moving among the people, touching them with the fire of excitement and idealism. The staff of José Arrocha, Octavio Pinto, Chacho Hernandez, and Eric De Leon was increased by two valuable additions. One was Gustavo Stumpf, a brilliant and articulate Bolivian who had spent more than half his adult life in prison or in exile as he relentlessly worked to promote his dream of a true, participatory democracy. Long after he left Panama his ideas were used by the Panamanian government in its large-scale reform of the Ministry of Education, with no credit ever given to the source of those ideas.

The other addition to the organizing staff came from the U.S. Peace Corps. A young man in his twenties, Thomas Block had completed a two-year tour of duty in San Miguelito but was excited by the vision of this systemic change; he asked to stay. I arranged for an extension of his visa. Tom had graduated with honors from Yale before entering the Peace Corps. While working with us in Panama, he applied for admission to four law schools, Yale, Harvard, Chicago, and Stanford, and was accepted by all four! Not only gifted with a high degree of intelligence, he was blessed with good looks and a smile that fascinated and won over everyone he met. What's more, he possessed an unassuming manner that disguised a remarkable sense of morality and integrity. He was of German-Jewish descent and belief, but I often saw him at the Sunday Eucharist.

I asked him once, "Tom, do you find it strange to be at Mass?"

"Not at all," he replied with a chuckle. "I just close my eyes and imagine I'm at a seder meal. It is really very much the same."

Looking back and feeling the pain of the tragedy and failure that was about to overtake us all, I think of Tom Block—one of the finest human beings I have ever known. We Christians believe that, in Jesus, God showed himself to be deeply and wonderfully human. In Tom Block, a blood brother of Jesus, I was privileged to look upon another young man who showed me once again that God lives in good human beings. Scripture uses the ancient Hebrew way of announcing a theophany, a divine appearance: "A voice from the heavens declared: This is my beloved Son." I learned to see the face of God through the young men and women whose eyes shone with goodness and idealism.

First," said Pinto, "we cannot get paid for any jobs that evolve in our design. Agreed?"

"Absolutely," the team echoed.

"Any appearance of building our own empire and taking over political leadership would destroy a basic democratic principle," Eric noted. The violation of this solemn oath would cause me, a year later, one of the deepest heartaches of my life.

"Any spokesperson must be Panamanian," added Tom. All agreed.

"Let's keep the name simple and call our plan, 'The Plan of San Miguelito,'" declared Chacho. And thus it was.

The first step in the making of a city in which the people would plan and own their own destiny was to educate and to organize them. The territory was divided into sixty-eight districts, each of which was to elect a representative to the General Assembly, an alderman, and a judge for minor matters of arbitration. We could feel the level of enthusiasm rising as classes and seminars were held in every sector to explain the new structure and its process.

A ll elections in Panama had been suspended since the military coup. When it was thought that the preparation had been adequate, the elections in San Miguelito were called. The day came on a Sunday, the customary day for elections in the country. All eyes were on San Miguelito. Observers came from the government and foreign press correspondents were in attendance. A remarkable 73 percent of the electorate voted in perfect order. Absent were the irregularities, the violence, the buying of votes with liquor or with money that had characterized previous elections.

Each of the sixty-eight sectors elected these persons, none of whom was to receive a salary. The structure was in place. Fifty-three of the seats in the General Assembly were won by persons who had taken part in the evangelization programs. Panamanian history had been made. It happened through the leadership of men who had allowed scripture to reform their lives, believed in themselves, and went forth to use their new strength to reform their government.

The spirits and pride of MUNDO couldn't have been higher. The fruit of education continued to ripen. Within two months, the people of one of the sectors, San José, presented a petition signed by 75 percent of the electors asking that their representative be unseated and a new one elected. They gave as reasons incompetence and indifference. The Assembly granted the petition and used the principle of revocation. The people were taking ownership and correcting their own mistakes.

A chief judge of the district was assigned to work with the local arbiters elected in each sector. The purpose of the new system was to reduce the impact of adversarial law—the extreme of which can be seen in countries such as the United States where everyone seems to be suing someone else, often on the flimsiest pretext. Such an abuse of the law is expensive, not only in terms of litigation but also in terms of community divisions that instead of being healed are exacerbated.

In the first stage, the mayor, the chief executive officer, was to be appointed by the central government. We proposed to Torrijos the name of Paulino Salazar—a man we knew to be honest, competent, and dedicated to the dream of a new democracy. Salazar resigned his post as president of his own company and became mayor at a salary way below what he had previously earned. He gathered a professional staff which, along with him, worked an average of seventy hours a week for many months.

Once inaugurated, the new city took over the property of the Ministry of Housing, which had formerly directed the fortunes of San Miguelito. A large warehouse was converted into a building cooperative —turning out cement blocks, windows, doors, and other building supplies. The people who bought there shared in the profits and provided work for many craftsmen.

The next step, a formidable one, was to establish a financial base for the new city. By law and custom, cities in Panama had no power to tax, to issue bonds, or to raise revenues. All they could do was petition for a share in the national budget. This meant that San Miguelito was not autonomous or independent. In fact, it meant living on welfare. Through Torrijos the new city received *some* funds from the Treasury but they were scarcely adequate.

Mayor Salazar went to the U.S.'s Point Four Program, which at that time was pouring incredibly large amounts of money into military and civic projects in Panama. But the U.S., partly because of its fear of Communism and partly because of its fear of losing the Canal, was committed to helping the central government, not a fledgling city within the country. This evolving loan had created an incredibly rich pork barrel on which the rulers of Panama had feasted for many years. Parceling more money to San Miguelito was not part of the program. I should have foreseen the effect that this economic control would have on any plans to raise money, but I plunged forward to help the new city.

Salazar approached me with concern. "Padre Leon," he said, "our city cannot grow without funds. Our resources are depleted. How do we advance democracy without funds? Would you ask Germany to help?"

I had previously obtained money from the Catholic church in Germany to help pay the budget of MUNDO. The German church and the German government contribute to the development of the Third World through their federal income tax. A percentage of a person's tax goes to the church of which one is a member unless one specifically requests an exemption. Consequently, the Catholic Church has ample funds for its clergy, its schools, and its charitable works. The bishops of Germany, in order to preserve a sense of voluntary giving, instituted two national collections, one in Advent which goes to an organization known as "Adveniat" and the other during Lent which goes to "Misereor." The funds of Adveniat are dedicated exclusively to religious works in Latin America and provide funding for such needs as religious education and retreat houses. The Misereor fund is open to requests for help with humanitarian projects in all parts of the world. It was the latter that had given us help in expanding the working budget of MUNDO.

I was not sure that either of the German Catholic agencies had the kind of money that San Miguelito needed, but we decided to ask anyway. I went to Germany accompanied by a young man, Pablo Vega. He was the embodiment of the gentility and integrity of the people of San Miguelito. The agency people were deeply impressed with Pablo and his story. We traveled to Essen and Cologne, the headquarters of Adveniat and Misereor. We were well received but, as I had suspected, there was no way they could help us. What we needed would have exhausted their entire year's budget and deprived other communities of assistance. The directors of Adveniat and Misereor suggested that we approach the government in Bonn. Armed with introductions and recommendations, we drove to Bonn and visited several ministries.

We were received with formality and circumspection, but beneath the courtesy I detected a genuine interest in the proposals. We were to come back with detailed proposals for specific projects. They sent us to Berlin to make plans for a film telling the story of San Miguelito. Each year, the church in Germany produced a television film of some significant project in the developing world. In conjunction with the appeal for funds, televisions across Germany showed the film. The San Miguelito story was filmed on location and produced in Panama. It turned out to be extraordinarily well done and was favorably received by the German populace.

S pace," Eric stated. "If we don't get more space, how can we ever urbanize?" The years of squatting had occupied every open piece of hill available. There were no roads or sewer systems. A park would have been unimaginable. Tin and cardboard shacks were still the dominant form of family shelter. Without new and open land, there was nowhere to move the people. A family named Jelabert made a large tract of vacant land at the very entrance to San Miguelito available. The cost of acquiring the land and developing it was set at $4,500,000.

"Transportation," added Tom and others simultaneously. The buses were old, few, and not municipally owned; workers and children going to school had to stand for hours waiting for a bus which, when it came, would be already bursting with an overabundance of passengers.

The plans completed, Salazar flew to Germany to negotiate the deal. Germany offered a grant of $300,000 to purchase new buses. The bus money was immediately put into operation and the people celebrated the arrival of new buses and an improved flow of bus traffic, especially in the busy times of the day.

Germany declared its willingness to loan the city of San Miguelito four and a half million dollars, at a very low rate of interest, to purchase and develop the Jelabert property.

However, we were unable to get the loan process completed, because many in Panama's central government thought that the money should be received by the national treasury and doled out to the city afterwards. "You can do what you want out there, but we control the money."

The German government refused to make the loan unless the money went directly to San Miguelito. The Germans argued that the whole point was to build an infrastructure that would enable the people to participate in their government, thus checking the power of the central government. It was as if we were in the middle of a family feud when dealing with the estate of a loved one's death. Love, friendship, and good will are set aside; greed, like an infestation of weeds in an open field, dominates. Our work was suspended, halted indefinitely by the government that had promised much but refused to facilitate reception of the aid we so desperately needed.

Revolutionary regimes have a tenuous hold on power anywhere. Unless they have an enormous military machine to protect their sovereignty, they must rely on popular approval. They often use "bread and circuses" to maintain their popularity. The military in Panama did just that—a new sports stadium, the Pan American Games, championship boxing matches, lots of building projects and hence construction jobs. Because of its incessant thirst for popular approval, this kind of regime does not easily tolerate anything that might rival or surpass its standing with the people. Control is its constant watchdog.

None of the pre-coup politicians were all that popular. Most had been discredited. Only Arnulfo Arias had any degree of populatity, and he was living in exile in Florida. The only ones around who presented a threat to the regime were priests—especially young priests who lived among the people and were able to communicate ideas and dreams. Consequently, there was tension between the church and the government. It was widely rumored—and rumors were as common and necessary in Panama as air itself—that a certain young priest was about to be arrested.

Worried by the situation, the bishops who had learned that I had an entree with the General asked me to see him and prevent the arrest. Torrijos was out of the capitol city, attending a fair in a rural area. I drove up there and surprised him by walking right up to him and saying that I needed to speak to him alone about an urgent matter. He consented. It was a private meeting, but he made sure that everyone could see us conversing—not only his military aides but also the townspeople.

"Look at the General talking to a priest—who is he anyway?" Torrijos liked to build controversy around himself.

I told him of the bishops' concern and my own. He knew all about the matter. He may even have instigated the rumors himself. It was an effective way of frightening people. We had a long talk that evening. He said to tell the bishops that he would see to it that no priest in the country would be touched without his consulting with me first—that I was to be the liaison person in these matters between the government and the church.

At the end of the evening he remarked, "Father, I figure I have about five years in this job. Then what shall I do? I think I would like to become a priest."

I looked at him sharply to see whether he was joking or mocking me. I saw that he wasn't, nor was he drunk. He never once took a drink in my presence although I knew that he took plenty when I wasn't around.

He saw my consternation and asked, "Well, a priest can do a lot of good, especially among the poor. Why not me?" The General happened to be a married man with small children at the time and the church would hardly set aside its rules for him. More than that, his lifestyle was hardly that of a type associated with the life of a priest, a good priest at any rate.

So I answered, "Omar, there are a lot of things in your life that would have to be changed even to consider such a thing."

Then I saw a slight smile cross his face as he said, "But I could change, couldn't I?"

"Yes, I guess so," I answered, wondering what it all meant and where it would all end.

On the following Christmas eve at around ten o'clock I was called to the door to see a young officer of the Guardia. He said politely, "*Felices Pascuas, Padre*" and handed me an envelope, "a gift from the General."

Suspicious, I opened the envelope immediately. Twenty hundred-dollar bills poured out. The messenger didn't look at all surprised. Who knows how many similar envelopes he had delivered that day? "This can't be for me," I said, handing the money back.

"Oh yes, Father, the General said I was to give it to you personally."

I tried to get him to take it back but he said that would only get him into trouble.

So I called two people who were working in the rectory to witness that I was taking the money and that I was stipulating that I would give it to the poor. The day after Christmas I instructed a committee to find the poorest families in San Miguelito. Each received a certified check for fifty dollars.

I asked for and received an appointment with Torrijos. Handing him a manila folder with the names of the families and the numbers of the certified checks, I said, "Thanks for the money, Omar, that's what I did with it."

He examined it for a moment and then said, "You are one shrewd son of a bitch!" It was the first and only time he used words like that in my presence, although his colorful language was legendary among those who knew him.

I smiled and said, "If you think you can buy me off for $2,000, you're mistaken!"

Lying on his desk was another manila folder, which he picked up and handed to me. "Read that," he said almost gloating.

"What's in it?" I asked.

"Go ahead, read it; it's a list of all the priests in trouble. Their women are listed, their crooked dealings, and so on."

"Is my name on it? Or any of the priests in San Miguelito?"

"No," he admitted, "we had you checked out but you're all clean."

Handing back the unopened folder, I said, "I don't want to see any of it. It's not any business of mine or yours."

He squinted at me but said no more.

That wasn't the last time I saw close up how he could control situations by buying people off or getting information on their secret lives. One day I was informed that another priest had been arrested. His colleagues asked me to help. I went to Army headquarters and asked to see him. They denied that the priest had been arrested or was in custody. I asked to see the General but was told he was not in the city. I stormed and ranted—all to no avail. Then I went over to the presidential palace where Torrijos had installed Demetrios Jimmy Lakas, his good friend and drinking partner, as the puppet president.

I was told that he too was not in. I sat down on the steps and told the guards that I was going to wait until he came back. They tried to persuade me to go home and come back in the morning. But I refused to budge. I sat there all night, watching the stars, questioning my sanity, and praying for some response. Dawn came and then the first hours of the morning. I was told to go home. Again I refused, stubbornly insisting that I had waited all night and I wasn't going home now.

At about nine o'clock President Lakas came out and talked to me on the steps. He denied that the priest had been arrested. I told him that simply was not true and said that I wanted to see him unharmed now and free in a matter of hours.

"Well," he said, "I'll check again to see if there is any news of him."

Not long after that he emerged with a grave mien and said, "Yes, they have him, but he's been charged with sedition for stirring up a counterrevolution. They have all the evidence."

"Nonsense. I don't believe a word of that and I want to see him," I retorted. With that, he said he would call Torrijos to find out if he would see me. Back I went to Army headquarters and after a good long wait I was ushered into the General's office. He waved another manila folder at me and said, "Here's the proof."

"Proof of what?" I asked. "That he was planning a coup?"

"No," he replied uneasily. "Read it."

I found a letter from this priest to his spiritual advisor about a personal problem. I gasped in horror, "Omar, this is a personal, confidential matter. You're trying to blackmail the man. That's horrible."

He attempted to justify himself by saying "*Dicen que es un mujeriego*" ("They say that he's a womanizer").

"*Dicen que!*" I must have been screaming. "If you want to trade *discen ques* (gossip), they say you are the biggest *mujeriego* in the country, though I've never seen you do it and have no reason to believe it. But that's what's said about you."

With that, I turned on my heel, walked out of the room, and drove back to San Miguelito, shaken by the vicious display of using people to gain one's ends.

Three days later President Lakas phoned me: "Please come down here immediately."

After I had been ushered into the president's private quarters, Lakas asked me, "What in the world did you say to Omar? He's been in a drunken rage for the past three days—abusing everyone, including his wife. He says you called him a *mujeriego*."

I explained what I had said, that I had told him he had the reputation of being one.

"Well, he *is* a *mujeriego*. Everyone knows that," groaned Lakas, "but you don't call him that to his face!" He went on to explain the enormous pressures Torrijos was operating under and how he felt that sometimes the General was close to cracking up.

He then suddenly stood up and said, "Let me introduce you to my wife." Motioning for me to follow, he led the way into the bedroom where I saw an enormous bed with a machine gun lying on the pillows. "That's my wife," he explained. "I sleep with it by my side every night. Now you know how nervous we all are."

Both Lakas and Torrijos had good reason to be apprehensive. There were always plots and rumors of plots against them, in the first few years anyway. One day I was in the executive mansion attending a Presidential Planning Commission meeting that was lasting way beyond its appointed time. Twice I went to a phone to inform the cook at the rectory that I would not be home for lunch. After failing the second time to get a line, I returned to the conference table and remarked that I could not get through.

"The lines are cut off; there is a coup in progress," said a colleague, very calmly, as though it were a minor interruption.

I stood up and hurried out. The last place I wanted to be during a coup was the president's palace. Once I was safely home, I joined everyone else in watching on TV the latest scene of what seemed to be a long complicated drama of upheaval. The coup had been staged by several younger officers of the Guardia, with the active encouragement and almost limitless funds of the CIA.

The rebel officers had taken over installations in the capitol while Torrijos and Lakas were in Mexico for a horse race! The conspirators called Torrijos in Mexico and told him not to return. The General thought his regime had been overthrown and his first concern was for his wife and children. He called up one of the district commanders for help in getting his family to safety. Fortunately, the rebellious officers had failed to shut down the military phone network. Torrijos proceeded to call each commander and get a pledge of loyalty. Finally he called the commandant at General Headquarters in Panama and got through to him. The conspirators were in the room when the call came through. The commandant dissembled so well they were unaware they had made a fatal mistake in not securing the lines.

Torrijos flew to his old base at David, near the Costa Rican border, and began a long march to the capitol city of Panama. It was all arranged by the Guardia, but it served to arouse a public enthusiasm which seldom had been seen in Panama. The conspirators fled into the night with what remained of their CIA funds. Torrijos entered the capitol city in triumph—the undoubted leader of his country.

I met with the General shortly afterwards. He asked me what I thought about the attempted coup and his triumphal return. I told him that now that he was solidly in power he had an unparalleled opportunity to do something great for his people and become one of the most illustrious personages in all of Panamanian history. He cocked his head slightly, a gesture that indicated interest as well as skepticism.

"How would I go about doing that?" he asked.

"Well, Panama has seldom had a leader of vision and of integrity, and never one with the kind of power you have now. If you had a vision of what this country could become..."

"Is that what you people call revolutionary theology?" he asked.

"Some call it that, but that's probably a pretentious title," I smiled.

He asked what I meant by integrity, this time with a grin on his face as if he knew well what the answer would be.

I said that he would need the self-discipline to avoid corruption, nepotism, and cronyism. He nodded his head several times and ended the conversation by saying, "I couldn't do that alone. Would it be possible to spend a few days together sometime? You could bring some of those laymen from San Miguelito and I would bring some of my people."

I agreed without hesitation. It was like seeing a shaft of light peeking through black clouds. It was never to be more than a peek.

There were more than a few people in Panama who claimed that I had enormous influence over Omar Torrijos. Why did he consult me so often? Why was he so enamored of San Miguelito and all it stood for? The real reason, I submit, is that he met fellow Panamanians there—such as Octavio Pinto and Chacho Hernandez—who were like himself. They could trade aphorisms with him or off-color jokes. They showed no fear in his presence. They refused to judge him but they demanded of themselves and of him integrity and honesty. They had a dream to which they were committed and they were clearly willing to sacrifice even their lives for their dream. Torrijos was deeply impressed by them. It may well have been that he had never met Panamanians like them. It was through them that he understood me, just as it was through knowing them that I came to understand Torrijos. No doubt he admired me, but it was for having something to do with the making and forming of his own countrymen as starry-eyed, earthy, but incorruptible leaders.

One reason for Torrijos's effectiveness was his ability to put people down—sometimes in a vicious way, at other times in an amusing way. One night, rather late, he called me at the rectory and said he had to see me right away.

"Aw, it's late. Are you sure it can't wait for the morning?" I asked.

"No," he said peremptorily. "I'm sending a car out there for you." Fifteen minutes later an official car arrived at our house. The car's red lights were flashing and it was accompanied by two motorcycles with outriders, their lights also flashing. I got into the car wondering where we would be going.

Torrijos had the habit of spending his nights in different houses, principally for fear of assassination but, I suspected, for other reasons too. The procession drew up in front of his own home where his wife and children lived, a house he seldom used.

The armed guards led me directly to his bedroom. Dressed in yellow silk pajamas, he was in bed alone, sitting propped up on pillows and reading the Panama city telephone directory, which was spread open on his lap. Though quite aware I was in the room, he did not look up but went on turning the pages of the book.

Irritated by being summoned late at night but also amused at the obvious game he was playing, I said, "Omar, what the hell are you doing?"

"Looking for a new cabinet," he replied.

I laughed and so did he. "Do you need me to go through the telephone book?"

"No, I need you to give me the names of the people who can serve the country well as ministers of state. You know their names, don't you?"

"Yes, I know a good many of them," I admitted.

"Then I want their names," he said.

"Omar, they won't work for you. You know that."

"Why not?" he asked.

"Because you won't give them the necessary freedom to do their job well and you'll saddle them with your relatives and cronies." By this time, at least a score of his relatives had good jobs in the government.

"I need those names, Leo. I'll tell you what I'll do. I'll appoint as minister without portfolio the man of your choice from San Miguelito." He simply could not resist buying a person off.

"Come on," I said. "You know very well that the only ones who can run this country well are the upper-class guys. They're the only ones with the necessary experience and skill. If you were to put a man from San Miguelito in the cabinet, no matter how intelligent he is, he would be doomed to fail. What you can do is put the young, intelligent people in as vice-ministers alongside the *rabiblancos*; they would soon learn how to do it."

"That's exactly what I want to do. I want the list from you within twenty-four hours."

I agreed somewhat reluctantly and left for home. I thought at first that he might be spotting potential opponents but that didn't seem to make much sense. I went to bed thinking that there was a lot more to this than met the eye; he seemed to be under a lot of pressure.

I made out the list and informed his office that it was ready. An officer came out to pick it up. The next week all the ministers of state were dismissed and replaced with new people. Not one of the persons I had suggested was appointed. Torrijos never gave me any explanation and I never asked.

Despite his obvious flaws, Omar Torrijos reflected more than most—certainly more than most—the spirit and mentality of the Panamanian people. He could speak their language and divine their thoughts and anticipate their desires. Was he an evil man? Was he a hypocrite? Was he a psychopath who had various personalities that he could take on or shed depending on the circumstances?

A perceptive anthropologist, Dr. Roberto De La Guardia, once told me that the key to understanding the Panamanian is to see him as the owner of a hotel. Panama is a small country in one of the world's most strategic places, where the Pacific Ocean is less than a hundred miles from the Atlantic. A hotel owner depends on the patronage of his guests. Unless guests are occupying the hotel and paying the bills, the owner will starve. Panama historically has had Spain, France, and the United States as its guests. Without them Panama would have starved or been foreclosed. Consequently, the Panamanian puts on a good act, is very friendly to those who pay the bills, and changes his line and even his language when other guests arrive.

If it turns out that some rough-looking characters with bulges at their armpits are his most regular clients, then he is likely to ignore the bulges. The hotel owner may want to run a respectable place, but if his best customers drink too much and occasionally bring in female friends, then he will defend his blindness as an act of benevolent tolerance.

Practically all that Panama has going for it is its strategic geography, and it has to use that asset unless it wishes to become once more the "mosquito capitol" of the world, saved from such infection by the hand of the gracious North.

Omar Torrijos, as *the* Panamanian of his time, understood that reality and tried to play his part well. Every once in a while, Torrijos flew over to see Fidel Castro in Cuba. Each time he did, the U.S. representatives would be thrown into a panic. Torrijos would come home with that big grin of his and get whatever he asked for from the frenzied North Americans.

The problem with those who use and manipulate, for whatever reasons, is that they, in turn, are also used and manipulated. Torrijos was used by the members of his family, by his military colleagues, and by his cronies in the government. No one rules alone. Torrijos was, by no means, an absolute dictator. I believe that he wanted the best for his people and that he saw in the experiment of San Miguelito, if not the model, a clear sign that things could be different, that people could rule themselves and be responsible for their own lives and future.

The experiment of building a model city was working well, too well, it appears for the Junta which wouldn't let go of power.

San Miguelito needed much of almost everything. The traditional way was to beg the central government for it, whereupon the aid was doled out in dribs and drabs. San Miguelito realized it could never organize itself well unless it controlled its own revenues and bonding authority. But the central government was saying the city could do all the voting it wanted for local offices but it could not have its own money to spend and repay to Germany. It was the worst sort of paternalism. Evidently Torrijos had real problems within his government on the matter.

Everything was put on hold. I tried several times to see him about the impasse but now he seemed to be very busy.

After weeks of frustration, I demanded an appointment and got one. I sat in his waiting room for twenty minutes past the appointed time. Then I stood up and asked his secretary if the General knew I was there. "Oh yes, he knows. Now be a good soldier and wait for him," she said sweetly.

Not so sweetly, I retorted, "I am not a soldier. So please tell the General I'm leaving in five minutes. If he's too busy, I can come back some other time."

She went into the inner sanctum to relay my message. She came back out and Torrijos emerged right behind her.

He motioned me into his office, explaining that he was just finishing up another matter. I recognized the other man in the office —a prominent labor leader from the banana plantations in the Chiriqui province.

"What were you saying?" Torrijos asked the other man.

"But General, I don't want to talk about this in front of a priest. Please, can't we talk privately?"

Torrijos brushed aside the plea and said, "You can trust Father Leo. He'll understand."

The man was extremely uncomfortable. I soon got the drift of the conversation. The labor leader was seeking a big job in the government. He was selling out! Torrijos offered him a consulate— specifically Kobe in Japan.

The man said he didn't know any Japanese, but the General said that didn't really matter.

The man then asked for a job in the Ministry of Public Works instead.

The General dismissed that request airily and said it was the consulate or nothing. The petitioner left the office with nothing, his eyes studying every tile on the floor as he left.

Without any reference to what I had just witnessed, Torrijos asked, "Well, what's the problem, Leo?"

"Look, Omar, I really don't know what's going on in your government. But it's evident that you are strangling San Miguelito. I won't have any more to do with the whole thing. I tender my resignation as liaison person with the government."

He replied, "You can't do that; everyone will know the revolution is a failure if you resign."

"As far as I can see, General, it's all over anyway. I'm not going to make any public statement or any attempt to embarrass you. I just wanted to tell you that I'm pulling out."

"Oh no," he said, "it can't go this way. I'll come out there along with my ministers and we'll get this settled."

The meeting in San Miguelito took place before a packed house. The government ministers talked first and one especially was arrogant and patronizing. It was rumored that he had been a Marxist and had converted. He and the other ministers of state made no secret of their opposition to the entire project. The people of San Miguelito rose to answer point by point. One man boldly told the ministers that he was willing to fight if necessary and, turning to Torrijos, added, "—and that goes for you, too, Omar."

The last person to speak was Torrijos, who looked tired and distracted: "I am as much behind this model of democracy as I was in the beginning, but as you can see, some of my ministers are not. We've got to work this out." With that enigmatic statement the meeting ended.

On his way out, he asked to see me. We moved into my office. We stood there for a moment—he discouraged and I perplexed.

Finally he said, "Remember that talk we were going to have about theology? Would two days be enough?"

"Sure," I said.

"You take two men with you and I'll come with two. It'll probably be at Farellon. I'll call tomorrow at noon to tell you when the helicopter will pick you up." The General and his party left. I was more intrigued than ever.

My hopes were dashed at eleven o'clock the next morning. A secretary from the Comandancia called to tell me the trip had been cancelled. No explanation, no apology, no word of an alternate date. That day was June 9, 1970.

9
FACING
THE UNFACEABLE

*J*une 10, 1970. The morning after Torrijos cancelled our spiritual retreat. The phone rang at about seven o'clock AM.

It was a long distance call from Santiago, the capital of the province of Veraguas, Panama. "Please, do something, Leo," pleaded one of the priests stationed there. "They took Hector away."

My heart sank because I knew I would get this call one day.

Hector Gallegos came from the province of Antioquia in Columbia, often called the Ireland of South America because it produced so many priests and religious. He was short and slight of build, friendly, but intense and dedicated. As a young seminarian, he had volunteered to work among the rural poor in Panama and had spent time with us in San Miguelito. We had become good friends.

After being ordained a priest, he had been sent to the town of Santa Fe. He was the first resident priest the people there had ever had. A peripatetic priest in the style of St. Paul, he had visited each village of his parish, staying for a week, sharing their poverty, gathering them each night to explain to them their dignity, and challenging them to strive for freedom. The people were enthralled by him and he soon had an entire community avidly seeking to learn the Word of God and willing to work together to bring the reign of justice and love to their community.

The principal crop in mountainous Veraguas was coffee, a fine coffee that brought a good price. Yet the people there were desperately poor. The storekeepers loaned the farmers money and supplies against the coming harvest. Once the harvest was in, the farmers were in debt, while the storekeepers prospered. It was a familiar story repeated in many parts of the world. With Hector's help, the farmers began two cooperatives, one for production of the coffee and the other a consumers' cooperative. Within two years, the cooperatives had amassed two million dollars. The people were proud and happy. They were not by any means wealthy, but they were making the gigantic step from destitution and despair to self-sufficiency and hope.

The storekeepers, on the other hand, were incensed and the object of their anger was the young interloper, Hector Gallegos. The storekeepers represented a formidable enemy, since they were also the local politicians and some of them were blood relatives of Omar Torrijos, who had been raised in the province of Veraguas.

Skirmishes were fought, most verbal but some physical, with the young priest and the farmers on one side and the local important people on the other, the same people who had begged the bishop to send them a more "traditional" pastor.

Months earlier, Hector had been arrested and jailed, accused of setting fire to the local radio transmitter, a patently trumped-up charge.

Informed of the arrest, I went to see Torrijos. He agreed to intervene, saying that he would bring the prisoner to our residence for a hearing. Once more the helicopter came down on the lawn. Torrijos was accompanied by Father Carlos Velarde, a native Panamanian priest who had accepted the position and salary of chaplain to the Army. The prisoner, Hector Gallegos, was put in a room under guard. The General, Father Velarde, several lay leaders, and I met in my study.

Torrijos began. "Some so-called popular leaders are causing unrest in the country."

"I have told you several times, Omar, that it is time to institute the *paredon* (firing squad) and eliminate the trouble-makers," Father Velarde asserted.

A few gasps came from the laymen present who were horrified at such a statement coming from the mouth of a priest.

Sensing the possibility of a nasty quarrel right there in the room, I intervened. "Let's get down to the business of Hector Gallegos."

Torrijos led off by saying, "Gallegos has been accused of a serious crime."

I answered "Omar, there is no evidence that he set that fire and no motive for doing so."

"But they tell me he's a Communist," continued the General.

I countered, "What proof do they have? Anyone who works with the poor and defends them, who cries for justice in this land, is accused of being a Communist. You know that and so do I. Besides, who told you all this about him? Your relatives?"

He looked at me as though he were about to curse me. Then he said, "The trouble with you is you know too much." That really was not the problem, because many knew of the situation in Santa Fe. What was different was that I said it openly to him.

Torrijos then ordered that Gallegos be brought into the room to speak for himself. Hector, seated in front of us, began to speak, and as he did, his nervousness settled. He related his efforts to bring the Word of God and justice to the people of his parish.

"From the very beginning I was harassed by a small group of powerful people." He spoke in a soft but even tone, working to connect with the people in the room, but not being overly bold. "They continually accuse me of things I do not do. I have spoken to the bishop and to the civil authorities, but neither have done anything. I am deeply worried about the situation, but am resolved to continue my work in the parish."

Torrijos seemed impressed with the young priest, and said to him in a tone that a father confessor might use, "Well, I'll look into it. But be careful, son. Stay here for a few weeks. Maybe things up there will cool down."

Then the General said he wanted to speak to me alone. After the others had left, he asked, "Couldn't you use your influence to get him transferred to another parish?"

"No," I said, "I can't do that. He's done a great job there and is loved by his people. He's done nothing wrong, so why should he be moved?"

"But there may be even more problems," Torrijos insisted.

I said, "Omar, it really isn't your place to recommend transfers of priests any more than it's my place to suggest changes among your officers. But I can tell you this. If anything further happens to Hector Gallegos, there's going to be big trouble. You simply don't attack a young, popular priest and not cause a big stir."

Hector remained with us under house arrest for several weeks and then was allowed to return to Santa Fe. Two months later, during the night, someone set fire to his house. He got out alive, but the fire destroyed the house, his books, his clothes, and all his Mass articles. He had possessed little, but even that was gone now. He moved into the house of the head of the cooperative. Like most houses in the rural areas of Panama, the house contained two rooms, a bedroom and a living room; all the cooking and washing were done outside. The owner, his wife, and his children slept in one room and Hector in the other.

At midnight on June 10 a military-style jeep pulled up in front of the house. A voice called out in the darkness, "Hector Gallegos."

In his skivvies, Hector opened the door and asked what they wanted. They replied they had come to take him to Army headquarters in Santiago. Hector, accustomed to such harassment, replied, "All right, I'll go down there in the morning."

"You must come now," one of the three men in the jeep said.

Hector refused to go.

"If you don't come now, we'll take you by force and we'll also have some fun with that family in there."

Under this threat, the priest donned a shirt and a pair of pants and climbed into the jeep, which then drove off.

The couple, awakened by the noise and listening from the other room, thought they heard a scream over the roar of the motor of the departing jeep. The man dressed hurriedly and rushed to the small truck owned by the cooperative, thinking to follow the jeep and round up some help along the way. But the motor would not start. Opening the hood, he found the ignition wires cut and removed. Without the truck it took him a long time to reach the neighbor's farm. By that time the trail had been lost.

How I dressed and got myself to the car was all a blur. I headed straight for Army headquarters. I'm known as a fast driver, but this day, apprehensive and angry, I drove excessively fast. I was disgusted with the Guardia and hoped that I would be stopped so I could take out some of my ire on one of them.

When I arrived at the Commandancia I asked to see the General. On entering his office I found him and the other members of the High Command sitting in silence, enveloped in an atmosphere of gloom. They told me they had heard the news, but vehemently denied that they or any of the Guardia had anything to do with Hector's disappearance. I asked them if they knew how serious this matter could become—that it could be the ground for a major confrontation between them and the church.

Colonel Manuel Noriega, then the head of Intelligence, answered, "Of course, we know it's serious. We've been on the case ever since I got the call at five o'clock this morning."

I asked them what they intended to do.

"What can we do?" responded Torrijos, "We didn't take him. We don't know where he is. What would you do?"

"I'll tell you what I'd do if I were in your position," I said. "I'd take a thousand men to Veraguas and I'd scour every yard of that province until I found him."

"I can't do that, Father," he replied.

"Why not?" I queried.

"Because they would only call me a priest-killer if I did."

"That's what they're going to call you anyway," I retorted, "unless you get to the bottom of this."

I went immediately to the office of the archbishop where people and clergy were already gathering. All the dioceses, religious orders, parishes, and lay organizations were sending representatives. There were observers from the other churches and religions, Lutherans, Methodists, and Episcopalians. All were concerned with the impact this government move would have on the church.

An executive committee was chosen. It marked the beginning of a campaign of pressure on the government, the strongest and most insistent campaign of this kind in the history of Panama. At that time all of us thought that Hector Gallegos was still alive. We speculated that they had injured him during or after the arrest and were too embarrassed to deliver him up. We refused to believe that they would have dared to murder him.

Late in the afternoon I returned to my own house and found a man waiting for me. He identified himself as a prisoner who had been released that morning. He told me that he had seen Hector Gallegos in the jail in the early hours in the morning. I did not know whether to believe him or not. I had neither the time nor the means to check out his story. But I was disturbed by the news that the officer in command at Santiago was claiming he knew nothing of the abduction until eight o'clock in the morning. If that were true, how then did Noriega learn of it at five o'clock? Who had called him?

I headed out again and drove back down to the Commandancia. Once again I was ushered into the General's office. I told him what I had heard.

Annoyed and angry, he said, "I told you, Father, that we don't have him. Don't you believe me?"

"Omar," I replied, trying to be as honest as I could under the circumstances, "the life of a man is at stake. We've been lied to before about priests being detained."

He then asked, "Would you like to see the cells?" Without waiting for an answer, he called a junior officer and ordered him to take me on a tour of the detention cells.

I felt foolish as I walked through a lower floor where political prisoners were held and interrogated by the agents of the dreaded Intelligence unit. This unit was known for its underhanded, manipulative maneuvers that usually sent anyone rationally trying to work with them in an out-of-control downward spin toward futility. Even if they had Gallegos, they would have moved him before I arrived. But I went through the motions of looking through the iron gates of the cells and found no one I knew, least of all Hector Gallegos.

The days and the weeks went by with no word of the young priest. The government said it was doing all in its power to find him. Few, if any, believed this, but all were outraged when the minister of justice appeared on television to explain the official investigation. He denied that the government was responsible and remarked blandly that it was altogether possible that the man was a fugitive that he had run off with a woman.

Insulted, the forces representing the church delegated Bishop Martin Legarra and myself to request, with Torrijos's permission, an independent investigator from abroad. Legarra was Hector's bishop, a lovable Spanish priest who quoted Don Quixote so often and so well we began to suspect that he himself had come out of the Cervantes masterpiece.

Torrijos received us politely, but not warmly. He told us that we were free to hire an investigator of our own, that neither he nor his government had anything to hide. He asked us about who we were planning to contact.

When the bishop mentioned the name of a well-known private investigator out of Miami, Torrijos said with a straight face, "Oh, I wouldn't hire him if I were you. My experience tells me that you can't trust a man who is not faithful to his wife!"

Neither the bishop nor I adverted to that amazing statement. It appeared that Torrijos could live a dual life and not even be aware of how foolish such comments could be.

We were delighted to have gotten the permission so easily. Too easily, as it turned out. A few days later an official communiqué came from the press office of the government stating that the request to bring in an independent investigator had been denied. Either Torrijos had changed his mind or else he had been overruled.

We planned a major act to force the government to release Hector or explain, at least, what had happened to him. It was to be a procession and liturgical act attended by every bishop and priest in the country, the papal nuncio, all the religious, and as many laity as possible. The government expressly proscribed the event, but we went ahead with the preparations anyway.

A week before the procession was to take place I was summoned to a private and secret meeting with Colonel Manuel Noriega, who would later be successor to Torrijos. We met in a spacious apartment in a luxurious high-rise building in Punta Paitilla.

He spoke earnestly, "Leo, you must cancel the march. It will only make matters worse."

I replied, "You are the ones who have done the harm and are responsible for the impasse."

When we both agreed that the conversation was getting us nowhere, he stood up to bid me good-bye with these words. "Father, someday the stone will be turned over, and the snake will be there all right, but its name will not be Noriega."

At the time I wasn't sure what he meant and, even after all these years, I am still unable to penetrate those words.

The procession and Mass took place on July 15, the feast of Our Lady of Mount Carmel, appropriately in front of the white church that looks like a giant wedding cake and is dedicated to Mary of Mount Carmel. Some fifteen thousand people marched in the blazing sun all the way from San Miguelito, a distance of some ten miles. The entire throng was estimated at approximately seventy-five thousand people from all over Panama. It was not only a show of strength and discipline, it was also the first time the church in Panama had acted and prayed as one body. Unfortunately, it was also the last time.

The government, having failed to stop the demonstration, was relieved when the huge crowd dispersed and wended its way home.

Had we turned left onto the Avenida Principal and marched to the government complex, we could have taken over the government buildings. Our numbers had increased that significantly. Friends in the cabinet later told us that Torrijos and others had their bags packed, ready to flee. But we did not march to topple the government. We wanted Hector Gallegos safe and sound, nothing more.

As the months burdened with conflict passed by, a dreadful picture began to take form and focus in our minds: Hector Gallegos was dead. There simply was no way he could have been kept hidden in a country as small as Panama without some word of him leaking out. To this day we are not certain what happened to him. The best guess on which most agreed was that he was killed the same night he was arrested, perhaps accidentally, and his body was thrown from an airplane into the sea where it became food for the sharks. Did Torrijos order his execution? Did he sign the order for his arrest? Possibly, but I rather suspect he did not.

What seemed most clear was that the General knew within hours what had really happened and that he decided to cover up the crime committed probably by his own relatives or the local Guardia or both working together.

Torrijos paid the price for his complicity in the affair. He was never again to enjoy the credibility he had once known. Further, the bloody secret put him into cahoots with his co-conspirators and robbed him of any possibility he might have had to lead his country to democratic and fiscal reform.

He did a masterful job of getting the United States to restore to Panama its most precious resource, the Panama Canal and its Zone. Yet, at the same time, he presided over the rape of the judicial system and of the national treasury from which millions upon millions of dollars that rightly belonged to the people were siphoned off to end up in the billfolds and foreign bank accounts of fellow officers and their partners.

After our encounters about Hector, the General and I had no further contact. Our relationship had been more than bruised. Trust had run its course. Torrijos had become the political power that he had so wanted to stop.

After I left Panama and was burrowing in comfortably as pastor in a Chicago suburban parish, I received a phone call. It was the General. He talked as though our friendship had never been severed. He thanked me for testifying before congressional committees in favor of returning Panama's patrimony to its rightful owners, something I had done since my return to the States.

He then asked a favor: "Leo, I know you are a friend of Cesar Chavez. Will you call him up and invite him down here? I'll pay all his expenses." It was part of his campaign to amass support for the Panamanian position on the treaty.

"But Omar, I don't think Cesar Chavez will have anything to do with you."

"I don't know about that, Leo. I'm not as bad as people say I am. Will you try?" I replied,

"Yes, I will ... and Omar, it's good to hear from you again."

"Yes, Leo, it should never have gone the way it did." That was the last time we talked. I did call Cesar Chavez, but, as I had expected, he declined the invitation.

Shortly after that, Torrijos was killed in an airplane crash. Some say it was an accident; others are not so sure it was.

The campaign to rescue Father Hector Gallegos went on, but it lost momentum. Pictures of him still hung on banners and posters all over Panama, not only in churches and homes but also in public squares. However, people had other concerns and worries. It is difficult to keep a one-issue movement going. The military regime, having survived the onslaught that had threatened its very existence, began to fight back. It had two powerful weapons in its arsenal: money and control of the bureaucracy. While always respecting the freedom of all religions, Panama has long recognized Catholicism as the faith of the vast majority of its citizens. In practice, that means the Catholic Church can, and often does, ask for help from the national budget in order to build churches, schools, and other facilities.

One prominent priest refused to have anything to do with the campaign to rescue Father Gallegos because he was waiting for a large grant from the government to build his parish church. As a reward for breaking ranks with the rest of the clergy, he did get the money. Some years later he was named and ordained the bishop of Santiago de Veraguas, ironically Hector Gallegos's diocese.

The government, whose life hung in the balance during the massive search for Hector Gallegos, slowly began to recover its nerve. Totalitarian regimes live on their popularity with the people, not on the solid ground of law. So it was decided that the anniversary of the Revolution would be marked by a gigantic celebration. Free transportation would be provided, T-shirts and machetes would be distributed, and free beer and liquor would be made available for all. There would be orchestras and entertainers. No matter what the cost, the military was bent on proving it was more popular than the church, that it—not the clergy—commanded the allegiance of the people. In pulling out all the stops for this massive gathering of people, the government leaders wanted, above all, the support of the people of San Miguelito.

Mayor Salazar was ordered to fill up scores of buses with people, but he calmly and decisively declined to cooperate. On the day of the mammoth celebration, only two hundred people from San Miguelito boarded the horde of buses awaiting them. However, there were plenty of others in the country who were willing to attend the gigantic fiesta—some hundred thousand persons crowded the streets of downtown Panama City.

Flush with success, the government began to act out its spite against the community that had refused to support the circus. That same night I got a telephone call from Dario Arosemena, chief of detectives. He uttered all sorts of threats, most of which were incoherent, since he had spent the day in drunken revelry.

The next day he ordered the arrest of Ramon Chacho Hernandez.

Once again I went to the jail at Army headquarters, but this time I was treated like a pariah. Eventually, Chacho was released and delivered to me personally by Lieutenant Colonel Arouz who, in the name of General Torrijos and the High Command, warned me that if I did not cease my activities there would be other steps, far more serious, against us.

The following morning, Paulino Salazar was dismissed from his position as mayor of San Miguelito. Had I been strapped into the electric chair and had the current been switched on, I could not have been more shocked by the appointment of the new mayor: José Arrocha, a close personal friend, a leader of the Christian movement almost from the beginning, and one of the staff of MUNDO, who had vowed never to accept a salaried position in the government.

I was numbed. I did not know whether to be angry or hurt, whether to cry or to take it stoically. José had been bought. The church and all José had stood for had been violated. It was hard not to believe that I had been sold out and that problems with the government were getting really "personal."

I received a call from Antonia, José's wife. "Please try to understand, Father. José still respects you. But he won't be able to talk to you now or see you at Mass. He has been instructed to stay away from you completely."

She asked, "You will forgive him someday, won't you, Father?"

I tried to reassure her, "Sure." I swallowed. "He'll always be my friend." Strangely, I meant those words. Long ago I had realized that mistakes, no matter how much they hurt, are never corrected by vengeance.

Our phones were being tapped. Within a few minutes the Secret Service notified the mayor's office of the call. The new mayor returned hurriedly to his house and furiously warned Antonia never to call me again.

The great political experiment was over. All the apparatus of the model city was in place, but gone was the spirit of freedom. The central government, after using and discrediting Arrocha, dismissed him a year later. The new city under the tutelage of Christian men had, like our cactus, bloomed for a brief time and withered much too quickly.

M oney was one puppet string, but there was another that, if pulled, could jerk the church into line. Most of the clergy and religious in Panama were foreign-born and came from countries such as Spain, Columbia, Holland, Belgium, and the United States. The proportion of native clergy to foreign clergy was low. During this time the major seminary was beginning to fill up with native candidates, half of them from San Miguelito, but it would be a long time before the church could staff its parishes and schools with Panama's own daughters and sons. Priests and religious from abroad were admitted to Panama under special visas— a practice that could be terminated or modified at a moment's notice. This control was the hanging sword that scared church authorities out of their opposition. The regime began to deny visas to incoming clergy, and worse, threatened to revoke the visas of those already in the country. The ploy worked. One by one, the bishops became neutral, some even forbidding their priests to engage in any more pressure tactics. In San Miguelito and in several other areas, such as the province of Chiriqui, the priests held firm in serious protest, but support was dwindling. The danger was clear.

As a stroke of propaganda, the regime informed the nation that President Lakas intended to visit the pope to complain of the church "meddling in politics." Worried by this move, the episcopal conference countered by sending two of its members to Rome to speak to the pope before Lakas could arrive.

Meanwhile, I received a call from Cardinal Cody asking that I come to Chicago for a talk. It had been quite a while since I had heard from him. He began the interview by inquiring in a friendly, solicitous manner whether I had given any thought to my career.

"What career?" I responded.

"Oh, you know, your next step after Panama. You're not getting any younger, Leo. How old are you now? Maybe it's time to come home."

I replied, "I have a lot of work to do in Panama and it is far from finished. Did you have something in mind that you want me to do here?" The church in Chicago was under high stress and priests were leaving in herds. The post–Vatican II changes had caused divisions between the traditionalists and the liberals. Perhaps Cody saw me as one who could help blend the differences and guide the future. Perhaps he saw me joining the ranks of bishop. Cody had never shown interest in my "career," or, as far as I knew, of the "careers" of any of my fellow priests, so I was befuddled by his solicitousness.

"No," he replied rather quickly, "but I think you should take a week or so to decide whether you should return."

I tried to search his gaze, but he averted my look. I didn't know why this request had required a visit to Chicago and I couldn't seem to get anything more from him. I responded, "I can tell you right now. My place is in Panama."

As he saw me to the door, he insisted once again that I give further consideration to leaving Panama and beginning a new career.

Once back in Panama I told Archbishop Marcos McGrath, a supporter of my work since my first days in Panama, of the conversation I had had with Cardinal Cody, adding that I couldn't understand it.

"Oh, I understand it all right," the archbishop said without hesitation. "I received a request from the government to remove you from Panama. I replied that such a move would have to be made by Cardinal Cody, not by me. The regime then made the same request to the Vatican and that's how the matter got to Cardinal Cody."

"Oh, I get it. Cody wanted me to leave Panama but was reluctant to tell me. He feared that I would create a ruckus."

McGrath nodded.

"Cody was perfectly right. I would have made the matter public immediately," I said. I did not leave Panama and heard no more about it.

A year later, I asked Cody's secretary what had happened. He said that the Cardinal had informed Rome that he would not remove me from Panama because doing so would have caused a storm both in Chicago and in Panama.

"If you want him transferred, then do it yourselves" was his final word. They didn't, of course; that's not the way Rome operates.

On my way back to Central America from visiting Cody, I changed planes in Miami. A few minutes after I boarded, a young man took the aisle seat adjacent to mine. He introduced himself as an exiled Cuban and a professor at Catholic University in Washington. He was interested in the situation in Panama and appeared to know a good deal about it. We began an energizing conversation.

"Do you think Torrijos and his group are Communists?" he asked.

"Goodness, no, they're not Communists. They are men who are getting to enjoy the feel of power and they are also getting very greedy," I answered.

We talked animatedly all during the two-and-a-half-hour flight to Panama. It felt good to engage with someone so scholarly and apparently so committed to our Panamanian efforts. It reminded me of my University of Chicago discussions and I felt revitalized in conversing with this intelligent young man who seemed so knowledgeable and sincere. I never doubted that he was anything other than what he had stated he was.

A month later Father John Kennedy, the pastor of St. Mary's Church, the American parish in the Canal Zone, called to ask me if I had been in an airplane recently. Kennedy had a good sense of humor, so I was expecting a joke or a funny story.

When I answered that, yes, I had lately returned from Chicago via Miami, he said in a serious voice, "Leo, you'll have to learn to keep your mouth shut."

"Why," I asked, "what's happened?" He told me that the chief of U.S. Army Intelligence had shown him a word-for-word transcript of my conversation with the "professor." The intelligence officer told Kennedy that he had received the transcript from Colonel Noriega who had thrown it on his desk, saying, "See what your people are saying about us?"

How had the transcript gotten to Noriega? Is it possible that our nation's principal security agency had shared it with Panama's intelligence agency? I do not have the answer to this, only dark suspicions. I am reasonably certain that my companion on the plane was a CIA agent and that his efforts to get information had put me in terrible danger.

Having neutralized and divided most of the church leaders, the military regime turned its attention to San Miguelito. Our phones were continually tapped. Luckily, the technician who tapped them happened to be a loyal parishioner who told us when the "bug" was operative. We discovered that our mail was being opened and so we arranged to have our correspondence sent through the Canal Zone, which had its own Postal Service. Far more serious were the personal attacks. Several times the newspapers, now either controlled or owned outright by the regime, printed scurrilous attacks and accusations against us. Once the headline blared "Mahon CIA Agent." I learned to live with the accusations. They did not fool the people.

The expulsions were what hurt. One day Gustavo Stumpf failed to attend an important meeting. Worried, I looked all over for him, starting at his home, but his family had not seen him all day. That evening I went to the Guardia to report his disappearance. They denied that they had him, but I knew that they did, since a parishioner had seen him picked up on the street. I found out later that they drove him to the airport and put him on a plane to Bolivia— with no clothes, no money, no passport.

Not long afterward, Tom Block was told that his visa had been revoked and he would thus be required to leave in a matter of days. I went to see a good friend who held a high post in the government to inquire whether there was any way to stop the expulsions.

His answer confirmed my own reading of the situation. "Father, the real object of their ire is you. But they don't dare expel you. It would cause them too much grief with the people and with Washington."

I was aware that my every move was being watched. Strangers were present at liturgies, taking notes on every homily. Men with tape recorders sat at the rear of many meetings. One day a secret service person called me and invited me out to lunch.

I recommended a very public restaurant where lots of people would be witnesses to any sudden moves.

I had geared up for the worst. He explained that he had been put in charge of San Miguelito and had eleven agents working under him on our case.

"What have you found?" I asked.

"Nothing. You and all your associates are clean. I reported that you are not involved in any conspiracy or in any immoral activities."

I responded by saying, "I could have told you that if you had asked. It would have saved a lot of money and time."

Two days later I saw the man's picture in the paper. He had been expelled from the country—the day after our luncheon meeting.

I wondered if the meeting had caused the exile. More probably, he knew he was finished and wanted somehow to relieve our fears.

The "persecution" continued. One night I returned late to the rectory only to find it ablaze with light and swarming with people. All the priests of San Miguelito were there as well as many more from the city.

"Leo, we were so worried."

"We thought you had been taken."

"Rumors have it that an order for your expulsion had been signed."

"Agents, we heard, are looking for you."

I barely had time to catch my breath as they fired messages of relief and of fear.

We made a hurried plan. Several cars left at the same time. I was hidden on the floor of the back seat of one of them. My driver took side streets and doubled back several times. Finally, convinced that we were not being followed, he delivered me to a "safe house" where I spent the night.

Thoughts came of my west-side Chicago home, my parents now deceased, and my team: John, Jack, the Maryknoll sisters, the lay deacons. Memories of forty some years came rushing at me. I saw Cardinal Stritch anointing me as priest, Cardinal Meyer sending me to Panama, and even Cardinal Cody and his plans to build an elevator and retire to Panama. Now I was fleeing for my life. I hardly slept that night.

In the morning, I looked out the window and spotted the Intelligence agents whom we were supposed to have lost the previous evening. They remained all day, watching my window and reporting by car telephone the visitors who came in and out of the house.

In the afternoon a man came to see me, a friend of the church but also an intimate of Torrijos. He was distressed by the conflict between the church and the government—particularly that between the General and myself. He asked whether I would be willing to sit down and talk it all out with Torrijos. I replied that I was willing, but I didn't think the General would agree. He asked me to wait next to the telephone because he was going directly to the General's office to set up an appointment. As I suspected, the call never came.

That same evening a rally was held at the Church of Our Lady of Mount Carmel. The church was packed with people. The purpose of the rally was to show support for me and force the government to back down. It succeeded. The next day the regime issued a statement denying any intention of expelling me from the country.

Although it did not succeed in getting rid of me, the government took its revenge by expelling a third lay person from the team of San Miguelito. This time there was a violent reaction. Jesus "Chu" Garcia, a young man born and raised in Mexico, had migrated to Chicago where he had worked with me in apostolic endeavors. He had expressed a desire to become a priest so he came to Panama to pursue his studies there. He changed his mind about priesthood, but stayed on to work as a lay missioner.

Some time later he married a girl who was active in San Miguelito's youth movement. His marriage to a Panamanian meant that he was no longer a foreigner living in Panama under a visitor's visa but rather a person with a legal right to residency and eventually to citizenship. Chu was popular, quiet, dedicated, and in no way embroiled in political controversy.

He was picked up on the street, handcuffed, and shoved into a plane bound for Mexico—again with no money, no change of clothing, and worst of all, no passport.

Upon arriving in Mexico, he was unable to prove he was a citizen of that country and consequently detained by the immigration authorities. Once released, he still had no identity papers. He could not return to the United States nor could he get a job in Mexico. He lived in hellish poverty and uncertainty for a long time.

The flash point of community anger was reached with the expulsion of Chu Garcia. Not only was it a cruel and demonstrably illegal act, but it was another in a long list of repressive actions.

The leaders of the movement in San Miguelito met and swiftly decided to issue a public document denouncing the regime for its cruelty and violation of the law and to march once more in protest.

The document was so strongly worded that it amounted to a direct challenge of the government's sincerity and legality; it was virtually a declaration of rebellion.

Copies of it were sent to all the parishes and priests still working together and to *Dialogo Social*—an outspoken magazine published by the Jesuit fathers. A copy of it arrived at the desk of Archbishop Marcos McGrath, who immediately foresaw decisive government action if the document were to be made public. He called the office of Colonel Noriega, chief of Intelligence, and was granted an appointment that very same day. The operatives who did the expelling worked for Noriega. The archbishop waited for two hours in an anteroom of the Commandancia and then was curtly told that the Colonel was too busy to see him.

McGrath, a native Panamanian despite his surname, proceeded to San Miguelito where he met with all of us. Deeply concerned about the consequences of publishing the document, he tried to convince the team that there were other ways to accomplish the same ends without risking a violent confrontation.

"What other means do we have?" asked the leaders of the movement. "They just humiliated you when you wanted to talk peaceably. What else can we do?"

McGrath was adamant in insisting that the document not be published. Finally a compromise was reached. He agreed to join the protest march the following day and we promised to withhold the written attack.

The next day he returned and asked to see me alone. He told me that after serious thought he felt his presence in the march might be misinterpreted and, therefore, he was not going to participate. He also asked me to explain this to the people.

"Archbishop, last night you gave your word to the people," I responded. "If you feel you cannot keep it, then you'll have to tell the people yourself."

As the throng was assembling for the march, McGrath went to the chapel to pray. When the starting signal was about to be given, the archbishop, tall and tense, emerged from the chapel and announced to the people he could not accompany them as he had promised.

His words were not well received; there were grumblings and mutterings of angry words.

Then Father Juan Alberto, usually called "Juancho" (Big John), jumped to his feet and said, "The bishop has spoken, what do the people say?"

A roar went up: "*A la calle!*" "To the street!"

The march began. The archbishop remained behind, alone. McGrath had pulled out.

Thelma, Chu Garcia's wife, led the march, holding high overhead the portrait of her missing spouse and followed by a great crowd of people. Once again the troops were out in force, armed and ready. They did not interfere or cause any disturbance. Perhaps they sensed we were beaten.

Our march received little news coverage. We got no call to come to headquarters and face Torrijos or any government official. The government didn't respond. Chu Garcia was never found.

To ignore another is one of the cruelest human acts. We were ignored, because we were no longer a threat to the government.

The Panamanian church, on the other hand, was paying very close attention and was strategizing its attack on us.

10

MUCKING
WITH THE MUCKAMUCKS

A few years earlier, before I got involved in the political scene
and when I was solely focused on building a church community, a
medium-size black Fiat sedan stopped in front of our little house.
The chauffeur opened the right rear door and out stepped Archbishop Antonino Pinci, papal nuncio to Panama, wearing a skull-
cap and dressed in a cassock with purple buttons and piping. We
had met many times before. None of the meetings had been
pleasant.

I greeted him at the door and he warmly grasped my right hand
in both his hands. "I have good news for you," he said. "You are
going to be made a monsignor."

My mind flashed back to seminary days when monsignors were
like the prancing roosters of the church. A monsignor, pronounced
monseñor and meaning "my lord," is a dressed-up version of a bishop
with all show and no substance. The title gives the individual the
right to dress in distinctive robes like a bishop, but entails none of
the duties and responsibilities of a bishop. The title is something
like an honorary degree in academia or some vice-presidencies in
the corporate world.

"No thank you," I said as politely as I could.

"You are too modest," he retorted.

"No one has ever accused me of being too modest," I responded and went on to explain that I was not interested. "But," I
added, "if you want to promote me to the real thing, that's another

matter." Becoming a bishop had been an expectation of mine for years and, with all the positive movement in Panama, I felt it was time that Rome recognized my leadership.

"But think of your people. They will be pleased," he added.

"My people know nothing of such things."

"Well, how about your mother? She'll be pleased, won't she?" He was raising the ante and I was becoming irritated.

"My mother?" I echoed, aware that my sarcastic side was rising. "My mother would be delighted. Why don't you make *her* a monsignor?"

Without another word, he stormed out.

Half an hour later, the same black Fiat pulled up again in front of the house. This time the nuncio didn't wait for the chauffeur to open the door, but climbed out and mounted the steps to our house.

"Now, young man, let's talk seriously."

"Okay," I answered, with no idea of what grave subject we were about to discuss. He had offered me an "honor." I had refused. End of story.

Short of stature, he raised himself on the balls of his feet and placed his nose no more than an inch from mine. He said, "I want you to pay for the landscaping for the new nunciatura." The nunciatura was the latest Panamian church palace being built in a wealthy neighborhood not far from the ocean.

Stepping back so as not to be overwhelmed with his episcopal breath, I said, "Your Eminence, I don't have that kind of money."

"No, I don't mean your money; I mean the mission money, the money Chicago sends you."

My words were like a door slamming shut: "That money belongs to the people and was never meant to build you a palace. Besides, Cardinal Cody would need to authorize this."

His next exit was more than furious. He turned apoplectic— this time leaving for good, never to return.

A short time afterwards I received a call from Cardinal Cody asking me to come up to Chicago.

"Leo, what in the world happened between you and the nuncio?" were Cody's first words upon my arrival. I wondered how the message had traveled, since no information had come from me. From Panama? From Rome via Panama?

I described the entire encounter to him.

"Well, how much would the landscaping cost?" he asked.

I gasped inside and responded matter-of-factly, "I don't know." With the implications dawning more clearly as his expression of discontent became more pronounced, I began to feel rage. "But you wouldn't really pay for it, would you?"

"Leo, you don't know how the ballgame is played!" he answered, treating me as one would treat someone with the naiveté to try to keep a bone away from a teeth-baring dog.

I don't know who paid for the landscaping, but I noticed that the new Panamanian complex was fully completed within a month after my return from Chicago.

Shortly after that the Panamanian church passed a law that no foreigner could become a bishop in Panama.

Cody's official visit to dedicate the church of Cristo Redentor had been put off for several years. During that time we had worked hard with a minimum of interference. We had completed another rather spacious church in Villa Guadalupe called Cristo El Hombre as well as smaller chapels in Monte Oscuro, Cristo Obero, and in San Isidro, Sagrada Familia.

Unlike his first visit, when the common people of San Miguelito had come out to greet him, this time he was met by a large entourage of bishops and military officials representing the institutional church and the government. He had been made a cardinal in the interim, and since cardinals are regarded in Catholic countries as visiting princes, he was received officially by the government with all the proper protocol.

His plane was met by the minister of foreign relations and the two of them made an inspection of the battalion of troops standing in perfect order on the tarmac, while the band played and the Vatican and Panamanian flags snapped in the swift breezes. All the bishops of Panama were on hand to greet him—Archbishop Pinci, the nuncio; Archbishop Clavel of Panama; and Bishops Serrano of Colon, Carrizo of Chitre, McGrath of Santiago, and Nuñez of David.

Cody was given the presidential suite at the Panama Hilton. A military honor guard stood outside during his entire visit. Several days after his arrival, a formal reception was held in his honor at the Palacio de las Garzas, the White House of the Republic. There the president presented the Cardinal with Panama's highest decoration, the Order of Balboa.

On the day of the Cardinal's arrival in Panama, the bishops had welcomed him in the V.I.P. room at the airport. At that time, Pinci had invited them all to a dinner in Cody's honor. This dinner was to be held on Saturday night at the Nunciatura, the very place that had been adorned with the finest landscape.

Pinci informed Cody that, because of "what was going on in San Miguelito," none of them—except Archbishop Clavel—could, in good conscience, attend the dedication ceremonies in San Miguelito on Sunday.

"What does he mean?" I asked Cody. No one had approached me about any issues or problems. I was confused. I felt rejected and didn't want to have anything to do with the muckamucks.

The Cardinal had no answers and changed the subject. He insisted that I join him for the banquet on Saturday night. In spite of all that I was feeling inside, I accompanied him.

The bishops were friendly and courteous, as though they had not taken a public action that spelled rejection and accusation. None but Clavel would be attending the dedication ceremony the next day and none of them would acknowledge that anything was wrong.

As I sat at the table I could hardly see. My eyes were filled with tears of anger and hurt. What was served and what was said that evening were all a blur. Evidently they regarded me as the Judas in their midst. To make matters worse, the Cardinal was enjoying all the attention, the pomp, and the pageantry so much that he didn't seem to notice the drama being enacted under his nose. I felt betrayed.

The next day, except for a few empty seats, there were no signs of the impending danger to San Miguelito. The liturgy of dedication was splendid. Cardinal Cody, assisted by Archbishop Clavel as well as Bishops Grady and Wycislo from Chicago, celebrated the Eucharist. What was most spectacular was the participation of about three thousand people from San Miguelito who sang the praises of God with a zest most of the visitors had never heard before. That evening was Cody's last in Panama.

Bishops Wycislo and Grady went to Cody's suite at the Hilton and upbraided him severely for leaving one of his own priests undefended. They told me later that they had had quite a row. It must have had some effect, because the next day the Cardinal sat down with me to talk over the situation.

That is when I broke down and began to cry. I cried the whole morning and on into the afternoon. Cody was shocked and asked why I was so upset. Through my sobs I tried to explain how much I loved the church and how I would never knowingly hurt it—and then to be treated like a Judas—to be charged publicly with misconduct! I had been accused, and I couldn't even defend myself, since I didn't know what the accusations were. He listened but was of no help. He didn't console or condole.

"What are the accusations about?" I pleaded for an answer.

He had none.

After the Cardinal's departure, I was still feeling lower than the little green lizards that crawl everywhere in Panama. A good number of parishioners noticed how down I was and came to offer help. They told me they didn't know what was going on in my life but since I was their friend they wanted to share whatever burden I was carrying.

We talked one starry night (all the good nights in my life seem to be decorated with stars) and I told them the whole sordid story, knowing, of course, that I didn't have many details to share. It was the vagueness that shadowed and haunted me. They listened with a remarkable intensity, as if they were hearing the Martin Luther story over again and I, for my part, told the story with same degree of self-pity Luther must have felt. After all, no one had ever suffered as much as I had! I was being abandoned by the church I had given my life to serve.

When I finished, there was a pause and then one man, with great sympathy but also with great strength, said: "*Y?*"

One word, one syllable, one letter—and yet it was enough to cure me. I knew exactly what he meant by saying, "And?"

They were the down-trodden and abused lower class of the world and I had preached to them so often that they must not stay down when hit, they must not die even when wounded. Now, gently but insistently, they were reflecting back to me the same message. I recognized it.

It took a while for the pain to go away, to reach a point where I felt I was able to pursue the case of misconduct put against me. I went to Bishop Marcos McGrath of Santiago, whom I had considered a friend.

"Marcos," I said, "what is this misconduct that I have been accused of?"

Somewhat embarrassed, since he was one who had boycotted the ceremony at San Miguelito, he advised me to see Bishop Lewis, the auxiliary of Panama.

Cody and now McGrath were unwilling to give me a straight answer! I was getting beyond hurt. I was mad.

When I walked into Lewis's office, he was seated at his typewriter, writing a whole series of accusations against us.

"Bishop Lewis," I began, "I want some answers."

He turned to me and said, "This isn't that big a deal. Let's straighten it out, just the two of us. Are you willing to listen?"

"It *is* a big deal. The bishops of Panama made it so," I reminded him. I added, "If there are charges of misconduct and heresy, then I want a written record of the charges and an opportunity to present my defense before all the bishops."

Lewis bridled at the word "heresy." "Let's just call it a hearing," he said.

I insisted on a bill of accusations.

I was in a restless, agitated state. The list was not forthcoming and the emotional pacing, the intensity of anger, the feelings of rejection and disgust mounted. Eventually the list of accusations was sent to me.

The accusations turned out to be a hodge-podge of disciplinary and doctrinal matters. We were charged with "not saying the breviary and teaching others not to say it," with not believing in hell, with not recognizing the authority of the bishop, and with not believing in the Real Presence in the Eucharist.

My initial reaction was to toss the whole document into the Gulf of Mexico and walk away. Once I was able to talk myself into dealing with it, I tackled my defense as if I was in the Super Bowl with seconds left to play, and it was all up me to achieve a victory.

I prepared a written defense, answering every question and charge and making sure to quote Denzinger numbers and noted theologians, such as Karl Rahner. It turned out to be a long document and I sent it to each bishop in the country.

I requested a formal hearing before all the bishops and, much to my surprise, they agreed. We met in the city of Colon.

I shouldn't have been surprised, but the bishops seemed to be very friendly, extending the same cordialness that they had demonstrated that night at the banquet.

I didn't feel "friendly." To me, a charge of public adultery would have been far less grave than one of heresy. Yet the bishops were treating me with urbanity, if not genuine charity.

They seemed to have ignored the document I had sent them. They either had not read it or really didn't care what doctrinal position I took. I was mystified by their method. The conversation began in a desultory, even joking fashion.

The elderly bishop of Colon, Bishop Serrano, began the questioning and it was as though a cold draft had crept through a partially opened door. "Young man," he asked quietly, "do you believe in hell?"

"Yes, I do," I answered.

He pressed on. "But do you *really* believe in hell?"

"Yes, Monseñor, I truly believe in hell, but I am not at all sure it's the same hell you believe in."

Banging the table, he said, "Now there's the problem; let me put it to you exactly. Do you believe that at this very moment there are dammed souls burning in hellfire?"

"Monseñor," I answered, "I have done my homework and have defended my positions with quotes from scripture, the Fathers, and the councils. Now I challenge you to show one single passage in any of our Catholic sources supporting the opinion you have just expressed."

"Why," he said, "everybody knows that is Catholic teaching."

I retorted, "Well, I don't, and I defy you to prove that it's Catholic teaching."

At this point, the other bishops, particularly Bishop McGrath, who was a good theologian, began to address their remarks to Bishop Serrano.

"You really can't say that, Bishop." The bishops huddled on the matter. One might have asked at that point who was on trial.

The subject of hell was dropped, but Serrano continued. "What catechism do you use?"

I answered that we didn't use a published catechism.

"And why not?" he asked, like someone suggesting that it would be illicit to repair an automobile without looking at the manual.

"Because, in this era of transition, we believe that it's more important to find the questions rather than the answers," I answered.

Seeing that he wasn't following my logic, I added, "Besides, what catechism would you have us use?"

He responded quickly, "How about the official catechism of Panama?"

I was incredulous at that point. "Bishop, that catechism was written long before Vatican II and is completely out of date." It was something like the Baltimore Catechism in the United States.

"You wouldn't seriously recommend that we use it?" I added.

The other bishops stiffened noticeably.

"Young man, do you know who wrote that catechism?" one rather quiet bishop asked.

"No," I responded. I really didn't know, but by that time I could offer a very good guess.

When Bishop Serrano said "I did," all I could do was purse my lips and groan inwardly.

The session ended, again with a remarkable degree of friendliness and courtesy on the part of the bishops. I was not shrewd enough to discern that the matter was not one of truth and falsehood, but rather one of control. They were in control, or at least they thought they should be, and my "not being under control" was the real offense.

During the entire session, my own archbishop in Panama, Tomas Clavel, sat listening intently, saying almost nothing. It took me a while to discover that the hearing, or the trial, was an oblique but not so subtle attack on him— for being too permissive.

When I got back to San Miguelito, the priests and sisters asked how it had turned out. I had to answer that I really did not know. Nothing was settled. I heard nothing more about it. The whole affair was destined to be played over in a much more formal and serious way down the road.

E arly on, Archbishop Clavel had appointed me episcopal vicar, a new post–Vatican II position that conferred on a priest in a given territory many of the powers of a bishop without actually ordaining that priest a bishop. Later on he extended the episcopal vicariate beyond San Miguelito to the entire eastern part of his archdiocese.

Clavel was earthy, perceptive, good-natured, and witty, a good man to work with and for. We had a mutually respectful relationship, something I desired since I had lost much respect for his counterpart back in Chicago.

As episcopal vicar, I was responsible for the largest portion of the Archdiocese of Panama, with a Catholic population fast approaching two hundred thousand. With me worked many sisters, priests, and lay evangelizers. They were dedicated women and men, hard-working and self-sacrificing, and yet they were becoming disillusioned. What we had experienced on our arrival in 1963 hadn't changed in almost a decade; in fact the military government reinforced the obvious disconnects between the needs of the people and the hierarchical authorities, church included.

Our weekly planning meetings were taken up with anger, impatience, and frustration over the bishops.

"The church is acting like Hector Gallegos never existed." After the immediate rush of activity ceased, the bishops did not speak of Gallegos or the injustice that was apparent in the government.

"Were their ears shut at Medellin?" A large bishop's conference had been held in Medellin, Colombia, in 1965. The most startling pronouncement to come out of Medellin had been the Option for the

Poor. The leaders of the Latin American church, the largest body of Christians in the world, decided to identify with and stand with the poor, the vast majority of their people, those without money or power.

What the Latin American church did in Medellin was summon up the courage to make a momentous historical turnaround and focus, not on the rich and the wealthy, the traditional response, but on the poor and the powerless. Panama did not respond.

When I quoted chapter and verse from the documents to defend our activities and methods, one bishop who continually criticized us said, "We shall rue the day we signed those documents in Medellin."

The outrage among our team continued. "When will they stop *selling* the sacraments?" The old way of external sacramentalism was still the modus operandi of many priests—couples were married with no premarital counseling and supermarkets were blessed by clerics in cassocks and surplices.

"Will they ever recognize the duplicity of their actions?" Perhaps the action that truly revealed the old church most fully was the ceremony of *Te Deum* at the cathedral on New Year's Day. The entire diplomatic corps as well as the leaders of the military government who were busy plundering the national treasury gathered in the ancient church in the presence of the papal nuncio, the archbishop, and much of the clergy to sing the official "thanksgiving" song of a "Catholic" nation. It was a living picture in miniature of a culture and society that had long since lost its meaning and its relevance and yet went on.

"Why don't we split from the institutional church?"

"We are one, here in San Miguelito. We can align ourselves with Medellin and Vatican II."

"Let's just let the old guard die off. There is a need for death, so that resurrection can take place."

The Catholic Church for centuries has been noted for permitting various theologies and spiritualities to co-exist within itself. In this sense, it has been truly catholic or universal. Yet there have been times when tensions between communities have become conflicts and serious quarrels have erupted. The result has been schism and separation and divorce. One kind of schism is what I would call "practical"—people get tired of the fight and walk away from the body of Christ; great numbers have done it recently. The other, of course, is "real" schism, a break between two communities. That type of schism is the worst of all ecclesial sins because it divides what by its nature is a sign of the unity of all human beings, one flock and one shepherd.

In San Miguelito there reigned a high degree of unity. One body, though, was beginning to rise against another. I could sense among many working with me a growing restlessness that could possibly result in schism.

It scared me. I had faced enough turmoil of civil as well as church infighting. I couldn't fathom a religious war. It went against everything I believed about working through—not against—issues.

To head off possible trouble, I convoked a meeting of all the priests, sisters, and full-time lay leaders. The meeting lasted almost a week. I figured it would be an opportunity to scream and complain. It would be an opportunity to discern our strategy moving forward. It would be an opportunity to view our relationship with the rest of the church in Panama and in the world.

It was time, perhaps past time, that I needed to reconnect with my pastoral duties, having walked away from the political scene.

I very much wanted the archbishop to attend the meeting. By then, McGrath had taken Clavel's place after Clavel had been forced to resign. I felt that McGrath should listen to the people who worked in the field and bore the heat of the day, that both he and I should listen to the pain and anger of those who had given their lives to the work of the church.

McGrath informed me that he would be unable to attend the meeting. He was scheduled to attend a meeting in Rome during the following month and he had a lot of work to do before leaving. Realizing that it was a bit much to have asked him for a week of his time, I accepted his declining the invitation. He asked me to keep him informed. Had I known the snowballing effect of his lack of presence, I would have insisted that he attend.

The meeting took place at the house called Emmaus in Las Cumbres. The entourage of priests, religious, and laity, most of whom I had personally recruited and trained and on whom I had depended for leadership of the parishes and the ministries, came dressed with multiple emotions. Some came armed for verbal battle. Others could barely camouflage their disappointment over my lack of attention to things religious. None came adorned with the simplicity of the peasant grateful solely for a place at the table.

All wanted voice.

All had hard questions.

"What is our future role in Panama?"

"Have we outlived our stay?"

"Now that the civic community is threatening to collapse, do we have credibility?"

"Do we want to survive within the duplicity of a two-church system?"

"Are you with us, Leo?"

"What does it mean to be a post–Vatican II Catholic in a medieval warped time zone?"

There were bitter statements and anguished cries.

There were moments of prayer when peace would descend upon us like the first snowfall of the winter. Each day as we gathered to celebrate the Lord's Supper, when we felt that mysterious unity through Him with all peoples and all times, our own confusions and anxieties would seem to fade along with the light of the setting sun.

Intermixed with the week's gatherings were talks by the most prestigiously astute among us. Most of the presentations were on recent documents of the church. Each was followed by a hearty discussion.

All the participants had attended the meeting clad in their own emotional wardrobes. Each left with a sense of revitalized energy and renewed willingness to work through our frustrations within, not against, the existing church.

First in our minds was to get at least one bishop to hear our concerns and work with us in resolving some of the issues. The natural choice was McGrath, who oversaw the eastern Panamanian church.

I asked Eric De Leon to transcribe the proceedings, since we had tape-recorded every word. He was trained psychologist, but not a theologian, and I discovered later that he had made a few errors in the transcription. I did not read the mimeographed pages. At the time I felt that I had been there for all the sessions and had heard it all. There was no need for micro-scrutiny; it was to remain an internal document. The distribution list was restricted to the participants and to the archbishop.

I gave the document to Bishop McGrath and asked him to read it, requesting time to discuss it. He agreed.

Not long afterwards, McGrath left for Rome. He had not had a chance to read the document before leaving but gave it to his friend, Bishop Daniel Nuñez of Chiriqui, to read in his absence. Nuñez, in turn, shared it with a few priests of his diocese.

One of the priests was an American Franciscan who had set up a minor seminary for the training of candidates for the priesthood. The candidates were of grammar school age. I remember his visiting me once to ask if I knew the manager of the Sears store in

Panama. I asked him why and he answered that he wanted to buy toys for his seminarians!

At the bishops' council I had objected strenuously to that kind of badly conceived plan for the formation of native Panamanian leadership. To my knowledge, not a single priest was ever ordained from that seminary! The rector, informed of my opposition, did not take kindly to me or to anything coming out of San Miguelito. It was he who read the copy of the Las Cumbres proceedings originally intended for the archbishop.

It was he who lifted the *most outrageous* statements and used them to create a separate document. He then prepared a charge of heresy based on those excerpts and appended it to his document. He got sixty priests to sign a statement requesting that the bishops and Rome convict us of heresy and expel us from Panama.

He did not inform me of his action nor did he give me an opportunity to explain.

By the time McGrath returned from Rome, the affair was public. Clerical circles across the land were buzzing with anxious curiosity.

Among the priests who had signed the accusatory document were, I thought, good friends of mine. I was both shocked and hurt. Meeting with some of them later, I asked them how they could possibly have been party to such an extreme action without talking to us first.

They answered: "Well, Leo, those were really heretical statements."

"Yes, what is put down in that paper you signed is heretical. But how did you know that is what we held or said? Did you read the original transcript from which the statements were supposed to have been taken?"

They admitted uneasily that they had not.

Archbishop McGrath felt he was in a bind. A good theologian himself, and a fair person, he had to act immediately or Rome would. His predecessor had been pressured to resign, with one of the charges against him being "failure to control the priests of San Miguelito."

There existed more than a possibility that the Vatican would send in an "apostolic visitor," a cleric from outside who would take over the diocese and investigate this problem. McGrath decided to set up a panel to review the charges. It would include, in addition to himself, three others appointed by him: Father Virgilio Sea, S.J., the dean of the theological faculty at the prestigious Xaveriana

University in Columbia; a Claretian theologian from Guatemala; and a prominent layman who would act as auditor.

I agreed to the panel representatives and so the business of investigating "heresy" began.

Some might think that such investigations took place only in the Middle Ages. Perhaps they should have ceased then, but they have not. Nor was ours the last of such trials in our own era. They continue on. Physical torture is no longer used and outright excommunications are rare. But the price is still too high in terms of shame, scandal, and hurt.

This time I personally was not accused of any error, but three of my associate priests were. In a way, that made me feel worse because I felt responsible for them. Knowing that they were by no means heretics, I was infuriated by the charges and the manner in which they had been made. I insisted that I be allowed to be present at every session held. So it was arranged.

The three priests were summoned to explain themselves and their positions. The first was Father José Martinez, O.P., a young, handsome Spanish priest who almost always had a smile on his face. He had given a presentation on the priesthood of the laity, teaching the people that they, through baptism, shared in the priesthood of Christ in its power and its responsibility.

Today this doctrine is a constant in Catholic tradition but, until recently, it has been widely ignored. Father Martinez, "Pepe," as we affectionately called him, was questioned as to whether he was teaching the laity that there was no difference between the ministerial priesthood, or that of ordained clergy, and that of the laity.

Such a distinction is of great importance to many in the church who wish to maintain and preserve intact the hierarchical structure. That distinction, therefore, is the theological foundation of clericalism. Some even maintain that the orders of the church that shape its hierarchical structure were instituted by Jesus himself—a proposition they would be hard put to prove from a reading of scripture.

Pepe answered that his intent was to convince the laity of their "priestly" vocation and nothing more. I can remember the sincere smile on his face when he added, "Look, I am not a professional theologian and have not reflected much on the niceties of such distinctions. I certainly did not intend to pronounce upon something I do not fully understand. But I refuse to sacrifice the dignity of the people to enhance or protect our own."

The members of the commission seemed to be satisfied and the second defendant was called.

Frans Beens had been trained at the Latin American College at the University of Louvain. Although ordained for the diocese of Bruges in Belgium, he—along with another priest trained in scripture—was sent to Panama as a gift to the missions.

Frans had the look of the people of the lowlands of Europe, a somewhat rounded physique, lively blue eyes, and dirty blond hair closed cropped in the style we used to call a brush haircut. Frans taught scripture in the National Seminary, but he lived and worked with us in San Miguelito.

I personally learned more scripture from him than I did in three years of formal study in the seminary. Like many Belgians, Frans spoke fluent French, English, and Spanish as well as his native language, Flemish.

When our phones were tapped by Army Intelligence, Frans used his Flemish connections to speak to other Belgian priests in the country, providing us with an impenetrable network. Much to the distress of the government, no one in the government could speak or understand Flemish.

When Frans Beens appeared before the court, he took his seat in the defendant's place. I saw in him, besides irrepressible energy and good will, a quality of innocence that I feared would render him vulnerable and hurt. Frans had given a major presentation to the assembly at Las Cumbres on the place of symbolism in sacred scripture, explaining in a simple but masterly way how important it was to get beyond the symbol to the meaning behind it. One of his examples was the virgin birth. During the question period, one of the lay people asked him: "Well, was Mary really a virgin?" It was the type of question that illustrated the point of his thesis, namely, that people so often get stuck on the symbol itself and never get to its inner meaning. Frans answered in a friendly but exasperated tone, "I couldn't care less whether she was physically a virgin or not. What I do care about is what does it mean to you, to your life—to this movement?"

It was that remark that had put Frans in front of a heresy tribunal. He would never have uttered such a throwaway statement in a formal address or written it in a serious article, but in the friendly, intimate environment of a question-and answer session he did.

"You do know, Padre Beens," said one investigator, "the clear, definitive teaching of the church has been from the beginning that Mary was a virgin. As the theological formula puts it, 'before, during and after giving birth to the child, Jesus.'"

"I had no intention of denying the traditional teaching," Frans responded. "I was trying to get my listeners past the physiological phenomenon to the actual meaning of the doctrine."

He continued without hesitation. "Although there are difficulties to be solved from the scripture scholar's point of view," he repeated, "I had no wish or intention to deny the traditional teaching of the church."

Then, caught up in the delivery of a scholarly response, he went on. "The symbol 'born of the Virgin Mary' appears in the earliest of Christian creeds. What does it point to—that sex is evil? That the state of virginity is higher than that of marriage?

"No," Frans said, "it means that nothing new, nothing good, nothing great, can be created without the Spirit of God. Men and women can go on coupling forever and they shall never produce a true image of God in the flesh, a wholesome human being, without an active union with and inclusion of the Spirit of God.

"Is it important to hold that Mary was physically a virgin in order to preserve the symbol and the teaching?" Frans asked. "Scripture seems to say both yes and no; there is debate among scholars.

"The infancy narratives of both St. Matthew and St. Luke state unequivocally that Mary did not know man before the birth of Jesus, yet, there are numerous gospel references to the siblings of Jesus." Frans opened the sacred book and read:

> And when Jesus had finished these parables, he went away from there, and coming to his own country he taught them in their synagogue, so that they were astonished and said, "Where did this man get this wisdom and these mighty works? Is not this the carpenter's son? Is not his mother called Mary? And are not his brothers James and Joseph and Simon and Judas? And are not all his sisters with us? Where then did this man get all this?" And they took offense at him. But Jesus said to them, "A prophet is not without honor except in his own country and in his own house." And he did not do many mighty works there, because of their unbelief. (Matt 13:53-58)

"The Catholic explanation has traditionally been that 'brothers' and 'sisters' are words that can mean 'cousins,' as well as brothers and sisters. Scripture scholars regard this as an evasion of the problem. They state that the context demands a different explanation. The question about his brothers and sisters generally comes up when neighbors claim they know who Jesus is because they know his parents, his brothers and sisters, and his entire background." Frans continued for twenty more minutes discussing the virgin birth.

I sat there in that cold and stark tribunal room, surrounded by the pompous and the righteous, and I listened to this scholarly, articulate, and humble man speak of the Virgin Mary. My fears of his inadequacy had been unfounded. Silent and proud, I heard Frans Beens expound on the most profound views, arguing from multiple sides on issues that have vexed scripture scholars and theologians for centuries. When he finished, I wanted to jump up and cheer as any fan of a most respected hero would do after a winning presentation.

The panel seemed to accept his arguments.

The third and last defendant called was Father Donald Headley, a young priest from Chicago who had been a recent addition to our team. Headley, a man of boundless energy and profound compassion, was well read in both theology and scripture. He was, in fact, the best theologian among the American priests of San Miguelito.

Having read his presentation on the Eucharist, the examiners asked him if he believed in the Real Presence of Jesus in the Eucharist.

"Yes, certainly I do," replied Headley, "but not in the presence of Jesus the Nazarene who died and was buried. He rose to new life. But He did not, as many seem to believe, return to his former life and existence, that which we live at this moment. If Jesus the Nazarene, restored to his former life, is present in the Eucharist, then there would have to be present there ten tiny fingers and ten tiny toes."

The panel members looked at each other. Headley continued.

"Jesus present is the Jesus who rose from the dead—the same Jesus, but clearly in a new mode of existence. The kind of body that can pass through doors and walls! The kind of person who can appear suddenly and just as quickly disappear! The kind of person who, upon appearing to his best friends, went unrecognized! They would have known him immediately if he had come as the familiar Jesus the Nazarene!"

Headley, like Beens, could speak for hours on church history and scriptural theology. He added, "The Risen Christ had to convince his companions that it was truly he, not a ghost and not a stranger. He was seen only by persons of faith who wanted to believe. He was recognized by his followers most clearly in the one act that characterized the Nazarene, in the breaking of the bread and the passing of the cup, in the act of loving, sharing, and forgiving. This is the Real Presence, a portent of how we shall live, move, and have our being after our own death and rising. A presence intimately related to community and to its most profound moments and experiences. Thus the followers of Jesus are the Body of Christ. 'Whenever two or three of you gather in my name, I shall be with you.'"

"Is the Risen Lord present in the Eucharist?" queried one of the panelists.

"Yes, absolutely," concluded Headley, "and therein lies the grand mystery of life and death and rising, the mystery of God's life and ours as well."

I was again proud. Headley spoke so clearly, with his heart as well as with his mind, of the mysteries he loved deeply.

The panel of theologians was impressed. Father Sea, the chairman of the commission, commented on all three defendants, but particularly on Headley: "This not only is not heresy but rather *la teologia mas actualizada* (the most dynamically relevant theology) I have encountered in Latin America."

Ten long days of hearings continued before the commission wound up its work. The proceedings were typed up, along with the opinions of the panel, and sent to Rome. Not long afterwards, the verdict came back from Rome. All three priests were censured for "imprudence," but the panel's judgment that there was no intent to commit heresy was accepted by the Vatican.

All the priests of San Miguelito were commanded to take an oath before the archbishop that we would not hold or teach heretical doctrines. To have to do this was humiliating, but we swallowed our hurt and pride and did as we were told.

Frans Beens received the harshest sentence. He was removed from the seminary faculty and forbidden ever to have more teaching contact with candidates for the priesthood. It was a severe and unjust blow to Frans—one from which he never fully recovered. A few years later he left the active priesthood. Thus the church, the people of God, lost a valuable and dedicated servant-teacher.

So it was over. Months and months of energy and enthusiasm wasted. I felt drained, more tired than I had been in my entire life. It wasn't the fatigue that comes from hard work, from doing something worthwhile or creative. Rather, it was the tiredness that results from a useless exercise that in its efforts to "defend and protect" the doctrine of the church creates distrust, anger, and disillusionment.

Then I discovered that the matter was not finished.

A friend with contacts inside the Vatican informed me that a new commission had been set up to investigate San Miguelito again, and that it was composed of five cardinals and the master general of the Dominicans. Such a body was by no means an ordinary committee and once more I began to feel the dreadful tics of anxiety.

One day I received a telephone call from the new papal nuncio to Panama. Pinci had retired and his successor wanted to know whether he could speak to me about an "important matter."

"Of course." I silently gulped. "When do you want me to come?"

He replied that he would prefer to come out to see me in San Miguelito. That sounded unusual, since nuncios typically summon simple priests to their residences.

The nuncio came out the next day. He and I sat down in the small room that served as my office, my parlor, and my bedroom. When he asked if I could give him all the files on the mission, from its very beginning, I knew that this was not merely a friendly visit.

I asked, "What makes you interested in these files?"

"I have heard so much about San Miguelito that I want to read all about it," he responded.

I trusted my inside information and blurted, "Monseñor, why don't you tell me the truth? A commission has been set up in Rome to investigate us and you have been asking to get the files."

He was visibly flustered. Shrugging his shoulders, and without denying the existence of the commission, he went on: "Well, will you give them to me?"

I thought for a moment and then answered: "Yes, I will, because we have nothing to hide, but under two conditions: first, that Cardinal Cody approve their transfer, and second, that we be given the right of representation in Rome."

Obviously agitated, he said, "Then you are asking for an apostolic visitation!" I knew well that such a procedure would mean a formal investigation of the entire archdiocese.

"I'm asking no such thing," I retorted. "I ask only that if we are to be investigated and tried again, it should be done openly and we should have the right of counsel."

He left my room with a polite farewell and without the documents. Never again did he speak to me on the subject, nor did I ever officially hear what the commission in Rome did while it existed.

That was 1973. I heard via the grapevine that the commission focused on three subjects—one generated by clericalism, one by scriptural fundamentalism, and the last by theological fundamentalism.

The outcomes were not reported to me or to anyone whom I have asked.

In the years since then I have had dramatic nightmares of being caught in a mud wrestle. The match seems to go on for hours. Several times I am close to drowning as my opponent, much stronger than I, holds my head down in the mud, but each time I manage to break his death hold. I am covered with slime, weakened, and very tired. Finally, I awake to find myself drenched in sweat.

By the early 1970s we had established a Pastoral Institute of San Miguelito where priests, sisters, and lay people came from all over the world to study, staying with us for three or four months at a time. They grew in their pastoral skills, interpreting scripture through lived experience. They became one with us, walking the streets of San Miguelito, living our mission, and extending theirs. The key message of the Institute was "Respect and honor the people, believe in them. If you don't believe in them, who's going to believe in them? They won't believe in themselves."

As the Institute was beginning to flourish, we lost the Maryknoll sisters. A decision was made in New York, their motherhouse headquarters, and it was hard to know the full reason for their withdrawal. Some would argue that the sisters offered an even greater and more lasting contribution than us priests. They touched the family: the women and children. They modeled and empowered the "dignity of woman," so that what we priests had initiated in the men was extended to the entire family.

Although our work did not include establishing or working in the school system, the sisters were instrumental in teaching native teachers how to teach.

"*Madres*, come and prepare the children for their first holy communion. We have almost two hundred children in our first communion class."

"We are but few," Madre Maria de la Cruz responded.

"Well, then, teach us so that we can teach them," requested the teachers. And so they did, modeling our Familia de Dios program. They prepared not lesson plans, but discussion groups—adult to adult.

Ingeniously they encouraged the teachers to get parents involved in the classroom, teaching gardening, sewing, and folk dancing, so that the teachers could be free once a week to discuss the catechism without adding hours to their day. They worked with the principals to schedule religious education at the same time each week so that the teachers could be supervised and guided as they taught. The spirit of working with the teachers clearly extended the sisters' influence in the community.

Our parishes flourished under the experimental co-pastoring. Without Madre Cecilia, my co-pastor, Cristo Redentor could not have sustained its ministries.

O ur political engagement, though, took its toll on the ministries. Perhaps that neglect was of more influence on Maryknoll's decision than I would like to believe. Many of us, priests, sisters, and lay leaders, became engaged in building and defending the civic community. For a time we lost some of the faithful and they fell back into non-practice.

With the increase in population, we didn't give the newcomers the attention that we had provided earlier. For a while, we let slip the need for advanced and specialized programs for the faithful who walked with us.

As we reflected on our loss of the sisters, we priests did much soul searching.

"Perhaps had I stayed pastoral, and not gotten involved in the socio-political scene..." I said aloud.

"Leo, you merely served as an advisor to the political movement," McGlinn said.

"The men of the community were the activists," added Headley. "Admittedly, the work of San Miguelito awakened their self-confidence, their sense of leadership."

"We did divert our attention. All of us did!" I reminded them.

"Isn't it our role to be prophetic, exposing injustices when those in power fail to do so?" continued Headley.

With the sisters' exit, we pledged to concentrate our attention on building the "common priesthood of the faithful."

On April 16, 1971, our parishes assembled and proclaimed the document, "The Proposal for the Constitution of the People of God in San Miguelito." When the later accusations of heresy came, no one questioned our constitution. I could never figure out what would catch the institutional church's attention and what wouldn't.

11

ENDING
THE UNENDABLE

*L*ate in the year 1974 I found myself with not nearly enough energy or spirit to do justice to increased responsibilities. I was vicar of San Miguelito, head of the Chicago mission and consulter to the archbishop. I was charged with interacting with Cardinal Cody in Chicago and both the archbishop and the papal nuncio in Panama —and dealing with them was no easy task. Cardinal Cody had grown increasingly capricious and our relationship was almost always testy.

The government of Panama harried me at every opportunity. Each time I left the country I feared I would not be allowed to return.

Working with me was a pastoral team of seven lay leaders, eleven priests, and seven newly arrived Belgian sisters. All were deeply committed and strongly motivated. And because our work was so intense and so intimately touched others, it also touched our own lives. My team needed to be affirmed, encouraged, and sometimes calmed and reconciled.

Salaries had to be paid, and while the subsidy from Chicago supplied the needs of the original Chicago mission and the municipality of San Miguelito, I had to raise the money to pay the salaries of the people who worked in the rest of the vicariate.

There were two *urbanizaciones* (suburban developments), both of which should have been made into parishes. I was temporarily in charge of these two developments, yet I was aware that I was not giving sufficient time to the thousands of families who dwelt in those communities.

I searched in prayer and reflection for an answer and thought I had arrived at a satisfactory solution. I announced to my colleagues that I intended to resign my posts as vicar and head of the Chicago mission, remain as an ordinary member of the team, and devote myself to being a pastor.

I added, "It is my fervent hope that living and working with people and not with the 'big shots' who were my superiors will renew my spirit."

Upon hearing my decision, my associates looked at me incredulously, as though my I.Q. had suddenly decreased by twenty points.

"Leo," they said with amusement, "there is no way you can stay without being the boss; no one could take over as long as you're here."

They added honestly, "It's either you stay as the boss or you leave Panama altogether." They meant no offense and I took none, for I knew immediately that they were right. So back I went to my personal drawing board.

I reckoned that if I were to stay any longer in Panama, I would have to make a life-time commitment. I would have to become a Panamanian citizen, despite the fact I did not know whether Panama or its government wanted me to stay. Furthermore, I would have to remain in office with all the tensions and aggravations that were sapping my spirit. Slowly the decision came into focus: I had to leave Panama.

My thoughts turned to the land of my origin and to the church of my ordination, Chicago. I had learned a great deal in my twelve years in Panama—about myself, about people, about the dynamics of Christian community.

Priests in Chicago had more than once said to me: "It's great what you've done down there among the poor. But it wouldn't work up here, especially not in the suburbs."

I remember not replying but thinking to myself that it could be done, perhaps even more easily than in Panama. I often visited the Chicago suburb where my brother, his wife, and their eight children lived. Most of my contemporaries lived in the Chicago suburbs. Moreover, if I had married and had a family myself, that is where I would have been. I knew enough about how faith in Christ can motivate and how pride in the Church can keep us together as Catholics to make a bet that it could be done and *done in spades.*

Something about returning to Chicago began to excite me and re-energize my spirits.

The team in San Miguelito accepted my decision with grace and realism.

Not so Cardinal Cody! After I wrote to him about my decision, Cody promptly sent back a cable stating that, "due to peculiar circumstances in this archdiocese, you may not return."

I had a notion of what he meant by "peculiar circumstances," and my suspicion was to be confirmed shortly.

I shot back a letter by the next post saying that I belonged in Chicago more than he did and named the date on which I was to return.

All that remained was to say good-bye. It was excruciatingly difficult. For years I had lived and worked with the people of San Miguelito. I loved them as I had never loved before and the affection was returned a biblical hundredfold.

I was leaving Panama with a deep sense of failure. Yes, we had done great things together, my companions, the people of San Miguelito, its leaders, and me. "Daughter" movements had come out of San Miguelito and had prospered in other parts of Panama and Central America. Some of them had even surpassed San Miguelito in effectiveness.

I personally had become a noted personality—famous in some circles, infamous in others. I'm sure there are thick files on me both at CIA headquarters in Langley, Virginia, and in Rome.

San Miguelito, however, was a failure in the sense that it did not end up as I had dreamed it would. Chacho Hernandez had once described the forces arrayed against us as too powerful, pointing out that the institutional church was no more willing to allow an experimental structure to thrive within itself than was the government to allow a democratic society.

That surely was a part of it, and indubitably there were other factors: we had made mistakes; we may well have moved too quickly; we probably hadn't mended our political and ecclesiastical fences.

San Miguelito did not become the glory of the Christian world that I had hoped it would be. Perhaps it is just as well. If my ideals had been achieved, then I would have a head bigger than one of those four-hundred-pound pumpkins one sees on rare occasions.

God has a way of letting us know that he (she) is the Lord of Creation and of the church and we are but the workers in the field. Jesus himself felt his failure at the end of his life. He had set his sights so high. If I may be forgiven the boldness of the comparison, so had I.

Each time I have left an assignment and a people, I have felt this same sense of failure, not the failure of a man who has accomplished nothing, created nothing, but rather that of the person who "shot for the moon" and did not reach it. Still, I know very well that if some of the people with whom I worked learned to dream great dreams and hold on tenaciously to high hopes, and if they had had a taste of glory of authentic community, then, in the long run, we did not fail.

On the morning of my departure they came at dawn to sing the "*Mañanitas*," that lovely Latin American tradition of serenading a loved one. I was so moved I was unable to cry. I felt numb, my body and spirit rendered powerless, incapable of action. I had to be nudged in order to board the plane.

From Panama I went to Bogota in order to take a few days of rest before departing Latin America for Chicago. Those days were quiet days: they were questioning, reflecting, dreaming, wondering, hoping, pacing, sleeping, suspended days.

Upon boarding the plan in Colombia for my homeward journey, I took my seat at a window on the starboard side. Sitting across the aisle from me was an elderly American couple.

A few moments before take-off, the couple exclaimed in unison: "There's a man out there walking on the wing."

I looked over but saw no one. The flight attendant was summoned and she asked others sitting nearby whether they had seen anyone. No one else had seen the man. The flight attendant calmed the couple by saying that she would relay the information to the captain.

The plane soared into the skies. During the flight every once in a while I looked over at the elderly man and woman who were wringing their hands and chatting nervously.

Several hours later we began our descent over the glistening waters of the Caribbean into the airport of Miami. When the bay doors opened and the landing wheels descended, the couple, once again looking out the window, let out a scream. Their reaction echoed through the plane as several more people spotted the same scene. A body had fallen from the port side of the plane. I rushed over and saw in horror something, later to be identified as a body, plummeting into the sea.

We were to learn that a seventeen-year-old boy had climbed into the housing where the wheels are stored. The airline officials said he had been crushed to death by the retracting wheels. Even so, during the flight he would almost certainly have been frozen to death.

That young boy was one of the teeming millions of Latin Americans who look to the United States as the fabled land of opportunity and work. Like many before him, he did not make it to the United States. Tens of thousands of Europeans died during the Atlantic crossing a century before. Who will ever know how many shackled blacks died traversing the same ocean?

As I contemplated the tragedy of that Colombian youth, I became aware of how close I was to indulging in self-pity. Yes, I was down and empty—a father without a family, a shepherd without a flock, a man alone, a priest going home to a home that didn't want him! Yet how my concerns paled in light of those of the destitute who fought simply to survive.

After my return to Chicago, I went to the archbishop's mansion on North State Parkway. Cardinal Cody's greeting was friendlier than I had expected.

He asked me what I wanted to do. I replied that after a little rest I wanted to be appointed pastor of a parish.

He countered: "Wouldn't it be better to be an assistant pastor for a few years? Lots of things have changed up here and that would give you some time to get used to them."

I answered that I did not think all that much had changed, that both my age and my experience fitted me to be a pastor, and that that's what I wanted to be.

"I kind of thought that's what you would say," he admitted. "In that case, you may have any parish in the archdiocese you choose."

"Any parish?" I gasped, not having expected such overwhelming graciousness.

"Well, yes, any parish you wish: after all, you did a good job down there." It was the first time he had complimented me on the work in San Miguelito.

But then he threw in a hooker, "Any parish, except a black parish or a Hispanic parish."

I had never served in any parish except a Hispanic and a black one and, therefore, one might think that that was where my greatest competence lay.

So I asked him why not a black or Hispanic parish, suspecting all along that his answer would probably have something to do with the "peculiar circumstances" he had mentioned in his cable a few months earlier.

"I'll tell you, if you promise to obey me," he said unflinchingly.

"All right," I said, "I'll do what you wish." It wasn't much of a sacrifice, since I was intrigued with the possibility of working with outer-city or suburban white Catholics.

"Well, if I name you a pastor in the inner city, then the movement is going to start again to get you named a bishop and I am not going to name you a bishop." Stamping his black shoe on the thick crimson carpet for emphasis, he repeated, "Never, never, never!"

Surprised by the vehemence, but not by the substance of what he was saying, I replied, "Your Eminence, I never asked you to name me a bishop. Even if you were to offer it to me, I'm not sure I would accept it. I would end up having my ass between you and the priests and the people. I've had enough of that."

My response did not seem to faze him. He instructed me to see the personnel board about a parish.

I could not resist the opportunity to make one more countermove. I had understood that the offer "any parish in the archdiocese" meant any parish now open or about to open in the near future.

So I said, "How about St. Joseph's in Libertyville?" I knew St. Joseph's was available.

"Oh, I'm sorry, Leo, I just promised that to someone." His generosity was not as fulsome as he had made it sound, but what mattered now was to choose a parish where the adventure could begin anew.

While I was looking for the right parish, Father William Clark invited me to reside at Mary Seat of Wisdom in Park Ridge, Illinois. "Uncle Bill," as he was affectionately called by his parishioners, had two young and dynamic associates, Fathers John Cusick and John Hoffman. It was a marvelous place for me to spend the interim time between peoples and parishes. The parish was truly alive—the liturgies were excellent; they made me want to leap for joy.

Lay leaders were involved in myriad ministries and organizations. Teenagers and college-age students were close to the parish priests and really had the run of the rectory. They made lots of noise but I enjoyed their vitality, their outrageous sense of humor, their innocent ideals that empowered them to think the world was out there for them to change and to transform.

While there I preached a mission—a week-long renewal in the faith. It was good for me and good for the people. Good for me because I learned that, even though I had been away for twelve years, I was able to speak to their hearts as well as to their minds. Good for them because deep in the heart of many middle- and upper-class Catholics is the instinct that there is much more to life than making money and having fun. But it's got to be put to them in such a way that "being church, following the Lord together," is far more adventurous than cocktail parties and sports and far more significant and thrilling than piling up money.

Every day of the mission saw the church packed with people. There are times in life when one is privileged to witness a truly spectacular event, when the Word encounters a people ready to hear and respond. This was one of those times—and the result was like a rainbow glistening with pearly moisture after the charcoal-colored clouds have moved away.

Still tired and working to regain my enthusiasm for ministry, I experienced a bright new world coming into being. Perhaps I could be a missionary in the suburbs. Father John Cusick described the experience: "We had blurry visions. You focused them into clarity; you took our dreams and put words on them, words as old as the ancient creeds." I felt a new sense of hope and was able to see the sign just as clearly as Constantine and his troops reputedly saw it etched in the sky.

One day, while I was still in residence at Mary Seat of Wisdom, a young man came to see me. He was a native of Oak Park and the father of many children. He had helped me with the Hispanic apostolate many years before. After bringing me up to date on what had happened in his life, he explained that he was a recovering alcoholic and a charismatic.

"I know, Leo, you are not all that impressed with the charismatic movement but that is why I came to see you. So please listen to me. Not long ago I received a vision in which the Cardinal was stricken by a heart attack. But you see it wasn't a real heart attack. He was dying of a broken heart because of his failure in Chicago. In this vision I was told that Leo Mahon was the only person who could heal the Cardinal and right the situation."

I loved this man and admired his zeal but, needless to say, I was skeptical about the vision. I promised him I would pray over the message. He smiled confidently as he left me.

"You'll see, Leo, you'll see." I wondered to myself if he hadn't gone mental.

Several weeks later, the news broke: Cardinal Cody had been taken to the hospital with a serious heart problem. I was incredulous. I called and asked the hospital's chaplain whether the Cardinal was receiving visitors. He answered, "No, only the vicar general. But, Leo, why don't you come down anyway and sign the register? He will appreciate it later."

So I drove to Columbus Hospital knowing that I would not be admitted to the Cardinal's room. On the other hand, I told myself that if I were to see him, I would deliver the message I was rehearsing.

When I emerged from the hospital elevator, I saw a policeman guarding the Cardinal's room. Only Chicago, I thought, would guard the door of a man of the church.

The policeman greeted me, asked my name, and had me write it down in the register, just as I had anticipated. The Cardinal was not having visitors.

A nun was passing by, overheard me, and stopped, "What did you say your name is?" she asked.

I told her and she said, "He may wish to see you. Please wait here."

Astonished by this turn of events, I waited nervously. The nun returned: "Yes, he wishes to see you. But, please, Father, don't stay more than two minutes. He's very ill."

When I entered the suite, the Cardinal was seated in a chair, looking weak and as pale as a gray winter sky. "How are you, Your Eminence?"

"Not very good at all, Leo, but thank you for coming to see me."

At that point, I summoned up all my courage and said to him: "Eminence, you usually do most of the talking when we meet, but the nurse says I have only two minutes. So please, let me talk this time. I know you are sick but it could well be you have a broken heart."

I swallowed hard and continued, "Since you came here, almost everything has gone wrong. You've pressed every button you could and still nothing happened. You think we don't like you. But you won't let us love you. It doesn't have to be this way. I know of five or six priests who can help you turn this situation round. I don't have to be one of them. There are others. But let us help you."

I could hear the torrent of words pouring out of my mouth and I stopped suddenly to let him react. He had no words. Tears came out of his eyes and flowed down his cheeks. Then he turned to the wall. I waited for a while but he did not turn to face me. The two minutes were up—and so was the strangest episode of my life.

A s I looked around at various parishes that were about to become vacant, I began to hear rumors that I was to be the new pastor of St. Victor's in Calumet City—a large, blue-collar community in the far southern suburbs. I had no particular feeling for or against going there, but I wondered how such a rumor had been generated.

So I asked my good friend and classmate, Father George Kane, if he had heard the rumor.

He replied, "Sure I have. I started it."

"You did?" I said. "Why?"

"Wait 'til you've seen it. It's just the type of place you would like. Besides, Bill Stenzel is going there as an associate and that alone should be reason to go there."

I knew well that George was very high on this newly ordained priest who had done his internship in George's parish in Schaumburg.

A man is foolish if he ignores the insights of his best friends because they know him in a way he often does not know himself. So I called Bill Stenzel at his parents' home. He had been ordained the previous Saturday. We made a date for the following Monday, the day after the celebration of his first Mass at his home parish.

Neither of us was about to waste time. After graduating from the Illinois Institute of Technology, Bill Stenzel had worked for General Electric. I had heard that he had been offered a high executive post in that corporation, but he declined it in order to study for the priesthood. He was a tall, trim, good-looking young man brimming with both ideals and ideas and more than enough energy to pursue them.

We traveled together to Calumet City. As we drove up and down its quiet streets, I was struck by the similarities to the west side

neighborhood where I had been born and raised: a town of bunga-
lows and two- and three-story houses in the older part of town and
ranch houses in the newer section of the city.

I instantly had my first feeling of "coming home."

We then drove around the square block on which the parish
plant was located. We saw a parish church, rather ordinary in style
and modest in size, as well as a large parish school which accommo-
dated some 550 children. The rectory was modern and spacious—a
definite plus in my mind, because a good staff needs spacious quarters in which to live and work. The building that truly attracted my
attention, however, was the convent—a handsome, three-story red
brick structure that had once housed twenty sisters who had taught
in the parish school. Now it had but a tiny group of nuns who lived
there but did no work in the parish at all.

I had resolved that if at all possible I would take a parish that
had a building that could be converted into a parish retreat and formation center. I was firmly convinced that access to a retreat house
was just as necessary for a parish community as access to a sanctuary
or a baptismal font. There it was. I could almost see the building
beckoning me to approach and hear it say "Here I am. I'm willing if
you are."

S oon afterwards I appeared before the priests who made up the
personnel board. They asked me what parish I wanted. I replied
that, since they knew the needs of the archdiocese better than I,
they might like to propose a place where my talents would be uti-
lized well. They said that it was not their policy to recommend
parishes to an individual. I did not agree entirely with the policy
and still do not, but what was one to do?

I stated that I was very much interested in St. Victor's, but that
I wanted two questions answered—first, was the Cardinal going to
divide the parish in two? (so went the rumors), and second, what
did they intend to do with the other associate pastor, a priest
much older than I and clearly of a different pastoral and theological orientation?

Weeks went by with no answers to my questions. I decided to fill out
an application for another parish, St. Pascal's on Chicago's north-
west side, another blue-collar neighborhood much like St. Victor's.

When the members of the personnel board received the written
application, they called me to ask whether I was still interested in

St. Victor's. I answered that I was definitely interested but I wanted answers to my two questions before I would take it.

One fateful day, I received a call from the board formally offering me the position of St. Victor's. There was no mention of the two questions; evidently they could be answered only by the Cardinal, who had regained his health but had refused to respond.

I had twenty-four hours to make my decision. I was apprehensive and filled with doubts. Once again I went to a close friend, this time Father William Goedert, a good listener and a perceptive counselor. I think I must have talked for about two hours, which is not unusual, especially when I'm not sure of what to do.

At the end of my rambling, I put the question: "What shall I do?"

Bill answered quietly and quickly, "Go to St. Victor's."

"Why?" I asked.

"Because that is where you want to go," was the response of my smiling, soft-spoken friend.

I wasn't as sure of that as he seemed to be, but I accepted his advice. I had learned that there are times when one must accept help in making decisions or end up in a debilitating state of indecisiveness.

Thus it was that I called back to say I would accept the assignment. When the matter went to Cardinal Cody for final approval, he was surprised and commented, "If Leo wants that place, by all means give it to him." The questions were left unanswered. Neither of us ever surfaced them again. The parish remained one and eventually the older priest left.

EPILOGUE

*T*he years between 1975 and 2005 have been grace-full years for me. I have been pastor at St. Victor's in Calumet City and at St. Mary of the Woods on Chicago's north side. Those are full chapters of stories where I learned, once again, of the richness of people, hungry for their faith and willing to build community in their daily lives.

I went into my United States ministry as I had my work with the Panamanians. I worked with the avowed purpose of getting to know the people, being fascinated by them and being fascinating in my own right—to not assume, as I could not in San Miguelito, that I understood them or that they understood me. I wanted to fall in love with them and I wanted them to admire and love me. I wanted to be one in love with them so as to produce a community of disciples of Jesus, to generate the true church that would be a sign of the kingdom of God—a family committed to love and justice, to peace and to healing.

And I fell as deeply in love as any young man who extends himself to a cherishable woman. Both at St. Victor's and St. Mary of the Woods, with the enthusiasm of a lover, I took time to get to know the people, reveal myself to them, dialogue about serious things, and build a dream of a future together. We did! We created community and the kingdom of God was within and with us.

Today, I reside at St. Mary of the Woods in emeritus. I turned eighty years old in 2006 and have a disease called chronic inflammatory demyelinating polyneuropathy, which handicaps my writing and walking capability. My body has slowed me down.

Years ago, Monsignor O'Grady of the National Catholic Charities Conference said to Cardinal Stritch, referring to me, "This young man has fire under his feet." The fire continues to burn, not so much under my feet, but in my heart. In telling my story, I trust that I will connect with the next generation and perhaps inspire them to create a San Miguelito that works and changes the world.

The only memento I brought back from San Miguelito is a small fresco that depicts Cristo Redentor, the first church of San Miguelito, built in 1965 by the Chicago archdiocese. The picture shows a simple dome-like structure, open on all sides so the tropical breezes of Central America can pass through.

Looking back thirty years later, that structure represents a powerful image for my life. I am passing through, many times bringing relief and comfort for the suffering, at other times hanging with them in the stifling air, wondering which way to go next.

A RENDEZVOUS
WITH TIME
An Editor Reflects

Leo Mahon describes himself as having embraced the role of pastor as a lover about to court his maiden. When he arrived in Calumet City in 1975, flowers were in bloom, the sun was bright in the Chicago sky, and the excitement of a new venture filled the air. In his hiatus at Mary Seat of Wisdom in Park Ridge, he had discovered that suburban Catholics hungered for the same faith development as the indigent in San Miguelito. He energetically spilled fervor into St. Victor's blue-collar community.

As in Panama, he assumed he knew nothing of who the people were and what they really needed. He visited; he listened and moved at their pace. He surrounded himself with a team of people who constantly took the pulse of the community and encouraged them to act in the interests of those in need.

When alcoholism affected his own family and, like a virus, seemed to be spreading in his parish community, he empowered teams to support those afflicted. Bill Stenzel, then a young parish priest, has since gained a national reputation for the work he has continued to do in ministry to alcoholics and their loved ones.

When the steel mills, the feeder industry for many Calumet City jobs, laid off thousands of employees, parish teams got involved in supporting the jobless.

About a year after Leo arrived at St. Victor's, he received what he called his "greatest compliment." A parishioner with the "rhetoric and ideology of the extreme right" stood up at a town meeting and exclaimed, "Father Mahon, you are destroying our parish. There never were any drunks or poor around here until you came." The crowd burst into laughter, as did Leo. He had made an impact; change had transformed St. Victor's.

He used real-world applications to connect people to the gospel. He preached like a troubadour, echoing a song of joyous news. His message was never scolding or moralizing, nor did he deliver syrupy sweetness. He described a powerful delivery of the Word of God occurring "when the great story of the past meets the story of the present in such a way as to cause an explosion—the moment when new worlds are created, new beings generated, broken hearts healed, dashed hopes revived, hidden meanings revealed, the moment when banalities become surprises."

While Leo Mahon fell in love with his new parish and they with him, San Miguelito remained graced for a few years with Chicago missionaries, Don Headley and John Enright. As is the case in any community vitally alive in the Spirit, ministry abounded. There were lay leaders to train, the unchurched to discover, the poor to love, and the faithful to serve—all in the spirit of setting people free to grow and organize themselves as people of dignity and of God.

Don and John, along with the Adelina, Pinto, Modesto, and scores of others, extended themselves to their communities. But forces against them tightened. Eventually the priests returned to the States, unable to feel safe or needed.

John Paul II appointed Vasquez Pinto to replace Leo as episcopal vicar. Vasquez, it appeared, was slated to get rid of anything that reeked of "liberation theology." He fired the lay leaders in all the parishes and forbade them to minister. He preached of sinfulness and the fall of man . . . and woman. By 1981, three people attended Christmas eve liturgy in one parish. Pinto prohibited any practice that would represent the essence of what Cardinal Meyer had begun—building an experimental church.

Of the individuals from El Salvador, Guatemala, Honduras, and Nicaragua who had been trained in San Miguelito and carried the message of liberation back to their people, more than 80 percent were murdered during their guerilla wars. Rome apparently did nothing to stop the slaughter.

In Panama, Manuel Noriega reigned with military force and no tolerance of democratic process. The people of San Miguelito participated in demonstrations against him until he was overthrown by a coup and captured by the U.S. in 1989. Noriega was tried for drug trafficking and remains imprisoned in Florida. During his final years in power he can be credited for five thousand casualties, mostly innocent village people.

Little by little the lay leaders went underground. Adelina became a leader in the Panamanian Red Cross and brought with her dozens of individuals who continued the social causes they had begun. Today the children of those daring leaders are doctors, lawyers, and respected citizens who have helped to rebuild the spirit of the San Miguelito mission. The priests describe the spirit as one of *conscientisados,* where social conscience has transformed how people think and act.

Leo's pastoral life began at St. Mary of the Woods on Chicago's north side. One of the blessings of being appointed to a large parish, Leo says, is that "they [the hierarchy of the church] leave you alone" unless there is scandal or open defiance. He felt an "awesome responsibility to be creative" and indulged in empowering the laity to take an active part in their faith development. This lively spirit carried through his seasoned years of active ministry.

In 2000, Leo published a reflective book, *Jesus and His Message: An Introduction to the Good News.* In it he calls for the embracing of the kingdom of God, on earth, in the here and now. He captures the messages he has preached all his life: the living out of one's faith in community, hating violence, striving for unity, respecting and caring for the less fortunate, and valuing people for all they are able to be.

Time has given this editor, and hopefully the reader, opportunity to reflect on the efforts of one of the church's "greats," a descriptive term Chicago priests use for their own in appreciation of the extraordinary among them. Leo Mahon is described among his peers as one of the last of the greats.

They must be wrong. There have to be many more greats to come. They may not be the clerics. The greats may rise from the laity, as they continue to do in Panama. The greats will be individuals who dare to look at each other with the freshness of those in discovery, not in judgment or in tyranny. The greats will support the will and empower the dignity of people as they find solutions to humanity's wrongs. The greats will ask questions, not provide answers. The greats will be believers in community working together.

The example set by Leo Mahon inspires us to trust that the next set of greats, as those who came before them, will not be those wrapped in clericalism, protecting themselves from the humanity that makes community live. Those greats will be men and women who dare to be humans among humans, who can dream and, as lovers, birth a new generativity.

In the final words of his 50th anniversary message, May 3, 2001, Leo said:

> I am grateful to God the future, both yours and mine. I believe in my deepest self that we haven't seen anything yet. There is far more to come. We shall all live to see a New World, whether in the body or out, that we cannot now imagine, one beyond our wildest dreams, one so great it will make all the pain of living and dying very much worthwhile.

Nancy Davis

ACKNOWLEDGMENTS

Many people made this book come alive and to them both Leo and I are grateful.

Thanks first to John Enright, who spent hours sharing his archived photos—more than a thousand of them—identifying people and helping me "see" the Panamaian mission. Thanks both to him and to Don Headley, who reviewed early manuscripts and met with me for hours at a time, offering more detail and describing from real-life accounts more of the story. Thanks also to Jack and Adela Greeley, who added richness from their memory of the ministry.

Others who provided encouragement include Leo Mahon's life-long friend Andrew Greeley, who wrote the foreword to this book; my husband, Harry; early reviewers: Bob Potter, Bob Eme, Jan Fogelsong, Barb Hrebic, and Joan Ross; and Catherine Stakenas, who introduced me to Leo: "He is a man you have to meet; he has quite a story to tell." Finally, I'd like to add Mark Dickerson, a fellow researcher who inspired me to make Leo's story come alive. Also I'd like to acknowledge the Archdiocese of Chicago's Archives and Records Center, which transferred the photos from slides and albums into usable pictures for the book.

Most of all, I thank Leo himself for having a story to tell. I appreciate his trust in allowing me to pull apart a document he had written in 1986 and hadn't published, and in encouraging me to put it together "in whatever form makes sense" so that his story now is told as *Fire under My Feet*.

Nancy Davis